MARTIN AND PARSON -PRESENT-

WORLD WAR
TANK ★ GIRL

TITAN
COMICS

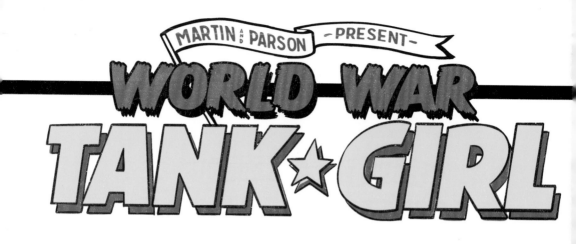

MARTIN AND PARSON -PRESENT-

WORLD WAR TANK ★ GIRL

WRITTEN BY
ALAN MARTIN

DRAWN & LETTERED BY
BRETT PARSON

COVER BY
BRETT PARSON

FORBIDDEN PLANET COVER BY
CHRIS WAHL

TITAN COMICS

COLLECTION EDITOR
LAUREN MCPHEE

SENIOR DESIGNER
ANDREW LEUNG

MANAGING EDITOR
ANDREW JAMES

EDITOR
NEIL EDWARDS

SENIOR PRODUCTION CONTROLLER
JACKIE FLOOK

PRODUCTION SUPERVISOR
MARIA PEARSON

PRODUCTION CONTROLLER
PETER JAMES

PRODUCTION ASSISTANT
NATALIE BOLGER

ART DIRECTOR
OZ BROWNE

SENIOR SALES MANAGER
STEVE TOTHILL

PRESS OFFICER
WILL O'MULLANE

MARKETING MANAGER
RICKY CLAYDON

ADVERTISING MANAGER
MICHELLE FAIRLAMB

ADS & MARKETING ASSISTANT
TOM MILLER

HEAD OF RIGHTS
JENNY BOYCE

PUBLISHING MANAGER
DARRYL TOTHILL

PUBLISHING DIRECTOR
CHRIS TEATHER

OPERATIONS DIRECTOR
LEIGH BAULCH

EXECUTIVE DIRECTOR
VIVIAN CHEUNG

PUBLISHER
NICK LANDAU

WORLD WAR TANK GIRL
ISBN: 9781785855269

FORBIDDEN PLANET EDITION
ISBN: 9781785865510

PUBLISHED BY TITAN COMICS,
A DIVISION OF TITAN PUBLISHING GROUP, LTD.
144 SOUTHWARK STREET,
LONDON, SE1 0UP

A CIP CATALOGUE FOR THIS TITLE IS AVAILABLE FROM THE BRITISH LIBRARY

10 9 8 7 6 5 4 3 2 1

WWW.TITAN-COMICS.COM
BECOME A FAN ON FACEBOOK.COM/COMICSTITAN | FOLLOW US ON TWITTER @COMICSTITAN
VISIT THE OFFICIAL TANK GIRL WEBSITE AT WWW.TANK-GIRL.COM

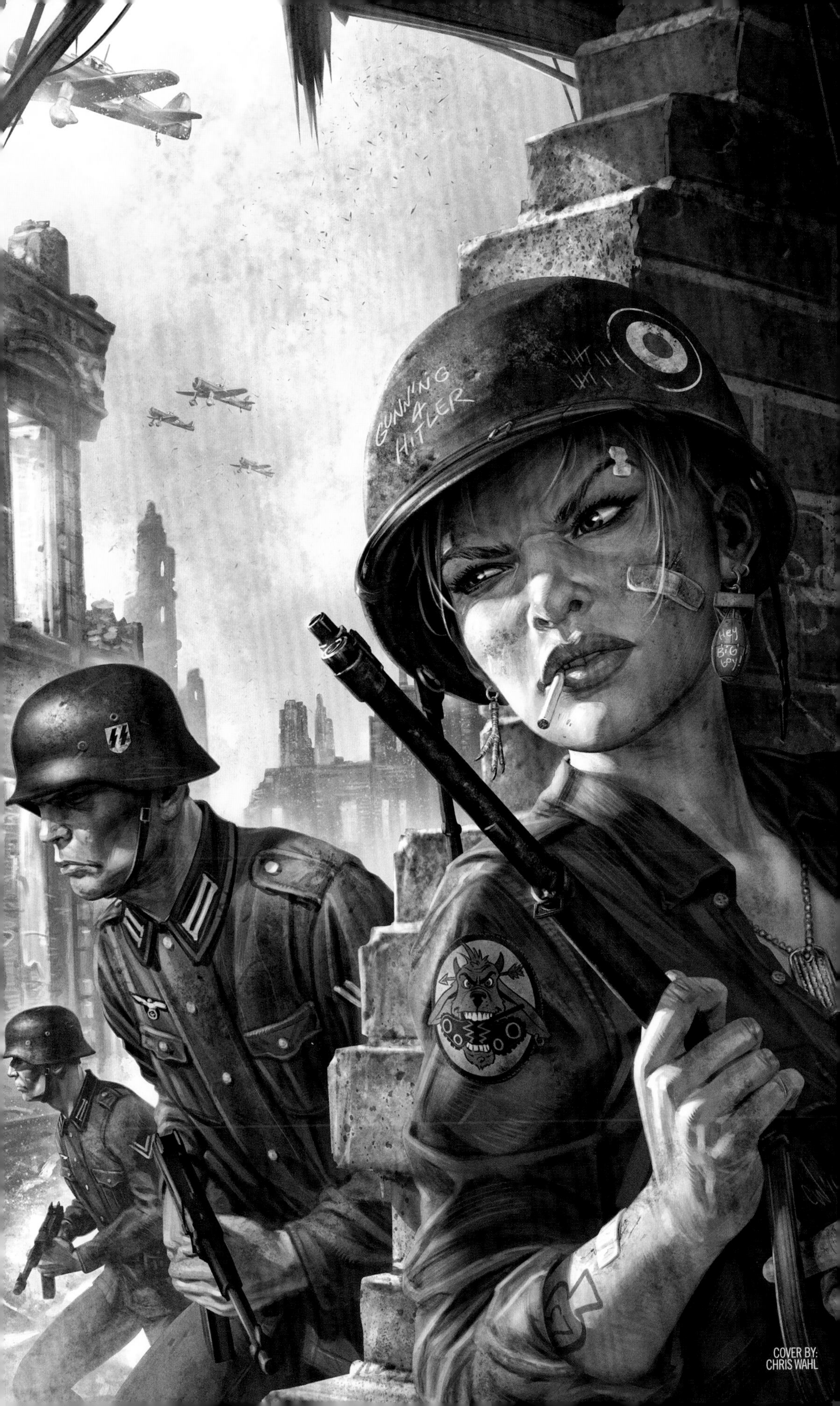
GUNNING 4 HITLER
Hey BiG boy!

COVER BY:
CHRIS WAHL

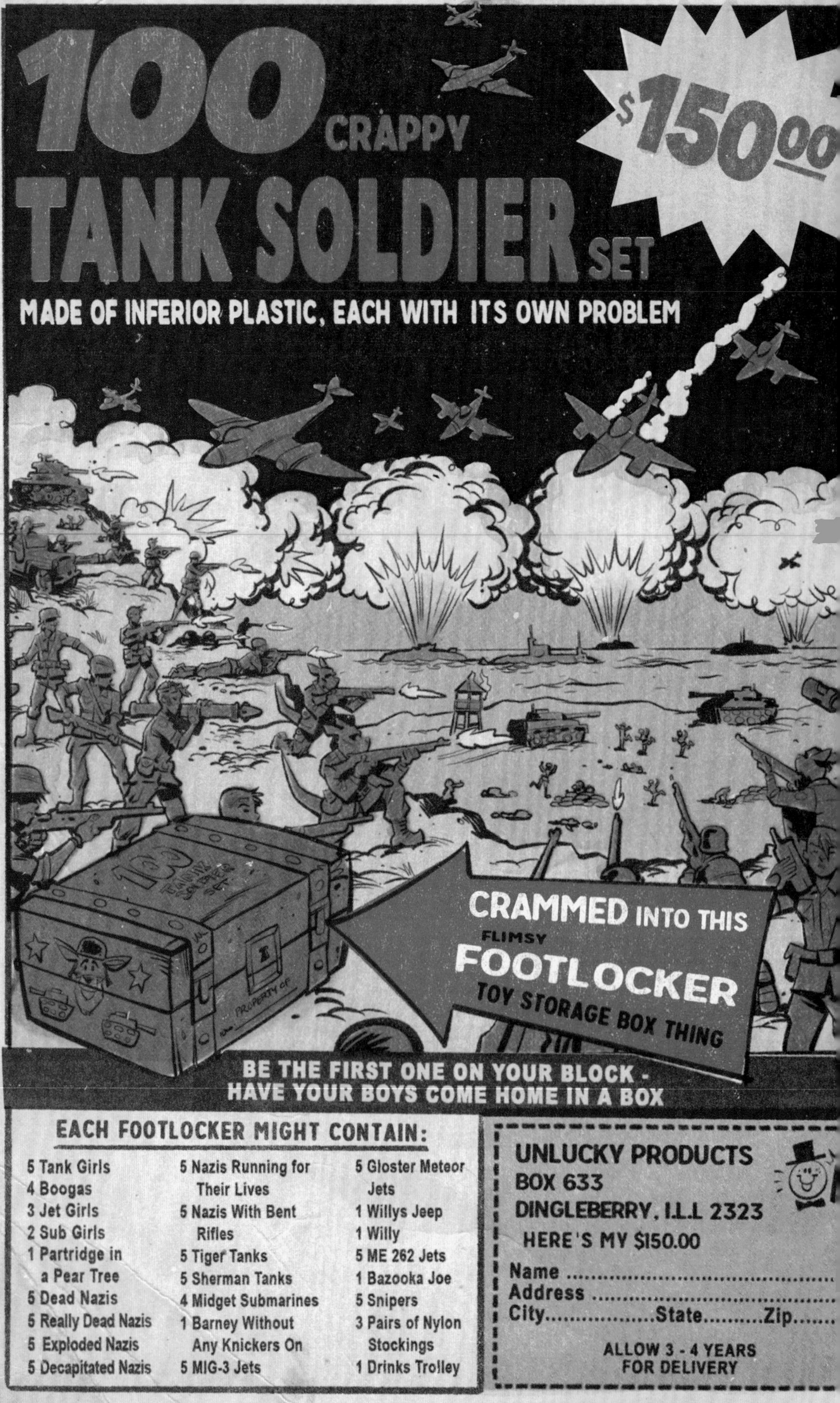

100 CRAPPY
TANK SOLDIER SET
$150.00
MADE OF INFERIOR PLASTIC, EACH WITH ITS OWN PROBLEM
PROPERTY OF
CRAMMED INTO THIS
FLIMSY
FOOTLOCKER
TOY STORAGE BOX THING
BE THE FIRST ONE ON YOUR BLOCK -
HAVE YOUR BOYS COME HOME IN A BOX
EACH FOOTLOCKER MIGHT CONTAIN:
5 Tank Girls
4 Boogas
3 Jet Girls
2 Sub Girls
1 Partridge in a Pear Tree
5 Dead Nazis
5 Really Dead Nazis
5 Exploded Nazis
5 Decapitated Nazis
5 Nazis Running for Their Lives
5 Nazis With Bent Rifles
5 Tiger Tanks
5 Sherman Tanks
4 Midget Submarines
1 Barney Without Any Knickers On
5 MIG-3 Jets
5 Gloster Meteor Jets
1 Willys Jeep
1 Willy
5 ME 262 Jets
1 Bazooka Joe
5 Snipers
3 Pairs of Nylon Stockings
1 Drinks Trolley
UNLUCKY PRODUCTS
BOX 633
DINGLEBERRY, I.L.L 2323
HERE'S MY $150.00
Name ....
Address ....
City.................State..........Zip.......
ALLOW 3 - 4 YEARS FOR DELIVERY

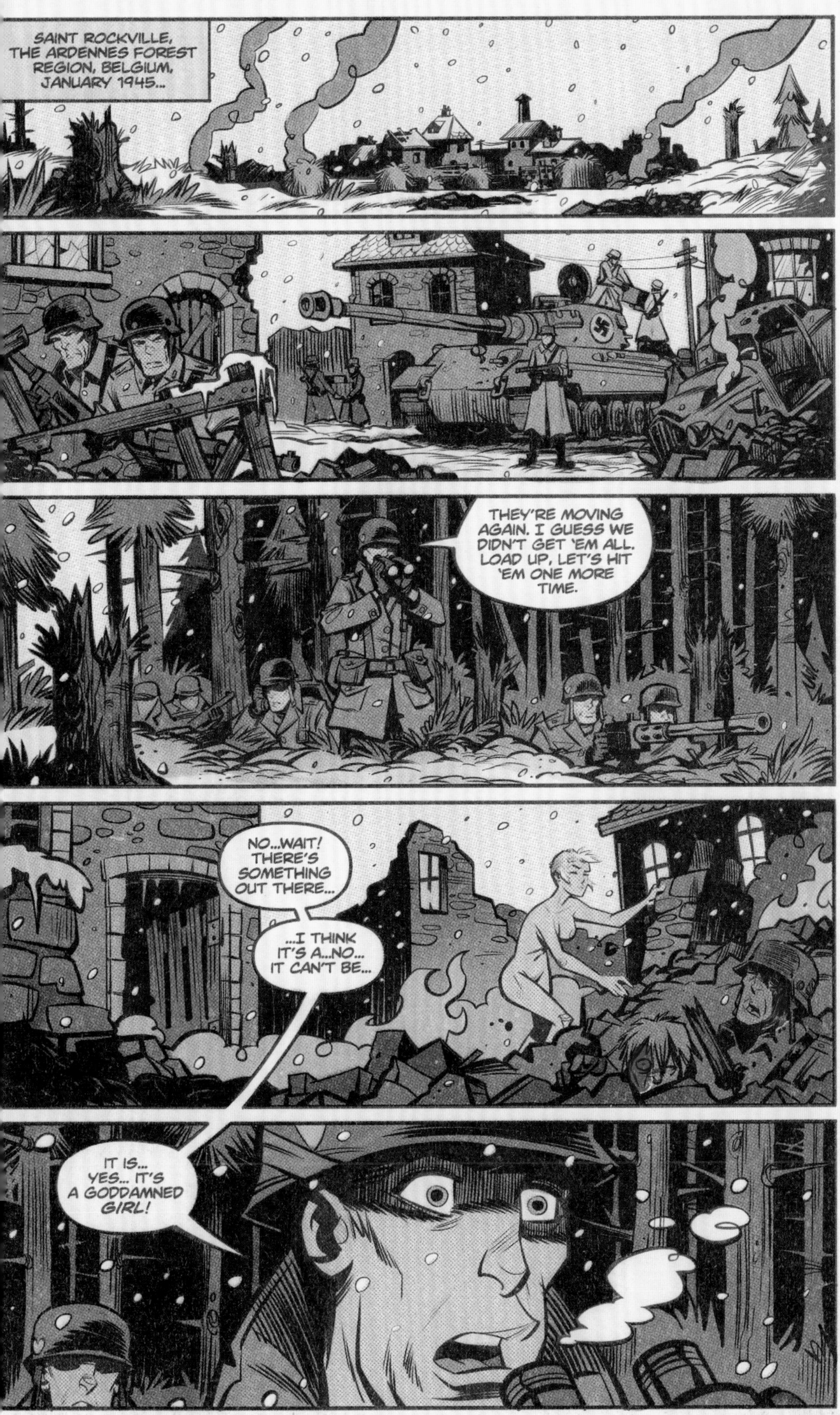
SAINT ROCKVILLE, THE ARDENNES FOREST REGION, BELGIUM, JANUARY 1945...
THEY'RE MOVING AGAIN. I GUESS WE DIDN'T GET 'EM ALL. LOAD UP, LET'S HIT 'EM ONE MORE TIME.
NO...WAIT! THERE'S SOMETHING OUT THERE...
...I THINK IT'S A...NO... IT CAN'T BE...
IT IS... YES... IT'S A GODDAMNED GIRL!

WRITER : ALAN MARTIN   ARTIST : BRETT PARSON

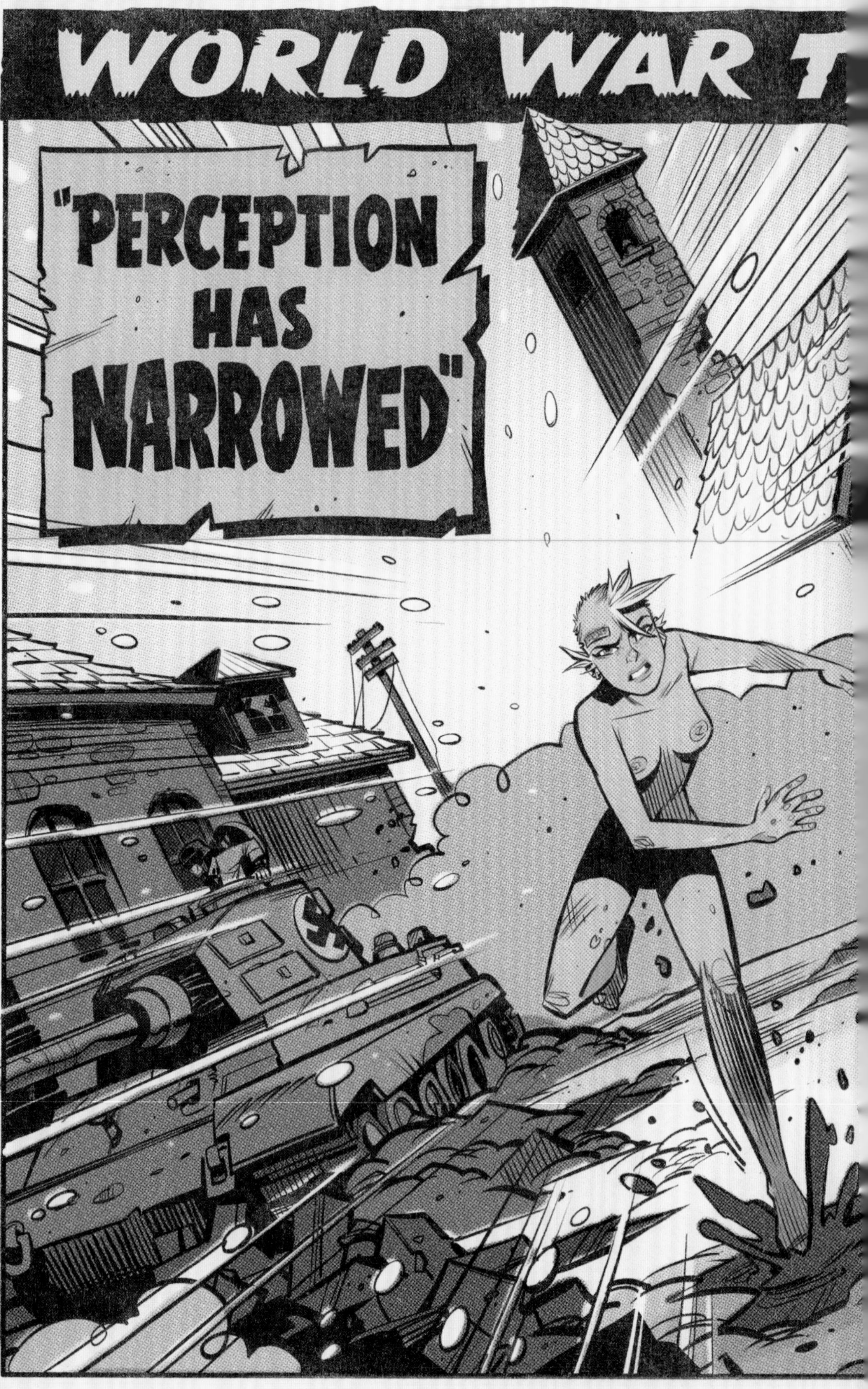
WORLD WAR T
"PERCEPTION HAS NARROWED"

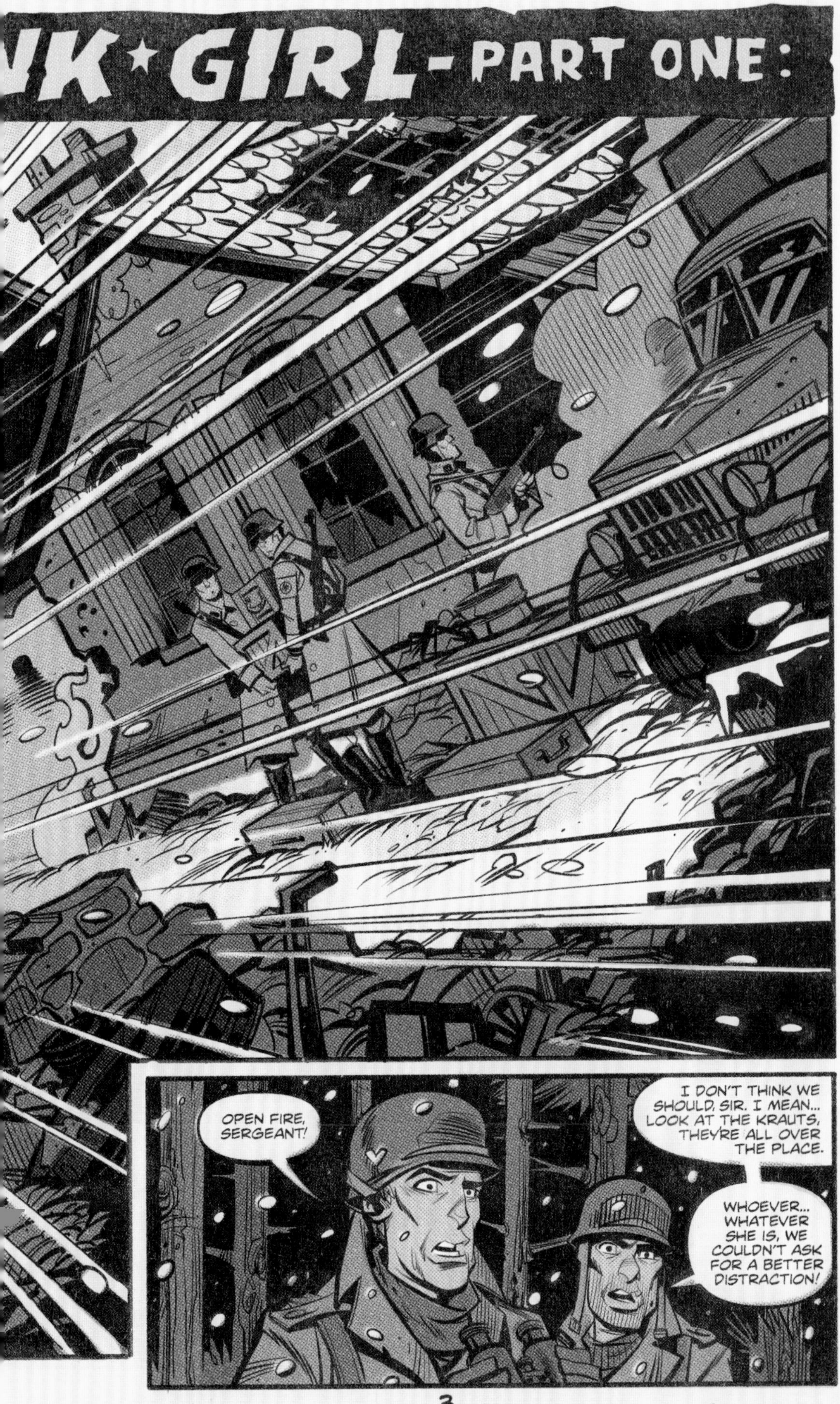

NK★GIRL - PART ONE:
OPEN FIRE, SERGEANT!
I DON'T THINK WE SHOULD, SIR. I MEAN... LOOK AT THE KRAUTS, THEY'RE ALL OVER THE PLACE.
WHOEVER... WHATEVER SHE IS, WE COULDN'T ASK FOR A BETTER DISTRACTION!

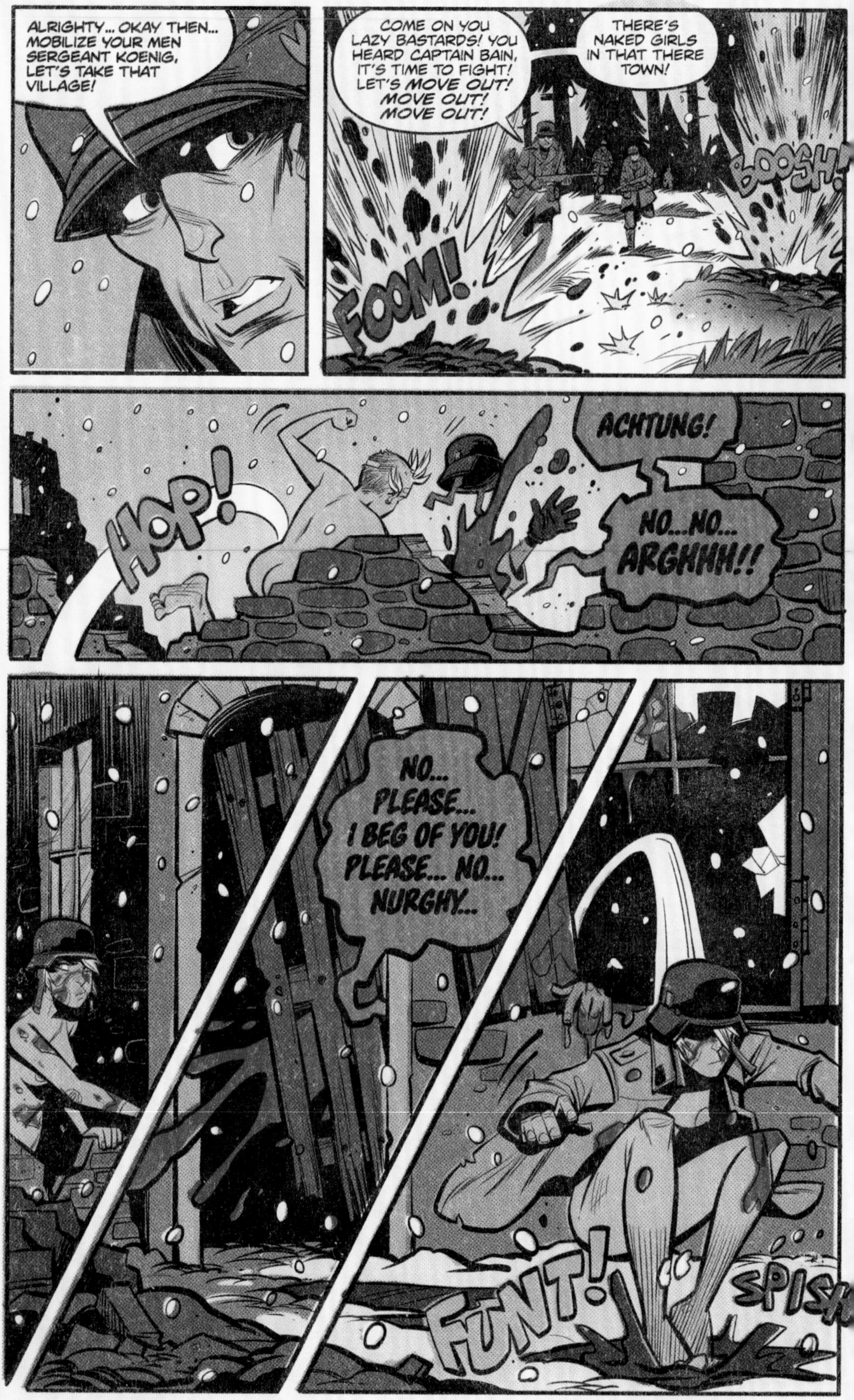
ALRIGHTY... OKAY THEN... MOBILIZE YOUR MEN SERGEANT KOENIG, LET'S TAKE THAT VILLAGE!
COME ON YOU LAZY BASTARDS! YOU HEARD CAPTAIN BAIN, IT'S TIME TO FIGHT! LET'S MOVE OUT! MOVE OUT! MOVE OUT!
THERE'S NAKED GIRLS IN THAT THERE TOWN!
BOOSH!
FOOM!
HOP!
ACHTUNG!
NO...NO... ARGHHH!!
NO... PLEASE... I BEG OF YOU! PLEASE... NO... NURGHY...
FUNT!
SPISH

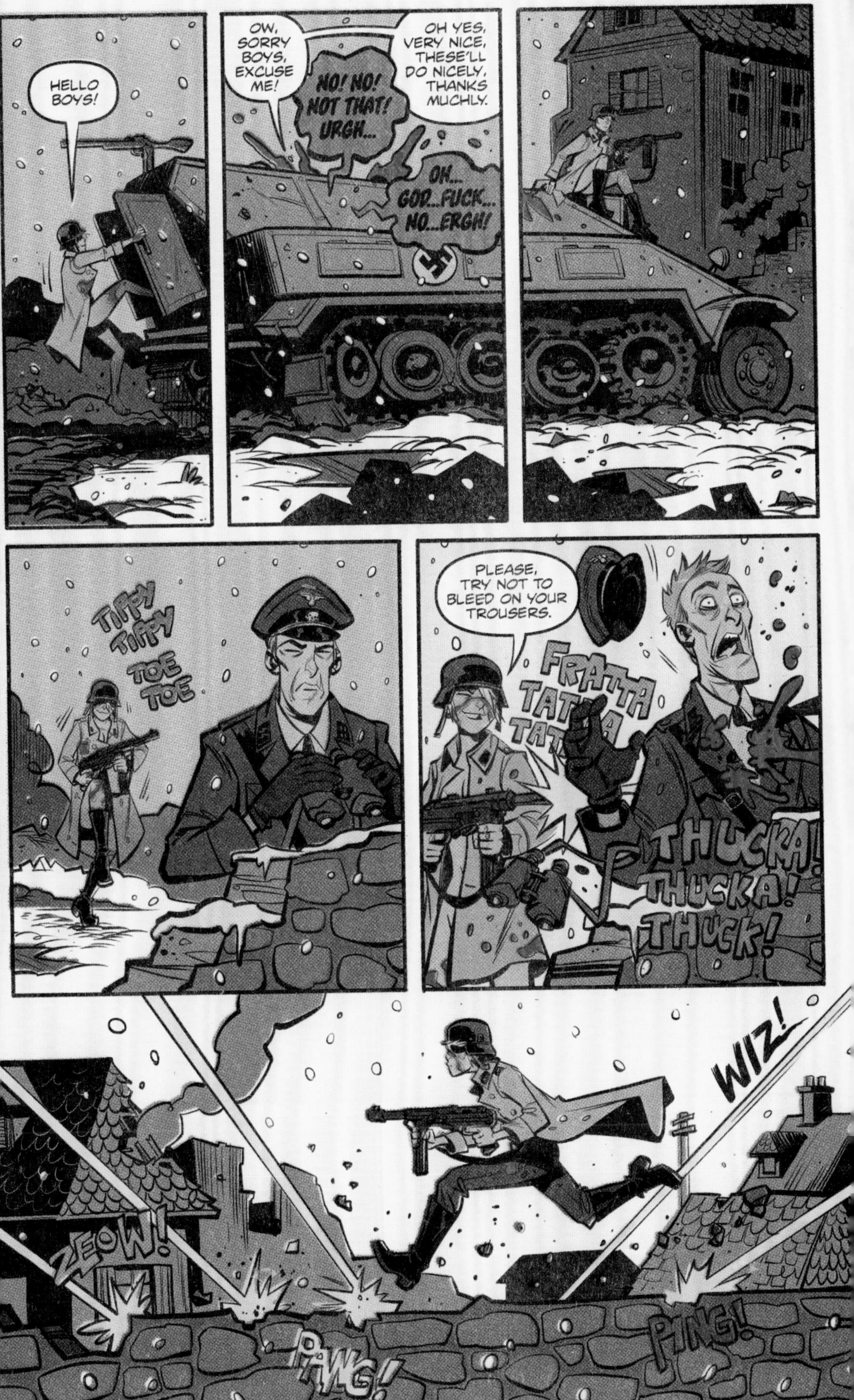
HELLO BOYS!
OW, SORRY BOYS, EXCUSE ME!
NO! NO! NOT THAT! URGH...
OH YES, VERY NICE, THESE'LL DO NICELY. THANKS MUCHLY.
OH... GOD...FUCK... NO...ERGH!
TIPPY TIPPY
TOE TOE
PLEASE, TRY NOT TO BLEED ON YOUR TROUSERS.
FRATTA TATTA TATTA
THUCKA! THUCKA! THUCK!
WIZ!
ZEOW!
PANG!
PING!

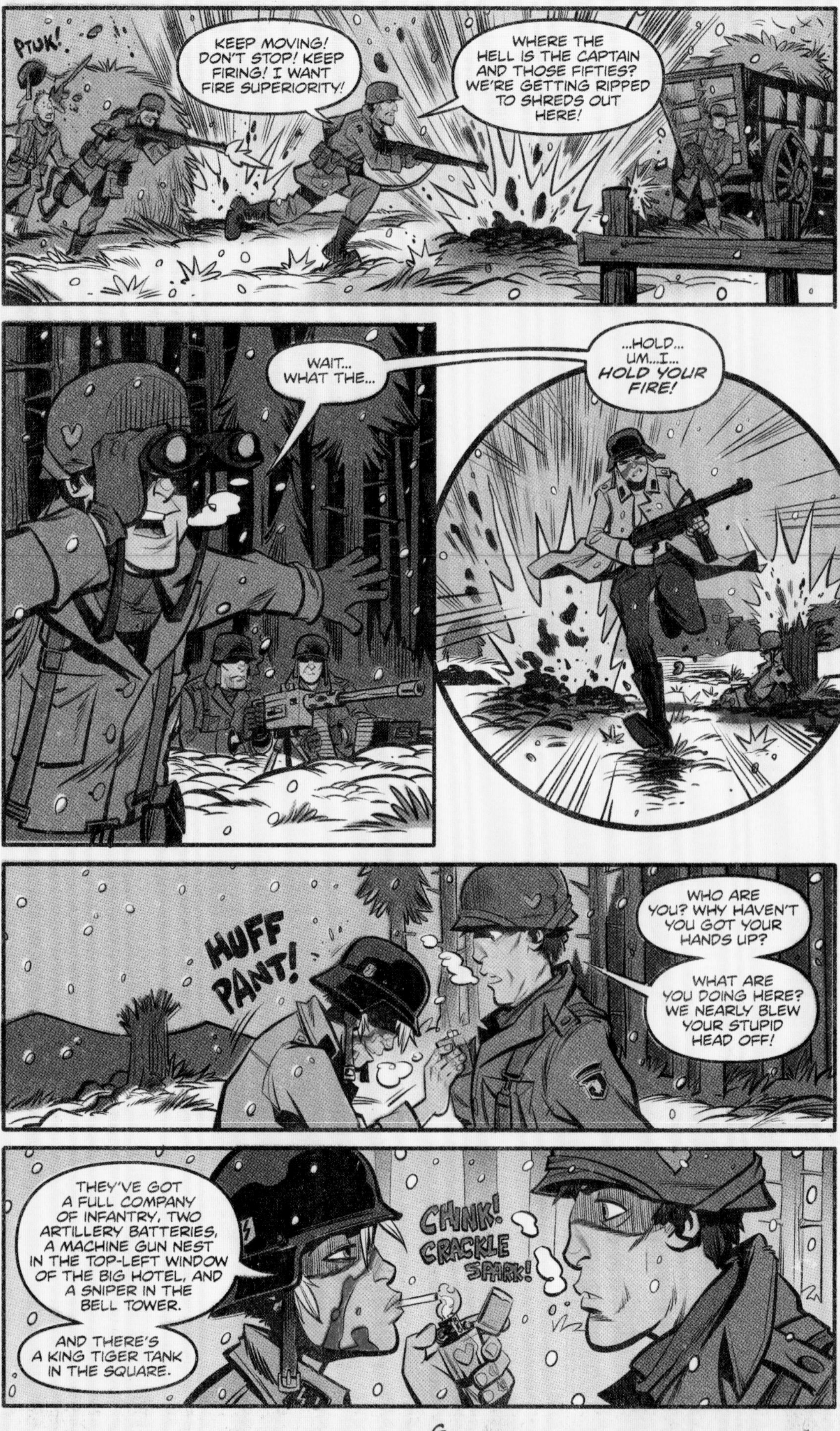
PTUK!
KEEP MOVING! DON'T STOP! KEEP FIRING! I WANT FIRE SUPERIORITY!
WHERE THE HELL IS THE CAPTAIN AND THOSE FIFTIES? WE'RE GETTING RIPPED TO SHREDS OUT HERE!
WAIT... WHAT THE...
...HOLD... UM...I... HOLD YOUR FIRE!
HUFF PANT!
WHO ARE YOU? WHY HAVEN'T YOU GOT YOUR HANDS UP?
WHAT ARE YOU DOING HERE? WE NEARLY BLEW YOUR STUPID HEAD OFF!
THEY'VE GOT A FULL COMPANY OF INFANTRY, TWO ARTILLERY BATTERIES, A MACHINE GUN NEST IN THE TOP-LEFT WINDOW OF THE BIG HOTEL, AND A SNIPER IN THE BELL TOWER.
AND THERE'S A KING TIGER TANK IN THE SQUARE.
CHINK! CRACKLE SPARK!

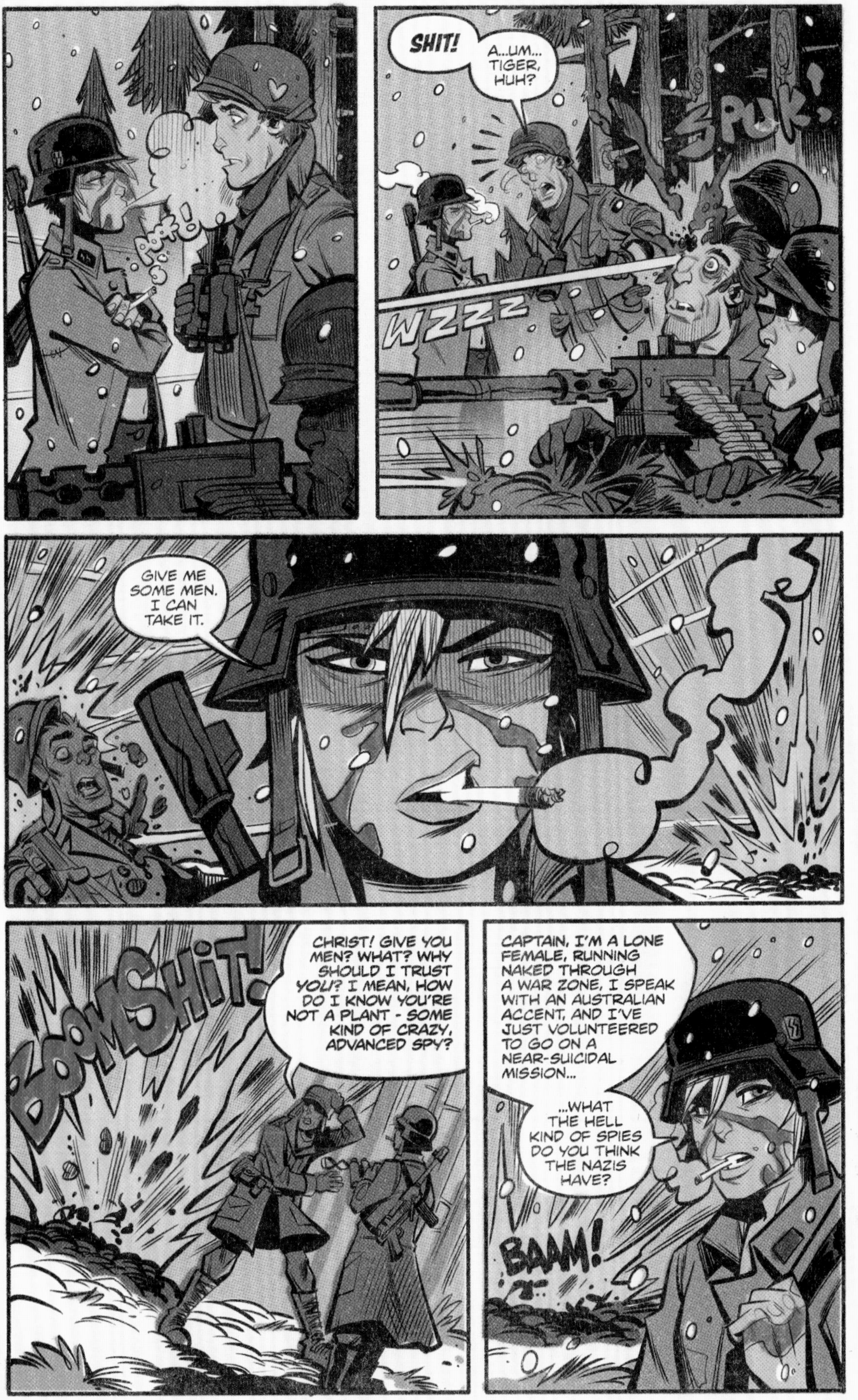
POFF!
SHIT!
A...UM... TIGER, HUH?
SPUK!
WZZZ
GIVE ME SOME MEN. I CAN TAKE IT.
BOOMSHIT!
CHRIST! GIVE YOU MEN? WHAT? WHY SHOULD I TRUST YOU? I MEAN, HOW DO I KNOW YOU'RE NOT A PLANT - SOME KIND OF CRAZY, ADVANCED SPY?
CAPTAIN, I'M A LONE FEMALE, RUNNING NAKED THROUGH A WAR ZONE, I SPEAK WITH AN AUSTRALIAN ACCENT, AND I'VE JUST VOLUNTEERED TO GO ON A NEAR-SUICIDAL MISSION...
...WHAT THE HELL KIND OF SPIES DO YOU THINK THE NAZIS HAVE?
BAAM!

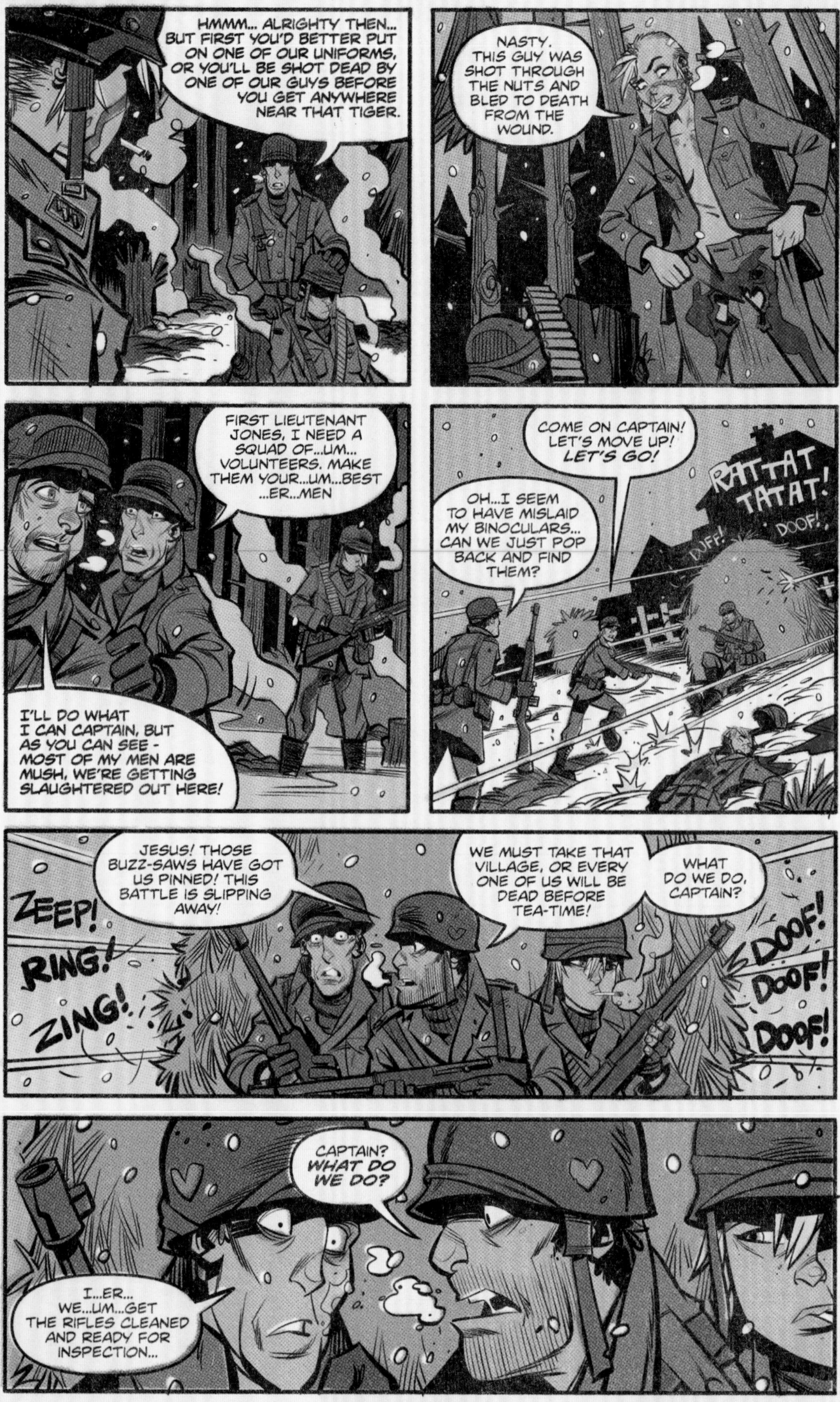
HMMM... ALRIGHTY THEN... BUT FIRST YOU'D BETTER PUT ON ONE OF OUR UNIFORMS, OR YOU'LL BE SHOT DEAD BY ONE OF OUR GUYS BEFORE YOU GET ANYWHERE NEAR THAT TIGER.
NASTY. THIS GUY WAS SHOT THROUGH THE NUTS AND BLED TO DEATH FROM THE WOUND.
FIRST LIEUTENANT JONES, I NEED A SQUAD OF...UM... VOLUNTEERS. MAKE THEM YOUR...UM...BEST ...ER...MEN
I'LL DO WHAT I CAN CAPTAIN, BUT AS YOU CAN SEE - MOST OF MY MEN ARE MUSH. WE'RE GETTING SLAUGHTERED OUT HERE!
COME ON CAPTAIN! LET'S MOVE UP! LET'S GO!
RATTAT TATAT!
DOOF!
DUFF!
OH...I SEEM TO HAVE MISLAID MY BINOCULARS... CAN WE JUST POP BACK AND FIND THEM?
JESUS! THOSE BUZZ-SAWS HAVE GOT US PINNED! THIS BATTLE IS SLIPPING AWAY!
ZEEP!
RING!
ZING!
WE MUST TAKE THAT VILLAGE, OR EVERY ONE OF US WILL BE DEAD BEFORE TEA-TIME!
WHAT DO WE DO, CAPTAIN?
DOOF!
DOOF!
DOOF!
CAPTAIN? WHAT DO WE DO?
I...ER... WE...UM...GET THE RIFLES CLEANED AND READY FOR INSPECTION...

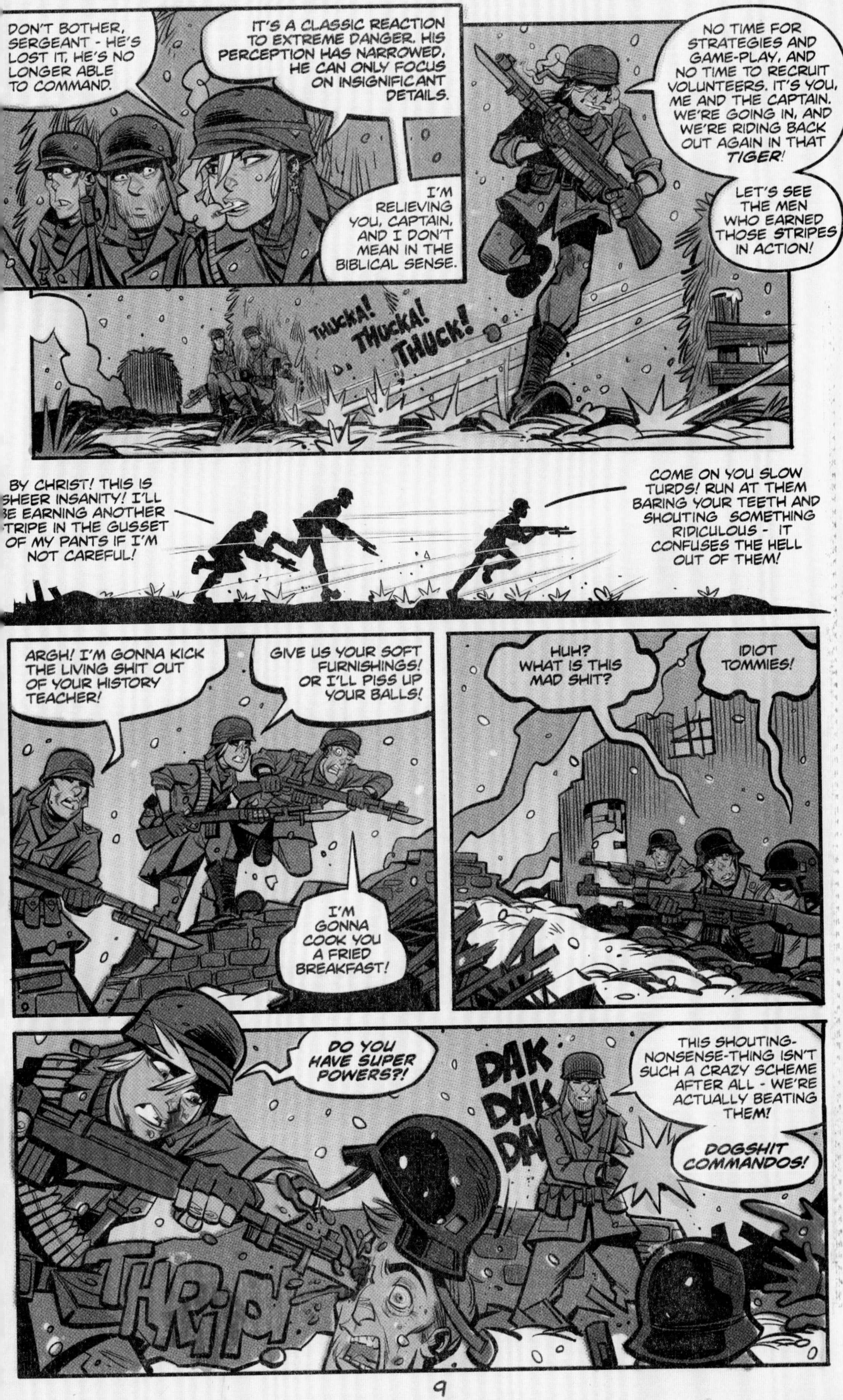
DON'T BOTHER, SERGEANT - HE'S LOST IT, HE'S NO LONGER ABLE TO COMMAND.
IT'S A CLASSIC REACTION TO EXTREME DANGER. HIS PERCEPTION HAS NARROWED, HE CAN ONLY FOCUS ON INSIGNIFICANT DETAILS.
I'M RELIEVING YOU, CAPTAIN, AND I DON'T MEAN IN THE BIBLICAL SENSE.
NO TIME FOR STRATEGIES AND GAME-PLAY, AND NO TIME TO RECRUIT VOLUNTEERS. IT'S YOU, ME AND THE CAPTAIN. WE'RE GOING IN, AND WE'RE RIDING BACK OUT AGAIN IN THAT TIGER!
LET'S SEE THE MEN WHO EARNED THOSE STRIPES IN ACTION!
THUCKA! THUCKA! THUCK!
BY CHRIST! THIS IS SHEER INSANITY! I'LL BE EARNING ANOTHER STRIPE IN THE GUSSET OF MY PANTS IF I'M NOT CAREFUL!
COME ON YOU SLOW TURDS! RUN AT THEM BARING YOUR TEETH AND SHOUTING SOMETHING RIDICULOUS - IT CONFUSES THE HELL OUT OF THEM!
ARGH! I'M GONNA KICK THE LIVING SHIT OUT OF YOUR HISTORY TEACHER!
GIVE US YOUR SOFT FURNISHINGS! OR I'LL PISS UP YOUR BALLS!
I'M GONNA COOK YOU A FRIED BREAKFAST!
HUH? WHAT IS THIS MAD SHIT?
IDIOT TOMMIES!
DO YOU HAVE SUPER POWERS?!
DAK DAK DA
THIS SHOUTING-NONSENSE-THING ISN'T SUCH A CRAZY SCHEME AFTER ALL - WE'RE ACTUALLY BEATING THEM!
DOGSHIT COMMANDOS!
THRIP

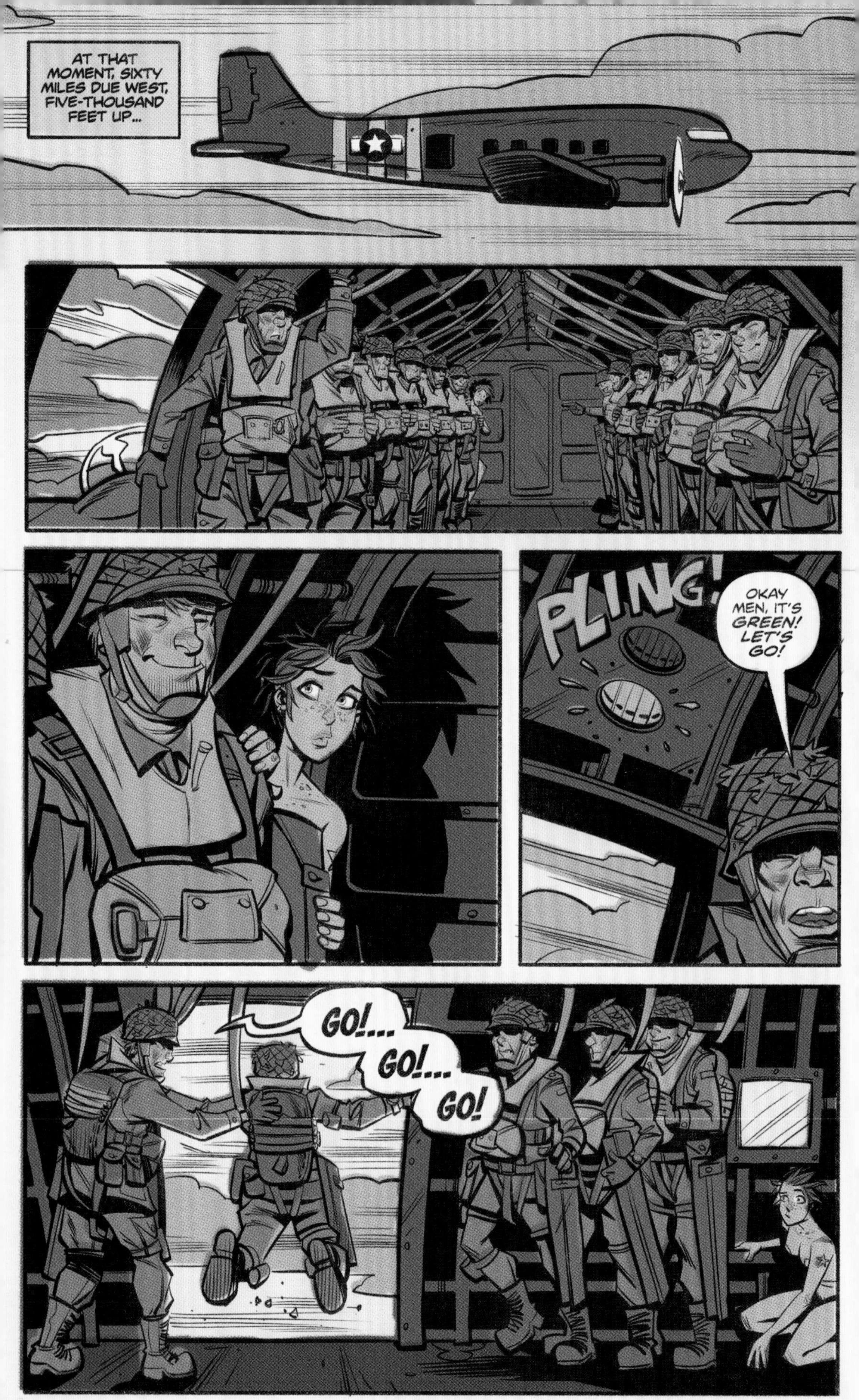

AT THAT MOMENT, SIXTY MILES DUE WEST, FIVE-THOUSAND FEET UP...
PLING!
OKAY MEN, IT'S GREEN! LET'S GO!
GO!... GO!... GO!

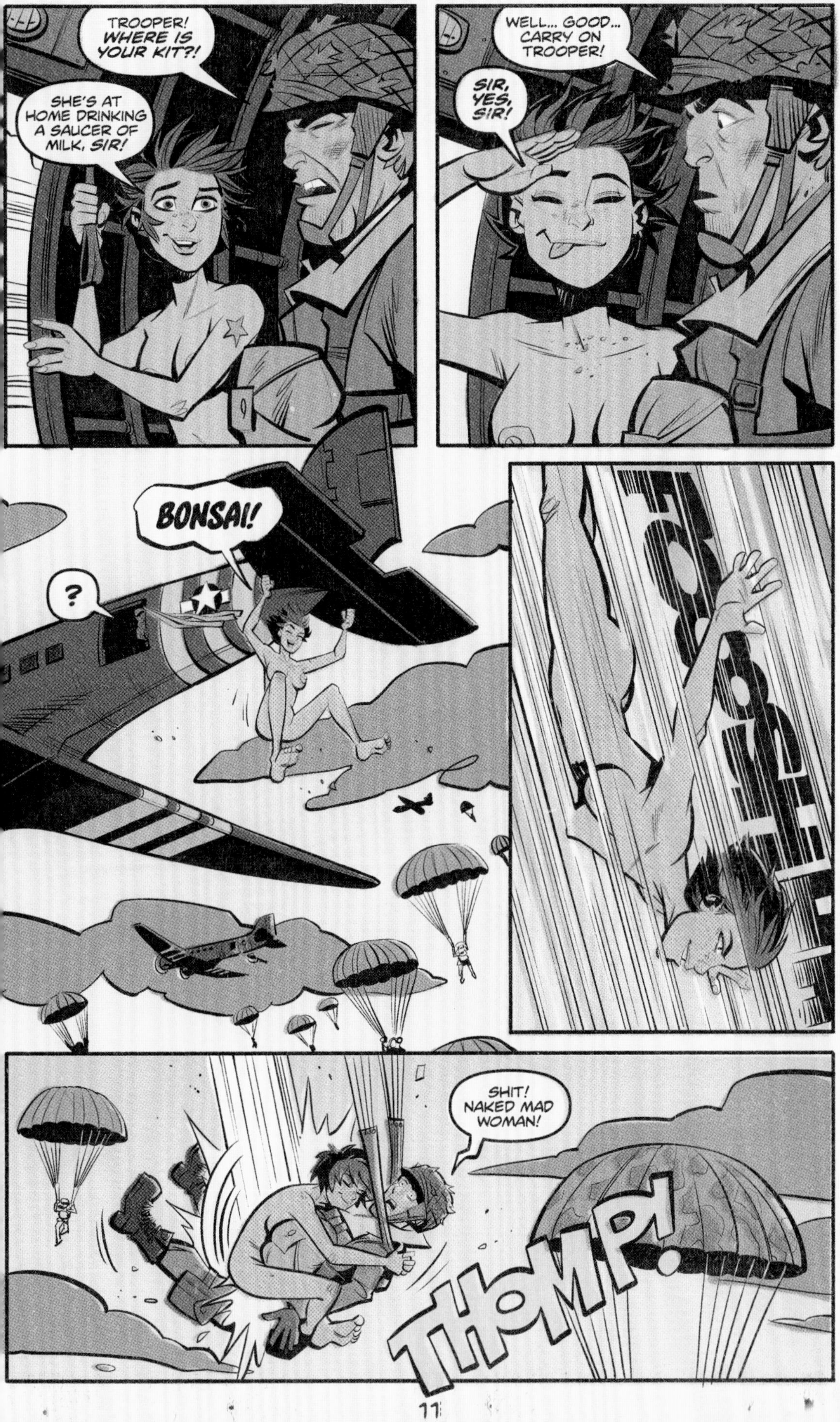
TROOPER! WHERE IS YOUR KIT?!
SHE'S AT HOME DRINKING A SAUCER OF MILK, SIR!
WELL... GOOD... CARRY ON TROOPER!
SIR, YES, SIR!
BONSAI!
?
SHIT! NAKED MAD WOMAN!
THOMP!

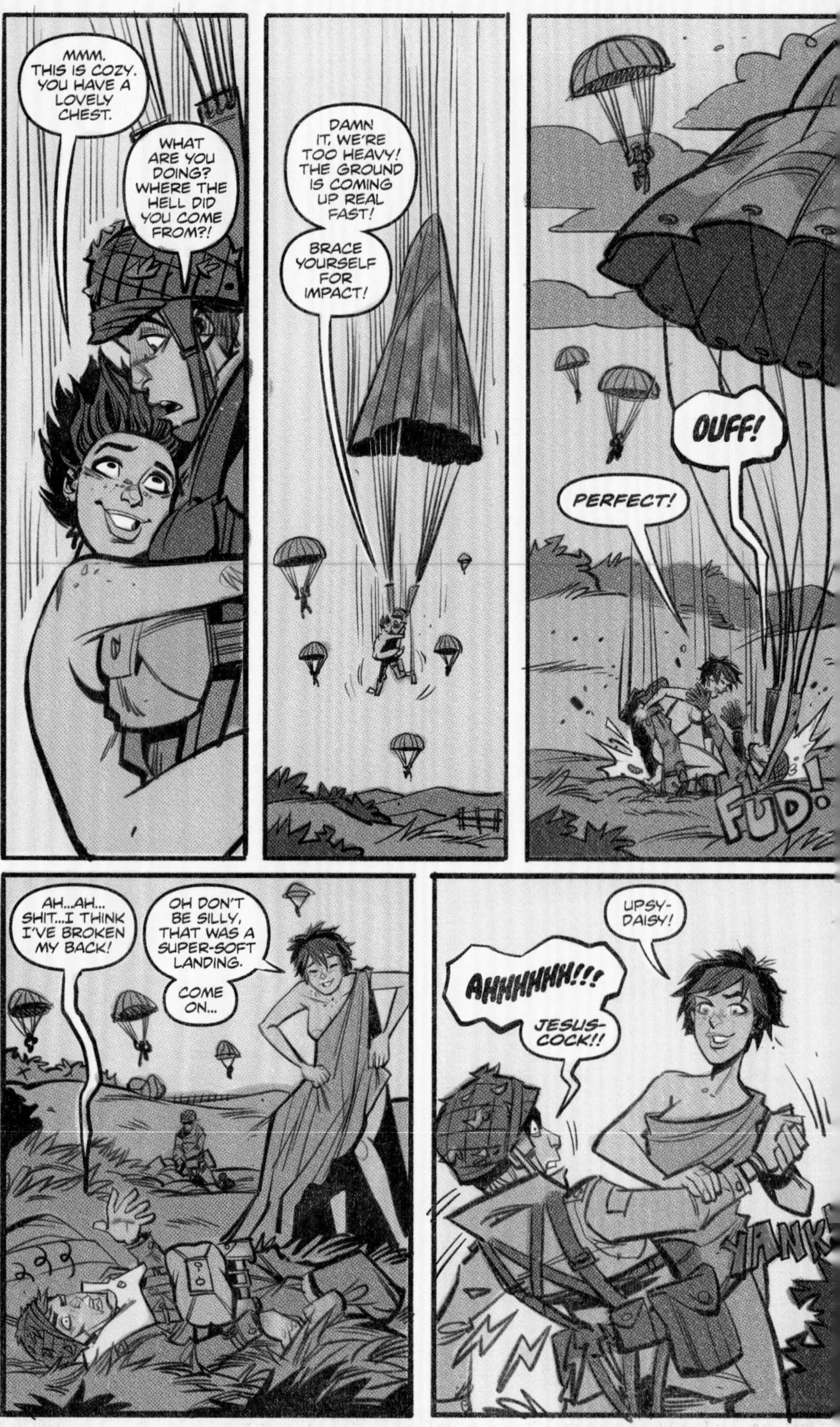
MMM. THIS IS COZY. YOU HAVE A LOVELY CHEST.
WHAT ARE YOU DOING? WHERE THE HELL DID YOU COME FROM?!
DAMN IT, WE'RE TOO HEAVY! THE GROUND IS COMING UP REAL FAST!
BRACE YOURSELF FOR IMPACT!
OUFF!
PERFECT!
FUD!
AH...AH... SHIT...I THINK I'VE BROKEN MY BACK!
OH DON'T BE SILLY, THAT WAS A SUPER-SOFT LANDING.
COME ON...
UPSY-DAISY!
AHHHHHH!!!
JESUS-COCK!!
YANK!

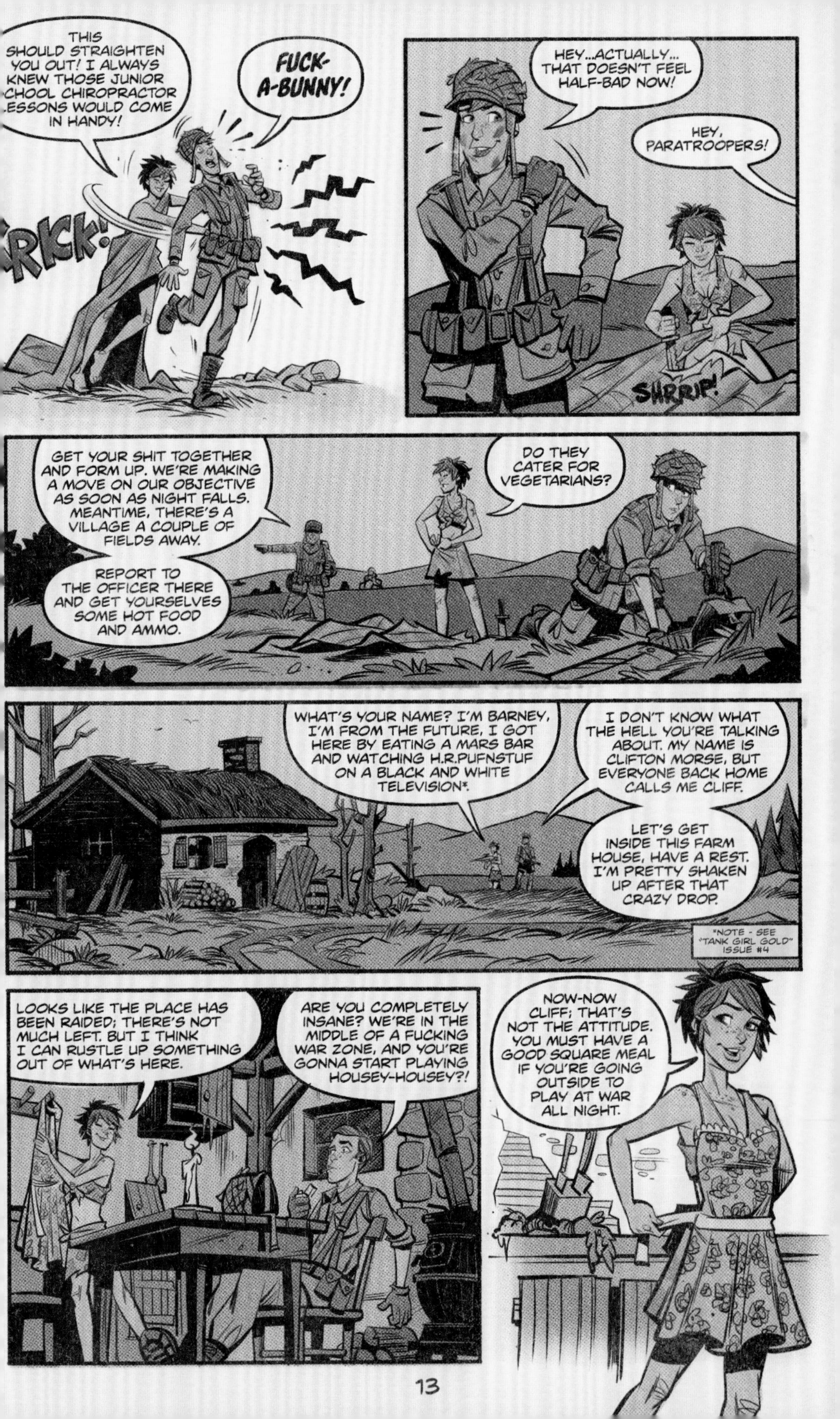
THIS SHOULD STRAIGHTEN YOU OUT! I ALWAYS KNEW THOSE JUNIOR CHOOL CHIROPRACTOR ESSONS WOULD COME IN HANDY!
RICK!
FUCK-A-BUNNY!
HEY...ACTUALLY... THAT DOESN'T FEEL HALF-BAD NOW!
HEY, PARATROOPERS!
SHRRIP!
GET YOUR SHIT TOGETHER AND FORM UP. WE'RE MAKING A MOVE ON OUR OBJECTIVE AS SOON AS NIGHT FALLS. MEANTIME, THERE'S A VILLAGE A COUPLE OF FIELDS AWAY.
REPORT TO THE OFFICER THERE AND GET YOURSELVES SOME HOT FOOD AND AMMO.
DO THEY CATER FOR VEGETARIANS?
WHAT'S YOUR NAME? I'M BARNEY, I'M FROM THE FUTURE, I GOT HERE BY EATING A MARS BAR AND WATCHING H.R.PUFNSTUF ON A BLACK AND WHITE TELEVISION*.
I DON'T KNOW WHAT THE HELL YOU'RE TALKING ABOUT. MY NAME IS CLIFTON MORSE, BUT EVERYONE BACK HOME CALLS ME CLIFF.
LET'S GET INSIDE THIS FARM HOUSE, HAVE A REST. I'M PRETTY SHAKEN UP AFTER THAT CRAZY DROP.
*NOTE - SEE "TANK GIRL GOLD" ISSUE #4
LOOKS LIKE THE PLACE HAS BEEN RAIDED; THERE'S NOT MUCH LEFT. BUT I THINK I CAN RUSTLE UP SOMETHING OUT OF WHAT'S HERE.
ARE YOU COMPLETELY INSANE? WE'RE IN THE MIDDLE OF A FUCKING WAR ZONE, AND YOU'RE GONNA START PLAYING HOUSEY-HOUSEY?!
NOW-NOW CLIFF; THAT'S NOT THE ATTITUDE. YOU MUST HAVE A GOOD SQUARE MEAL IF YOU'RE GOING OUTSIDE TO PLAY AT WAR ALL NIGHT.

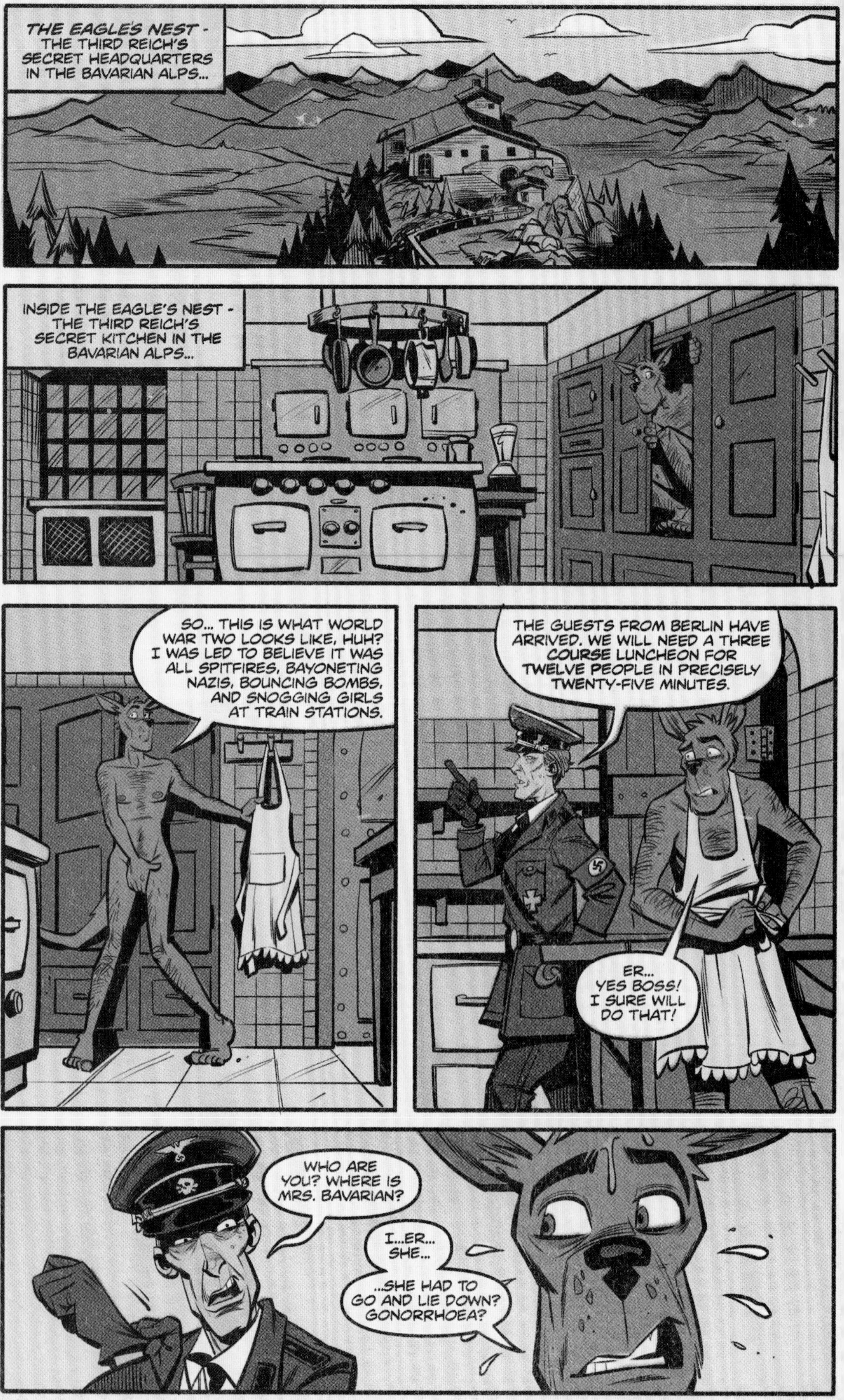
THE EAGLE'S NEST - THE THIRD REICH'S SECRET HEADQUARTERS IN THE BAVARIAN ALPS...
INSIDE THE EAGLE'S NEST - THE THIRD REICH'S SECRET KITCHEN IN THE BAVARIAN ALPS...
SO... THIS IS WHAT WORLD WAR TWO LOOKS LIKE, HUH? I WAS LED TO BELIEVE IT WAS ALL SPITFIRES, BAYONETING NAZIS, BOUNCING BOMBS, AND SNOGGING GIRLS AT TRAIN STATIONS.
THE GUESTS FROM BERLIN HAVE ARRIVED. WE WILL NEED A THREE COURSE LUNCHEON FOR TWELVE PEOPLE IN PRECISELY TWENTY-FIVE MINUTES.
ER... YES BOSS! I SURE WILL DO THAT!
WHO ARE YOU? WHERE IS MRS. BAVARIAN?
I...ER... SHE...
...SHE HAD TO GO AND LIE DOWN? GONORRHOEA?

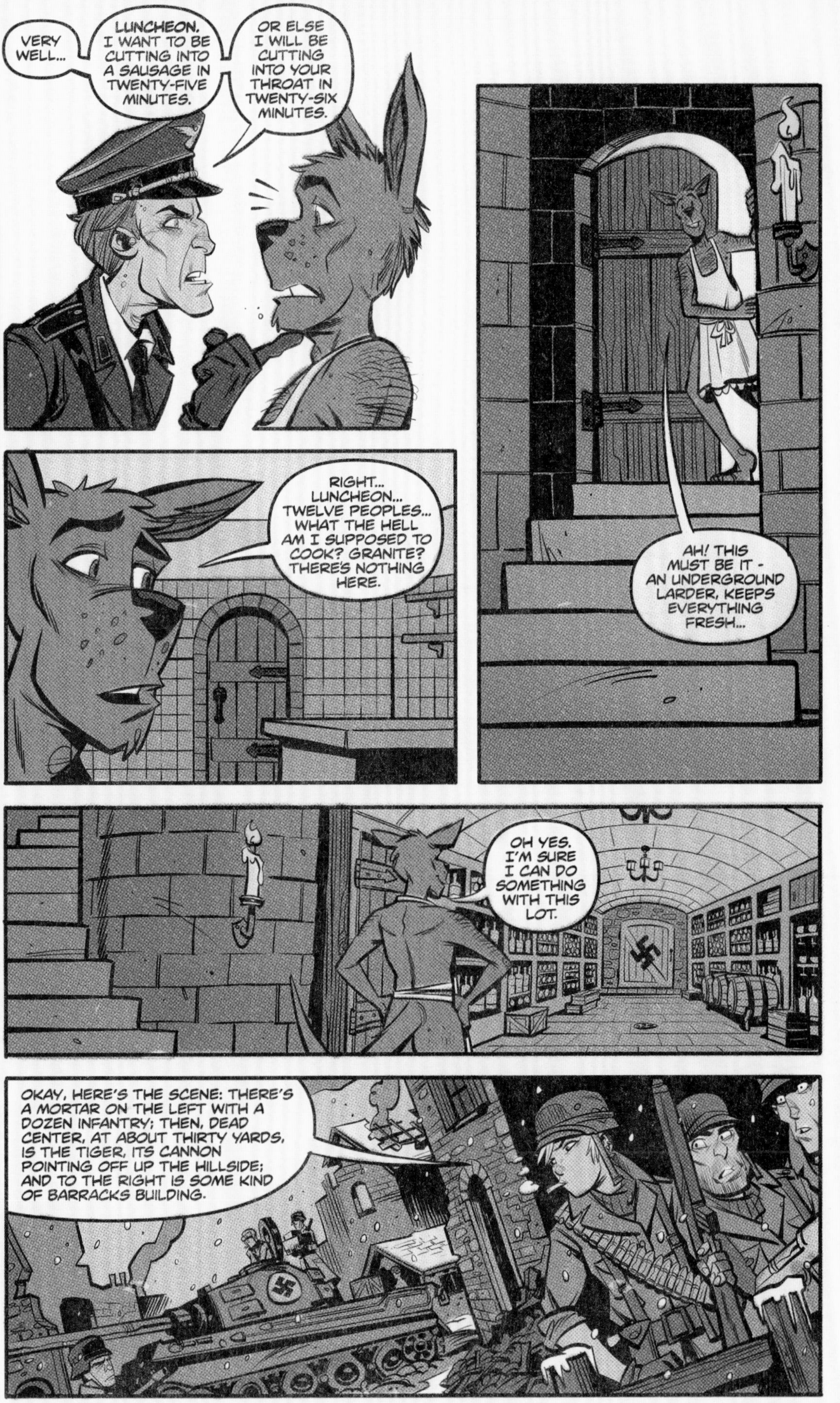
VERY WELL...
LUNCHEON. I WANT TO BE CUTTING INTO A SAUSAGE IN TWENTY-FIVE MINUTES.
OR ELSE I WILL BE CUTTING INTO YOUR THROAT IN TWENTY-SIX MINUTES.
RIGHT... LUNCHEON... TWELVE PEOPLES... WHAT THE HELL AM I SUPPOSED TO COOK? GRANITE? THERE'S NOTHING HERE.
AH! THIS MUST BE IT - AN UNDERGROUND LARDER, KEEPS EVERYTHING FRESH...
OH YES. I'M SURE I CAN DO SOMETHING WITH THIS LOT.
OKAY, HERE'S THE SCENE: THERE'S A MORTAR ON THE LEFT WITH A DOZEN INFANTRY; THEN, DEAD CENTER, AT ABOUT THIRTY YARDS, IS THE TIGER, ITS CANNON POINTING OFF UP THE HILLSIDE; AND TO THE RIGHT IS SOME KIND OF BARRACKS BUILDING.

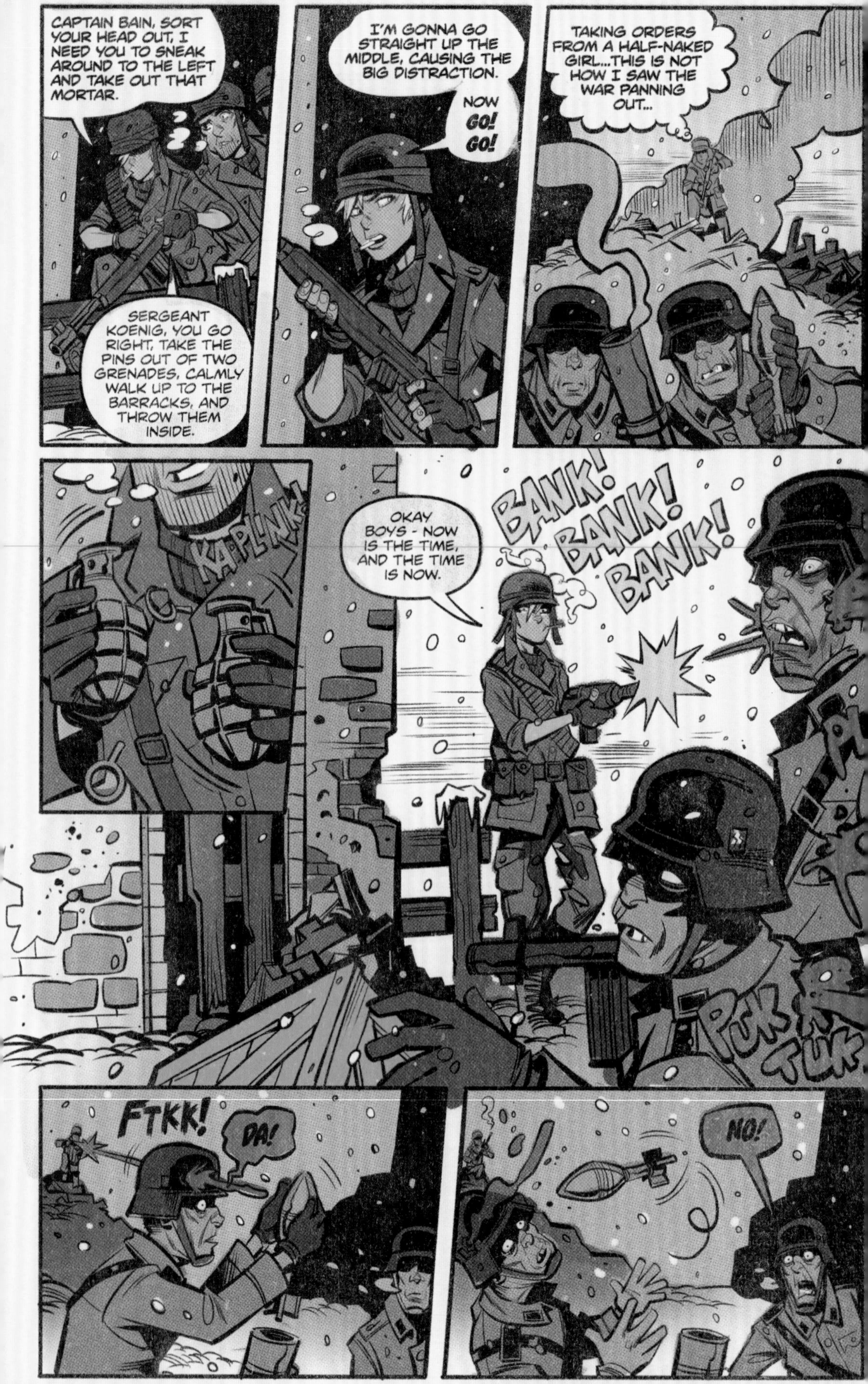
CAPTAIN BAIN, SORT YOUR HEAD OUT, I NEED YOU TO SNEAK AROUND TO THE LEFT AND TAKE OUT THAT MORTAR.
SERGEANT KOENIG, YOU GO RIGHT, TAKE THE PINS OUT OF TWO GRENADES, CALMLY WALK UP TO THE BARRACKS, AND THROW THEM INSIDE.
I'M GONNA GO STRAIGHT UP THE MIDDLE, CAUSING THE BIG DISTRACTION.
NOW GO! GO!
TAKING ORDERS FROM A HALF-NAKED GIRL...THIS IS NOT HOW I SAW THE WAR PANNING OUT...
KAPLINK!
OKAY BOYS - NOW IS THE TIME, AND THE TIME IS NOW.
BANK! BANK! BANK!
PUK TUK
FTKK!
DA!
NO!

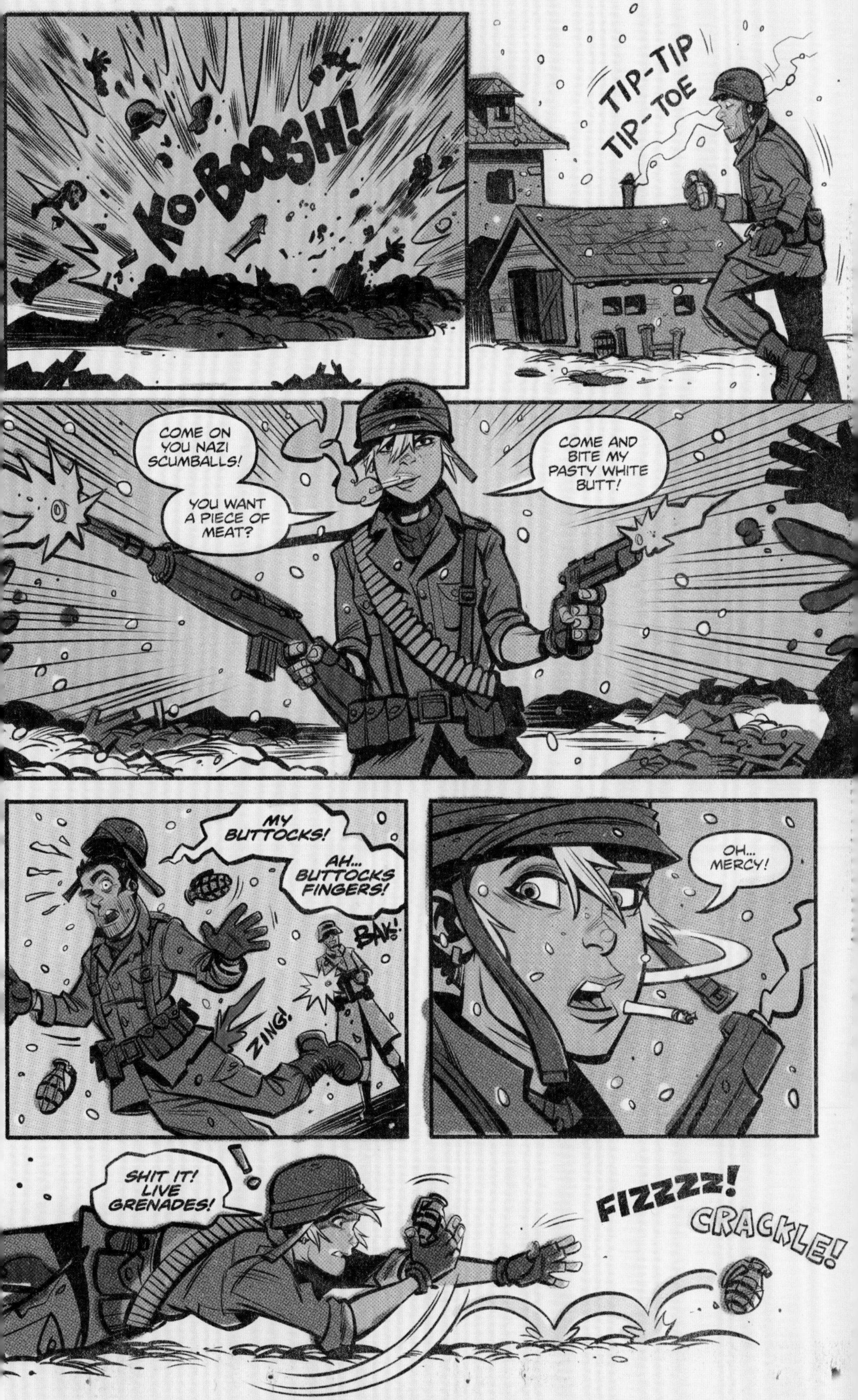
KO-BOOSH!
TIP-TIP
TIP-TOE
COME ON YOU NAZI SCUMBALLS!
YOU WANT A PIECE OF MEAT?
COME AND BITE MY PASTY WHITE BUTT!
MY BUTTOCKS!
AH... BUTTOCKS FINGERS!
BAK!
ZING!
OH... MERCY!
SHIT IT! LIVE GRENADES!
FIZZZZ!
CRACKLE!

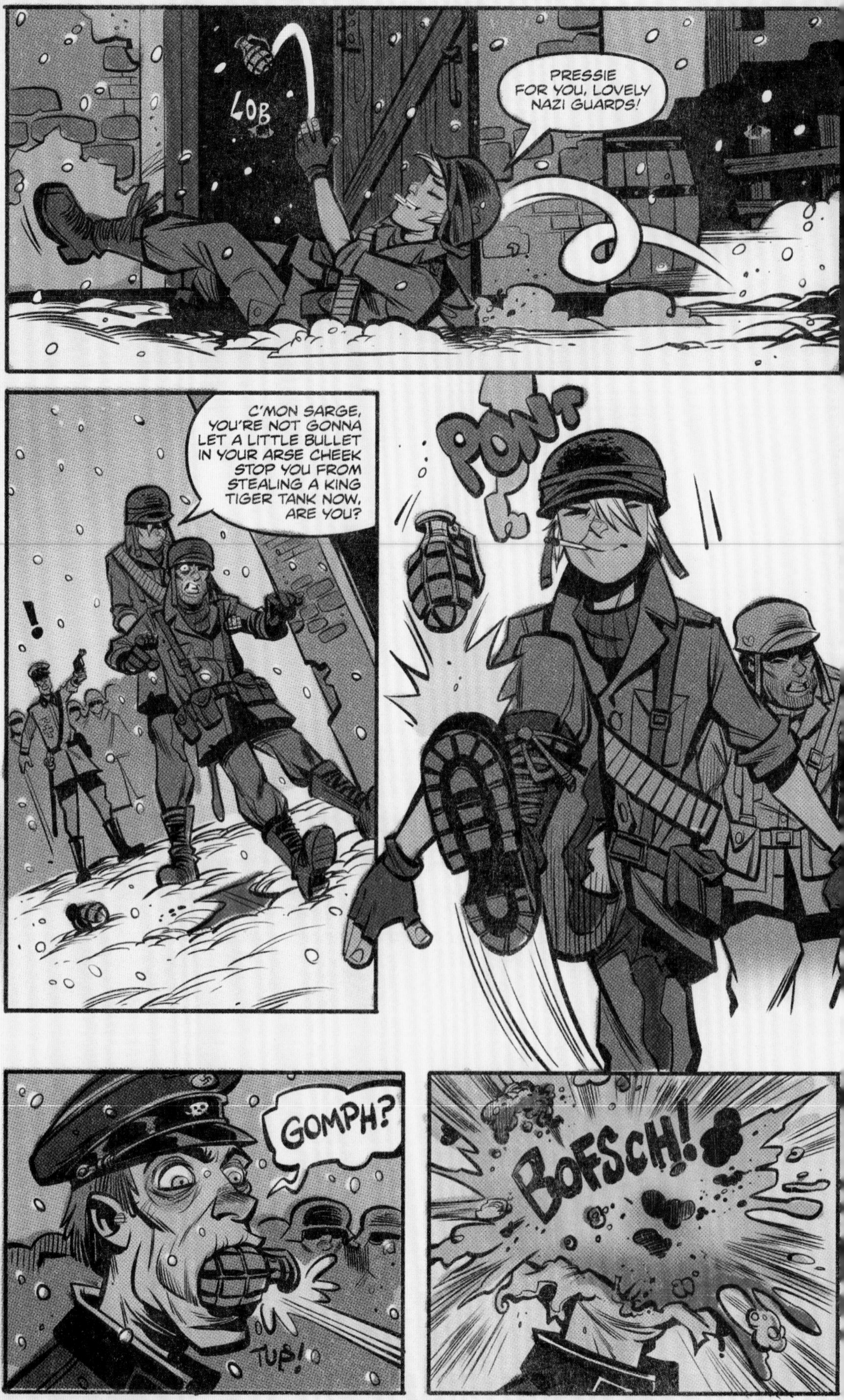
LOB
PRESSIE FOR YOU, LOVELY NAZI GUARDS!
C'MON SARGE, YOU'RE NOT GONNA LET A LITTLE BULLET IN YOUR ARSE CHEEK STOP YOU FROM STEALING A KING TIGER TANK NOW, ARE YOU?
!
PONT
GOMPH?
TUP!
BOFSCH!

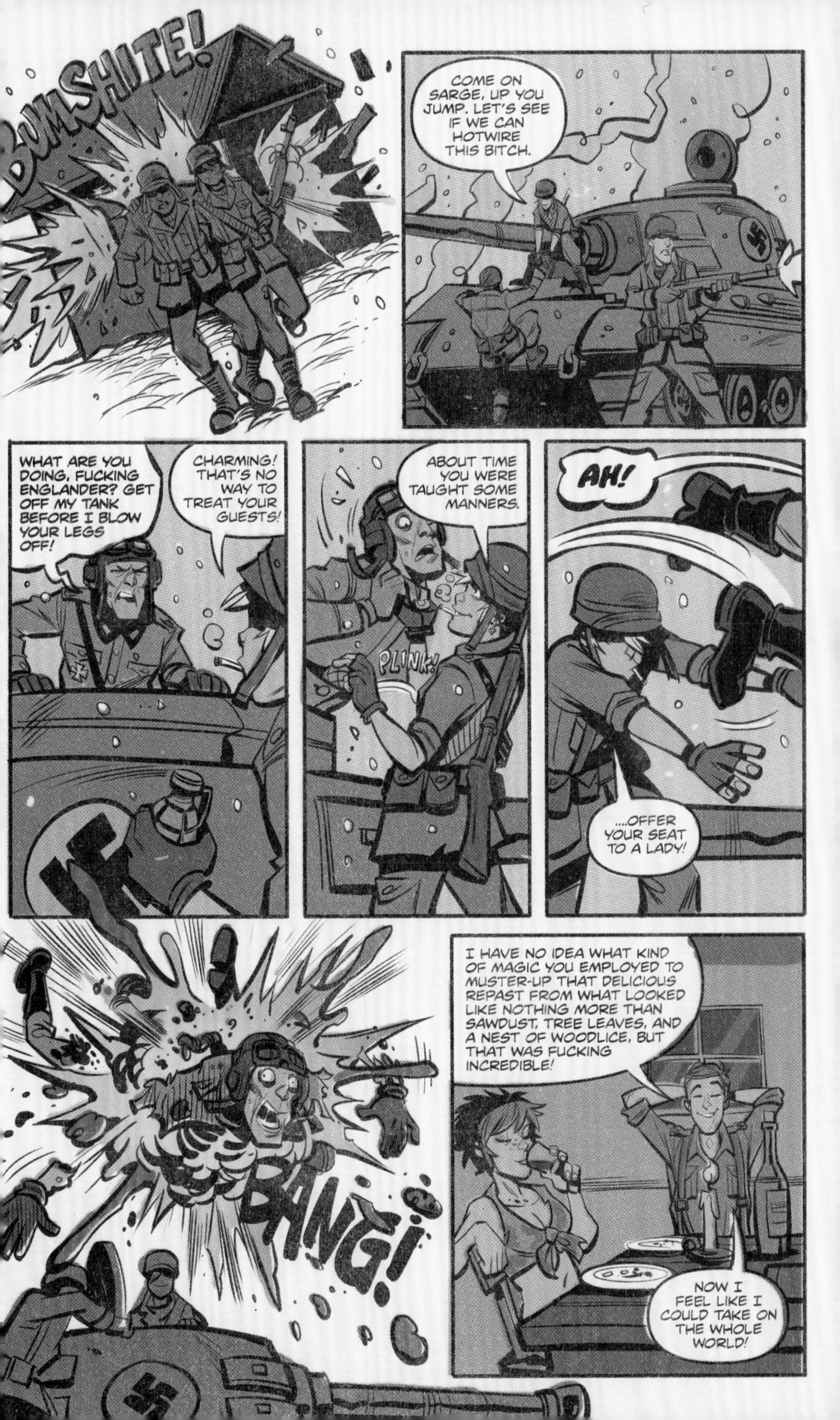
BUMSHITE!
COME ON SARGE, UP YOU JUMP. LET'S SEE IF WE CAN HOTWIRE THIS BITCH.
WHAT ARE YOU DOING, FUCKING ENGLANDER? GET OFF MY TANK BEFORE I BLOW YOUR LEGS OFF!
CHARMING! THAT'S NO WAY TO TREAT YOUR GUESTS!
ABOUT TIME YOU WERE TAUGHT SOME MANNERS.
PLINK!
AH!
....OFFER YOUR SEAT TO A LADY!
BANG!
I HAVE NO IDEA WHAT KIND OF MAGIC YOU EMPLOYED TO MUSTER-UP THAT DELICIOUS REPAST FROM WHAT LOOKED LIKE NOTHING MORE THAN SAWDUST, TREE LEAVES, AND A NEST OF WOODLICE, BUT THAT WAS FUCKING INCREDIBLE!
NOW I FEEL LIKE I COULD TAKE ON THE WHOLE WORLD!

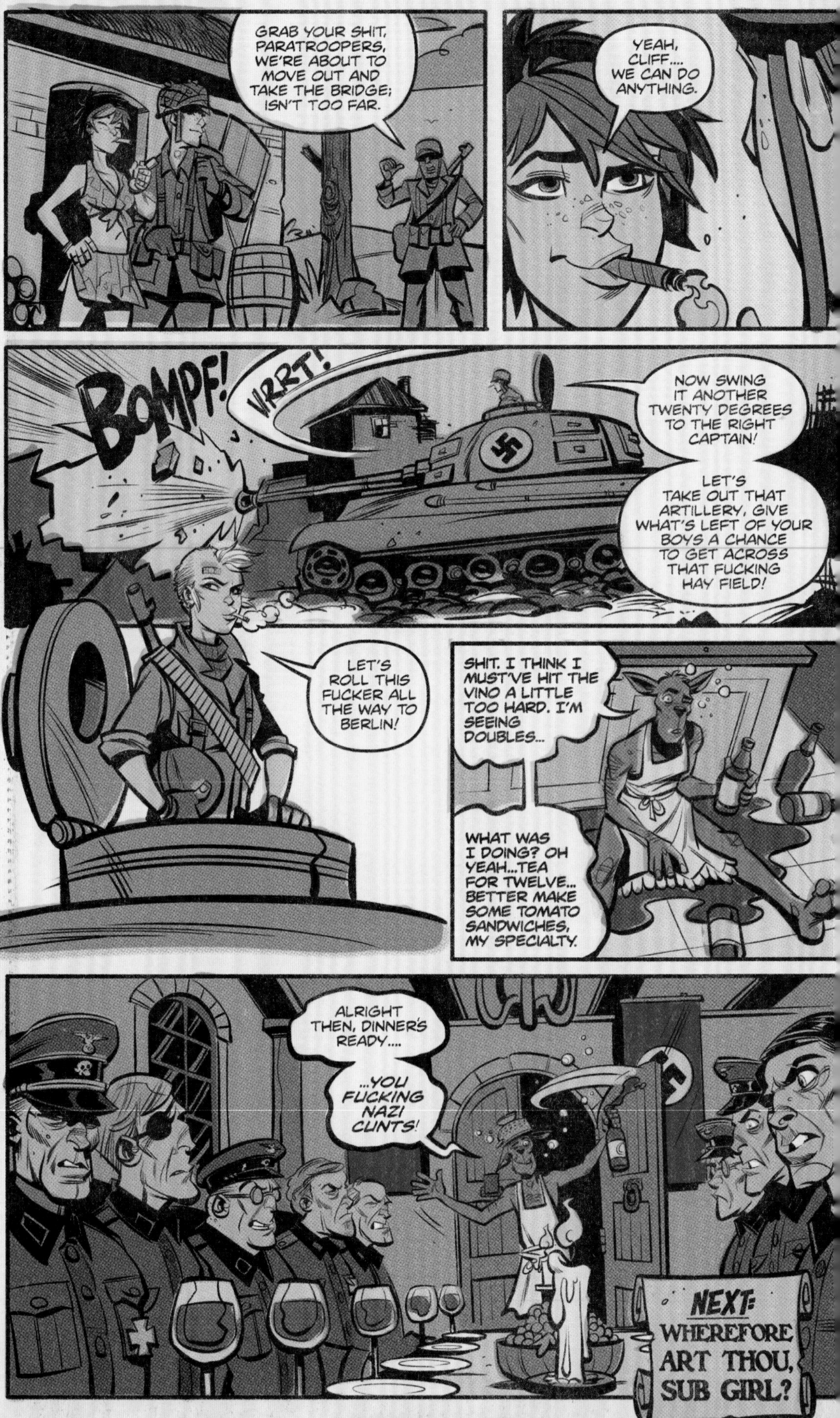

GRAB YOUR SHIT, PARATROOPERS, WE'RE ABOUT TO MOVE OUT AND TAKE THE BRIDGE; ISN'T TOO FAR.
YEAH, CLIFF.... WE CAN DO ANYTHING.
BOMPF!
VRRRT!
NOW SWING IT ANOTHER TWENTY DEGREES TO THE RIGHT CAPTAIN!
LET'S TAKE OUT THAT ARTILLERY, GIVE WHAT'S LEFT OF YOUR BOYS A CHANCE TO GET ACROSS THAT FUCKING HAY FIELD!
LET'S ROLL THIS FUCKER ALL THE WAY TO BERLIN!
SHIT. I THINK I MUST'VE HIT THE VINO A LITTLE TOO HARD. I'M SEEING DOUBLES...
WHAT WAS I DOING? OH YEAH...TEA FOR TWELVE... BETTER MAKE SOME TOMATO SANDWICHES, MY SPECIALTY.
ALRIGHT THEN, DINNER'S READY....
...YOU FUCKING NAZI CUNTS!
NEXT: WHEREFORE ART THOU, SUB GIRL?

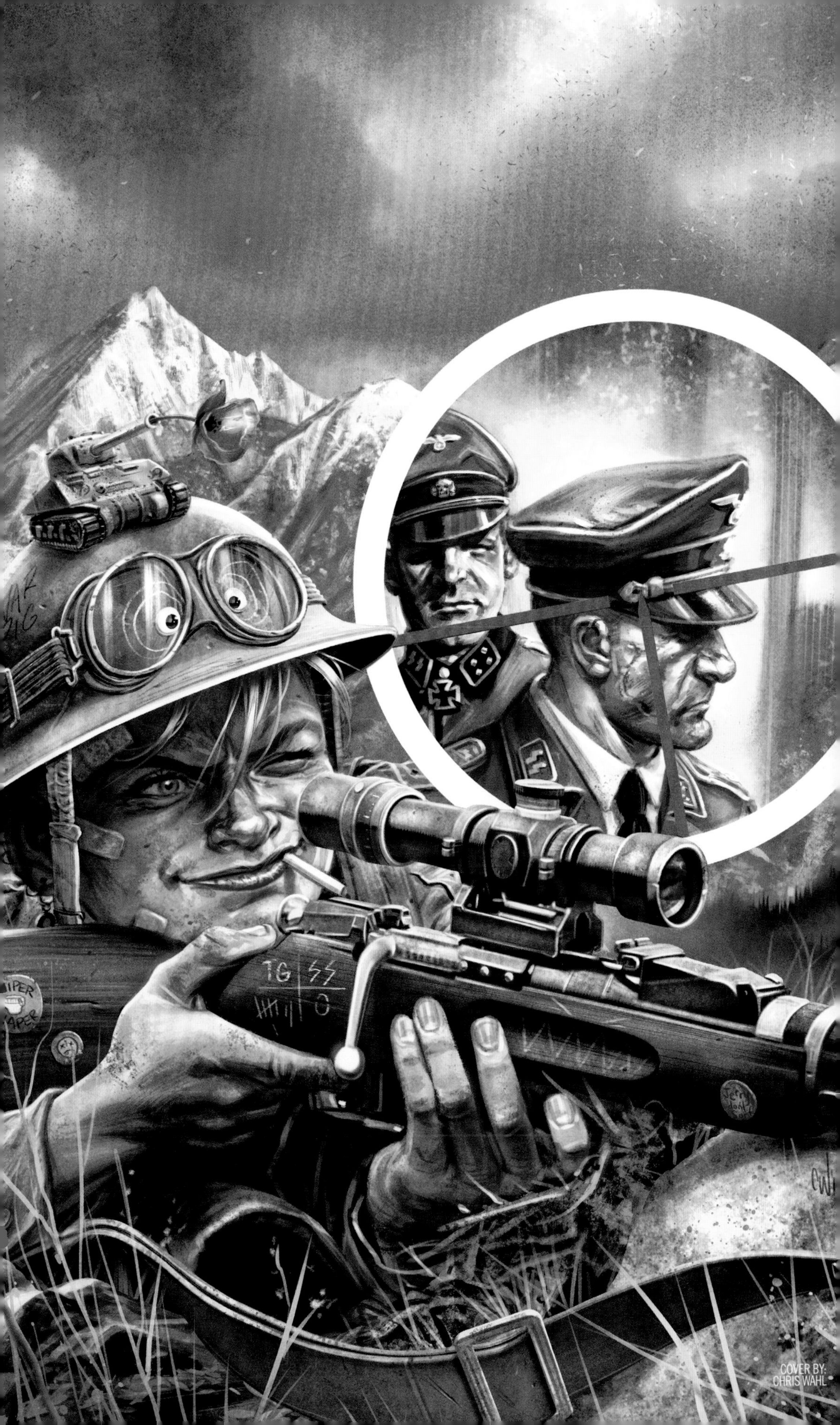
COVER BY:
CHRIS WAHL

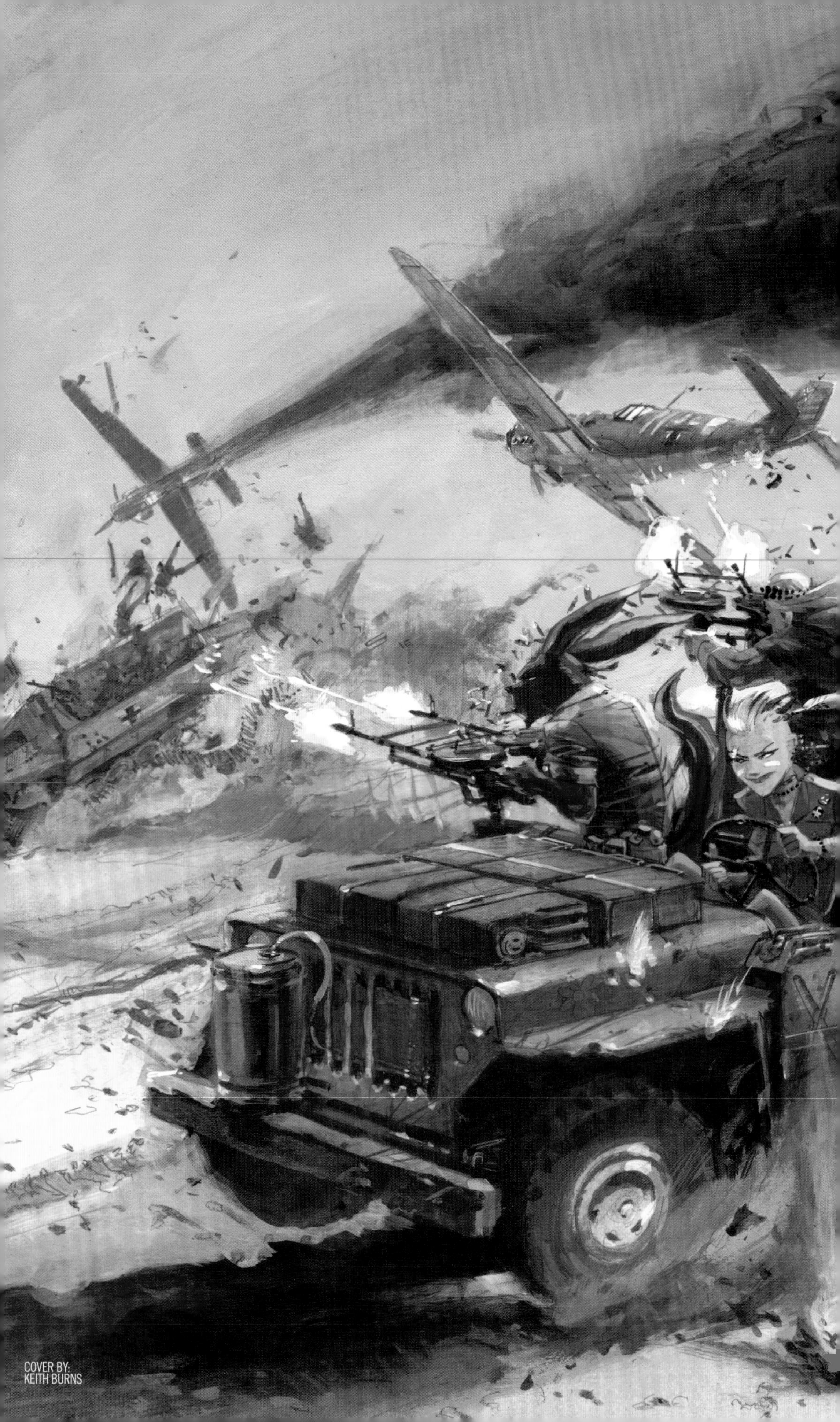

COVER BY:
KEITH BURNS

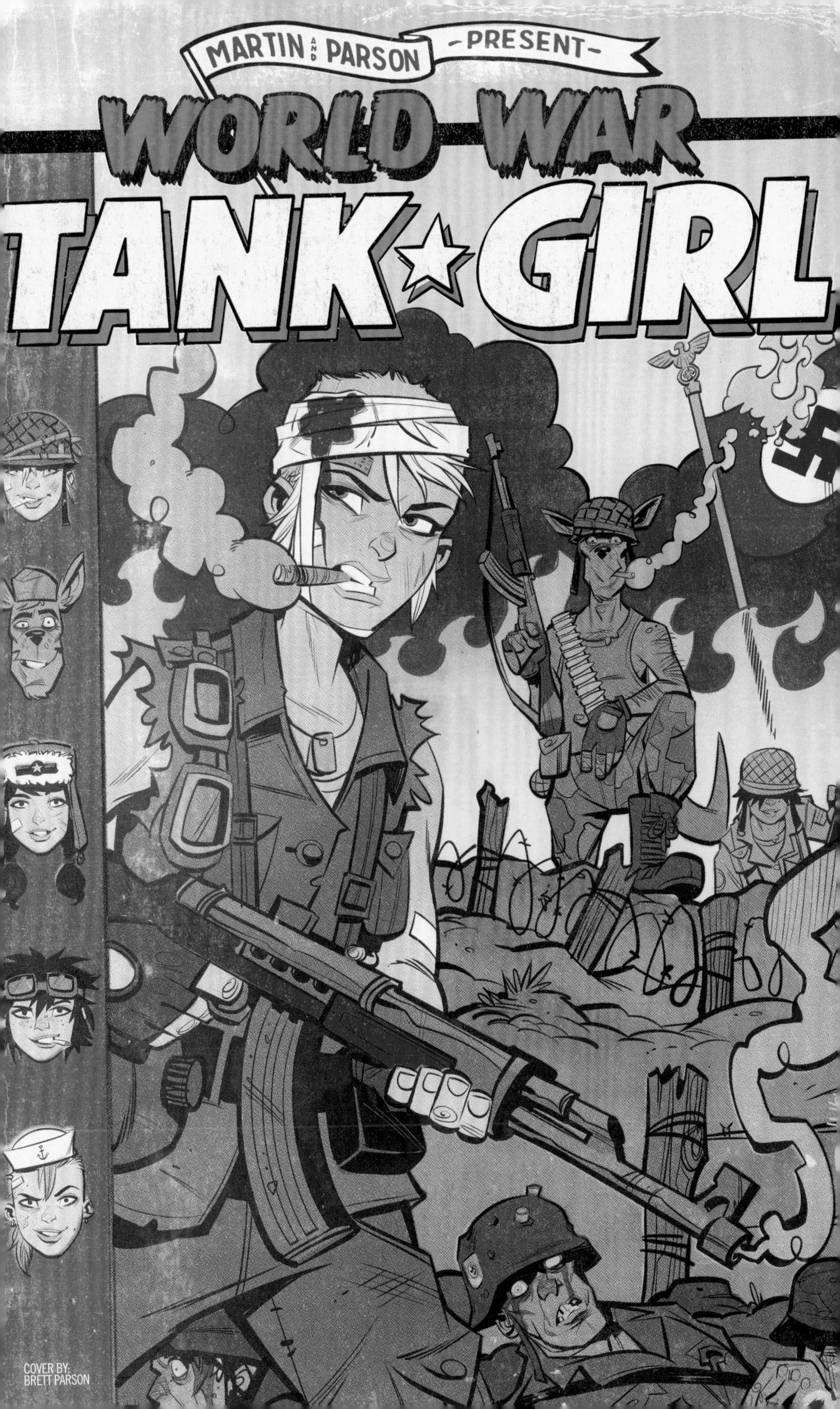
MARTIN AND PARSON
-PRESENT-
WORLD WAR
TANK GIRL
COVER BY:
BRETT PARSON

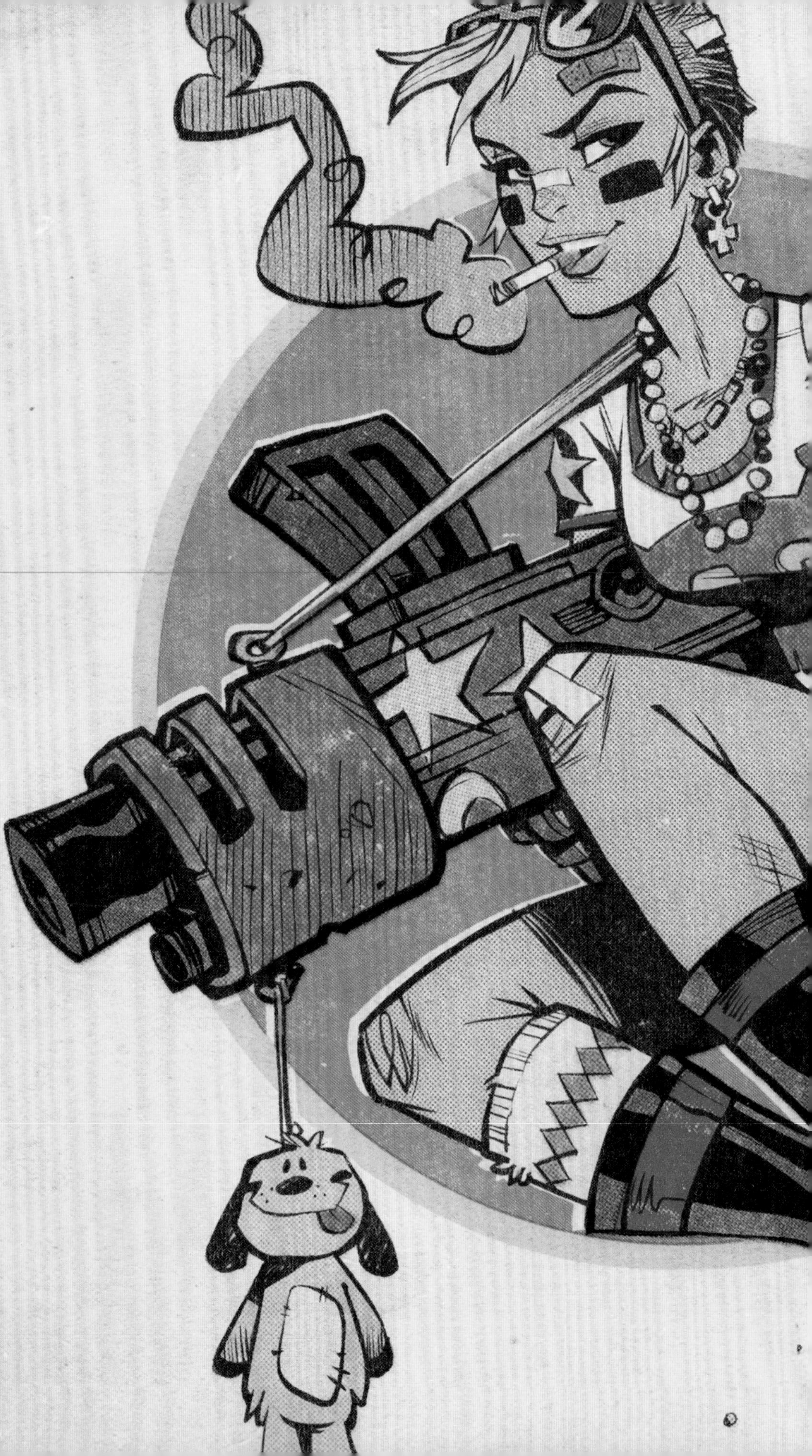

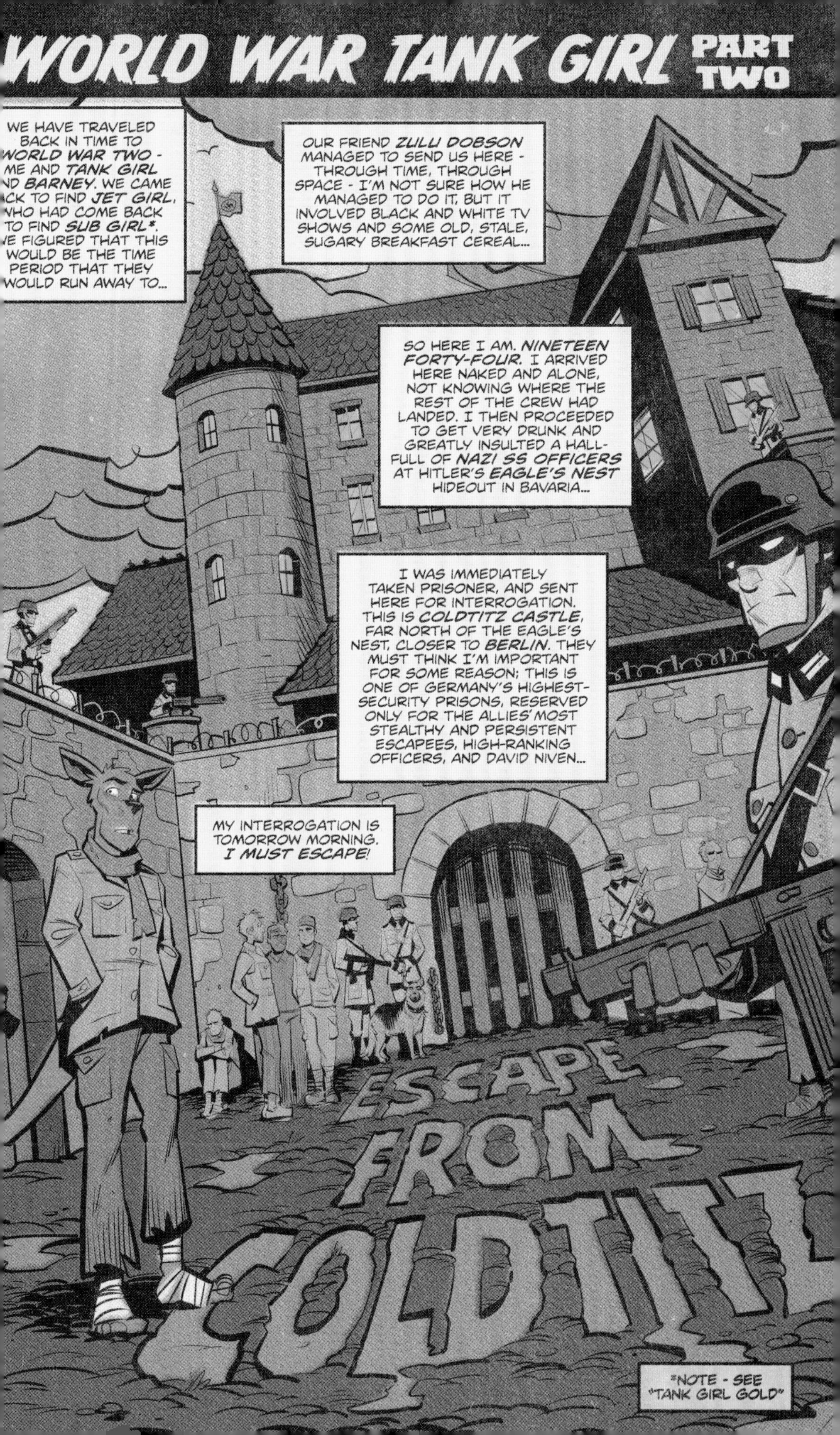
WORLD WAR TANK GIRL PART TWO
WE HAVE TRAVELED BACK IN TIME TO WORLD WAR TWO - ME AND TANK GIRL ND BARNEY. WE CAME CK TO FIND JET GIRL, WHO HAD COME BACK TO FIND SUB GIRL*. WE FIGURED THAT THIS WOULD BE THE TIME PERIOD THAT THEY WOULD RUN AWAY TO...
OUR FRIEND ZULU DOBSON MANAGED TO SEND US HERE - THROUGH TIME, THROUGH SPACE - I'M NOT SURE HOW HE MANAGED TO DO IT, BUT IT INVOLVED BLACK AND WHITE TV SHOWS AND SOME OLD, STALE, SUGARY BREAKFAST CEREAL...
SO HERE I AM. NINETEEN FORTY-FOUR. I ARRIVED HERE NAKED AND ALONE, NOT KNOWING WHERE THE REST OF THE CREW HAD LANDED. I THEN PROCEEDED TO GET VERY DRUNK AND GREATLY INSULTED A HALL-FULL OF NAZI SS OFFICERS AT HITLER'S EAGLE'S NEST HIDEOUT IN BAVARIA...
I WAS IMMEDIATELY TAKEN PRISONER, AND SENT HERE FOR INTERROGATION. THIS IS COLDTITZ CASTLE, FAR NORTH OF THE EAGLE'S NEST, CLOSER TO BERLIN. THEY MUST THINK I'M IMPORTANT FOR SOME REASON; THIS IS ONE OF GERMANY'S HIGHEST-SECURITY PRISONS, RESERVED ONLY FOR THE ALLIES' MOST STEALTHY AND PERSISTENT ESCAPEES, HIGH-RANKING OFFICERS, AND DAVID NIVEN...
MY INTERROGATION IS TOMORROW MORNING. I MUST ESCAPE!
ESCAPE FROM OLDTIT
*NOTE - SEE "TANK GIRL GOLD"

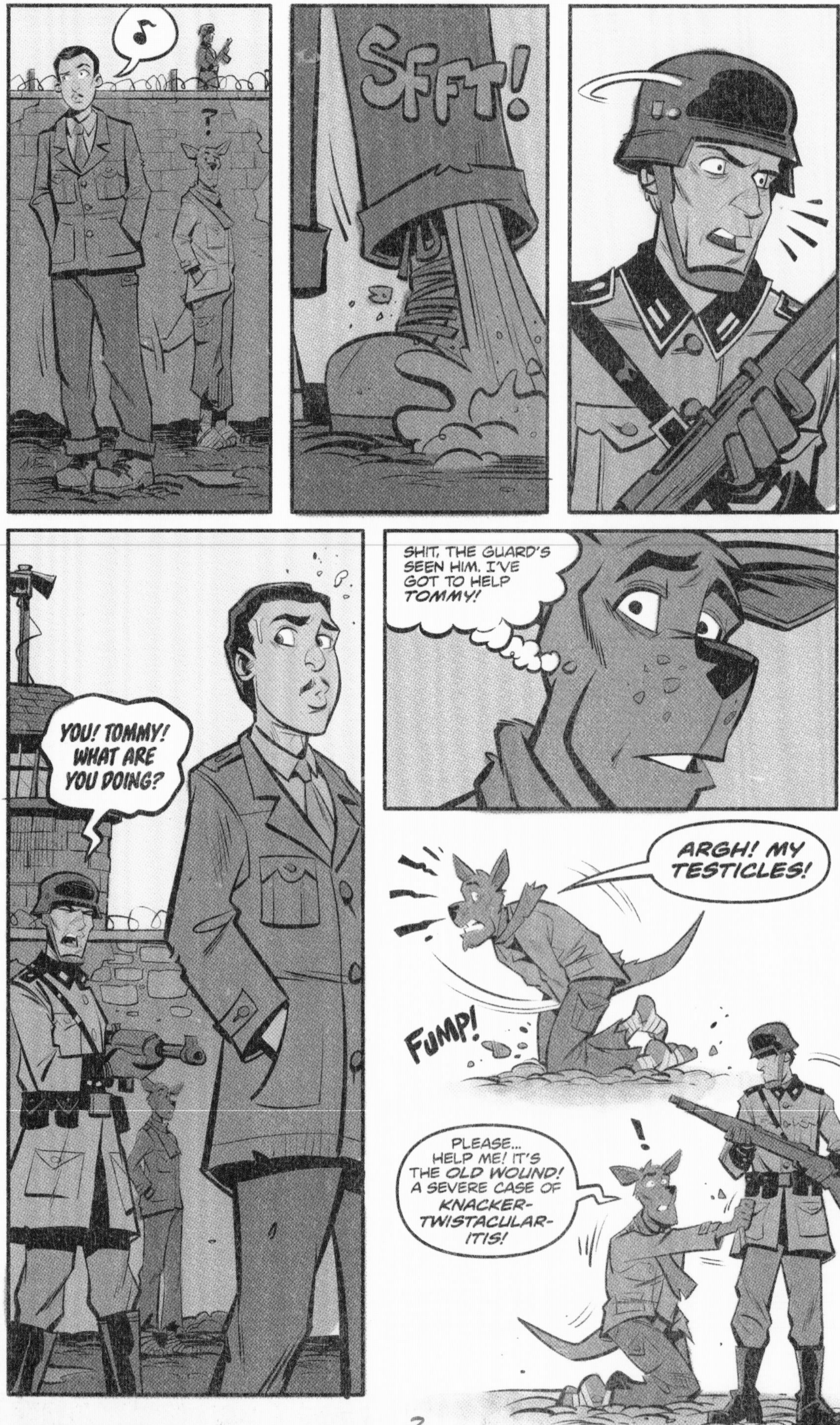
♪
?
SFFT!
YOU! TOMMY! WHAT ARE YOU DOING?
SHIT, THE GUARD'S SEEN HIM. I'VE GOT TO HELP TOMMY!
ARGH! MY TESTICLES!
FUMP!
!
PLEASE... HELP ME! IT'S THE OLD WOUND! A SEVERE CASE OF KNACKER-TWISTACULAR-ITIS!

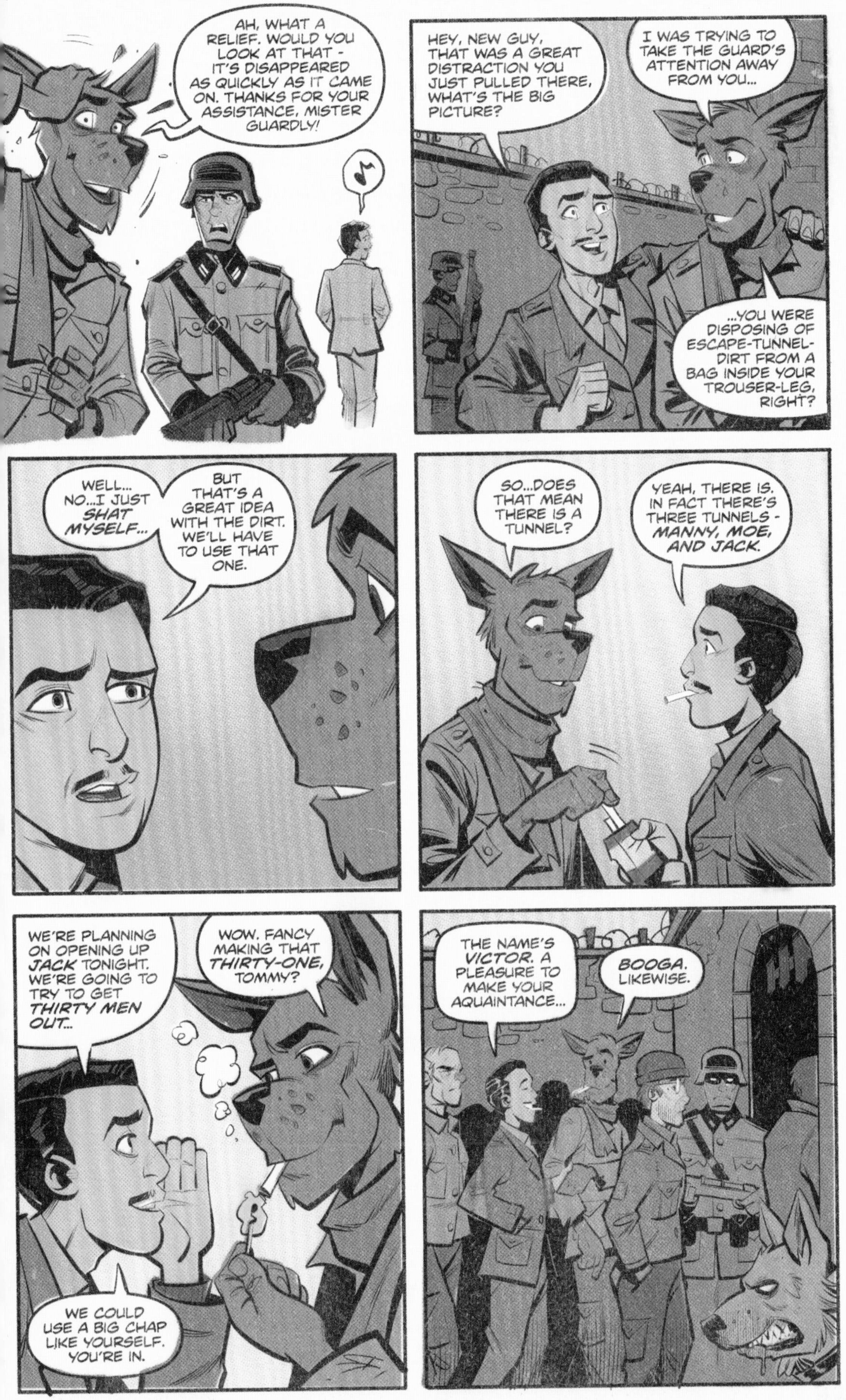
AH, WHAT A RELIEF. WOULD YOU LOOK AT THAT - IT'S DISAPPEARED AS QUICKLY AS IT CAME ON. THANKS FOR YOUR ASSISTANCE, MISTER GUARDLY!
HEY, NEW GUY, THAT WAS A GREAT DISTRACTION YOU JUST PULLED THERE, WHAT'S THE BIG PICTURE?
I WAS TRYING TO TAKE THE GUARD'S ATTENTION AWAY FROM YOU...
...YOU WERE DISPOSING OF ESCAPE-TUNNEL-DIRT FROM A BAG INSIDE YOUR TROUSER-LEG, RIGHT?
WELL... NO...I JUST SHAT MYSELF...
BUT THAT'S A GREAT IDEA WITH THE DIRT. WE'LL HAVE TO USE THAT ONE.
SO...DOES THAT MEAN THERE IS A TUNNEL?
YEAH, THERE IS. IN FACT THERE'S THREE TUNNELS - MANNY, MOE, AND JACK.
WE'RE PLANNING ON OPENING UP JACK TONIGHT. WE'RE GOING TO TRY TO GET THIRTY MEN OUT...
WOW. FANCY MAKING THAT THIRTY-ONE, TOMMY?
WE COULD USE A BIG CHAP LIKE YOURSELF. YOU'RE IN.
THE NAME'S VICTOR. A PLEASURE TO MAKE YOUR AQUAINTANCE...
BOOGA. LIKEWISE.

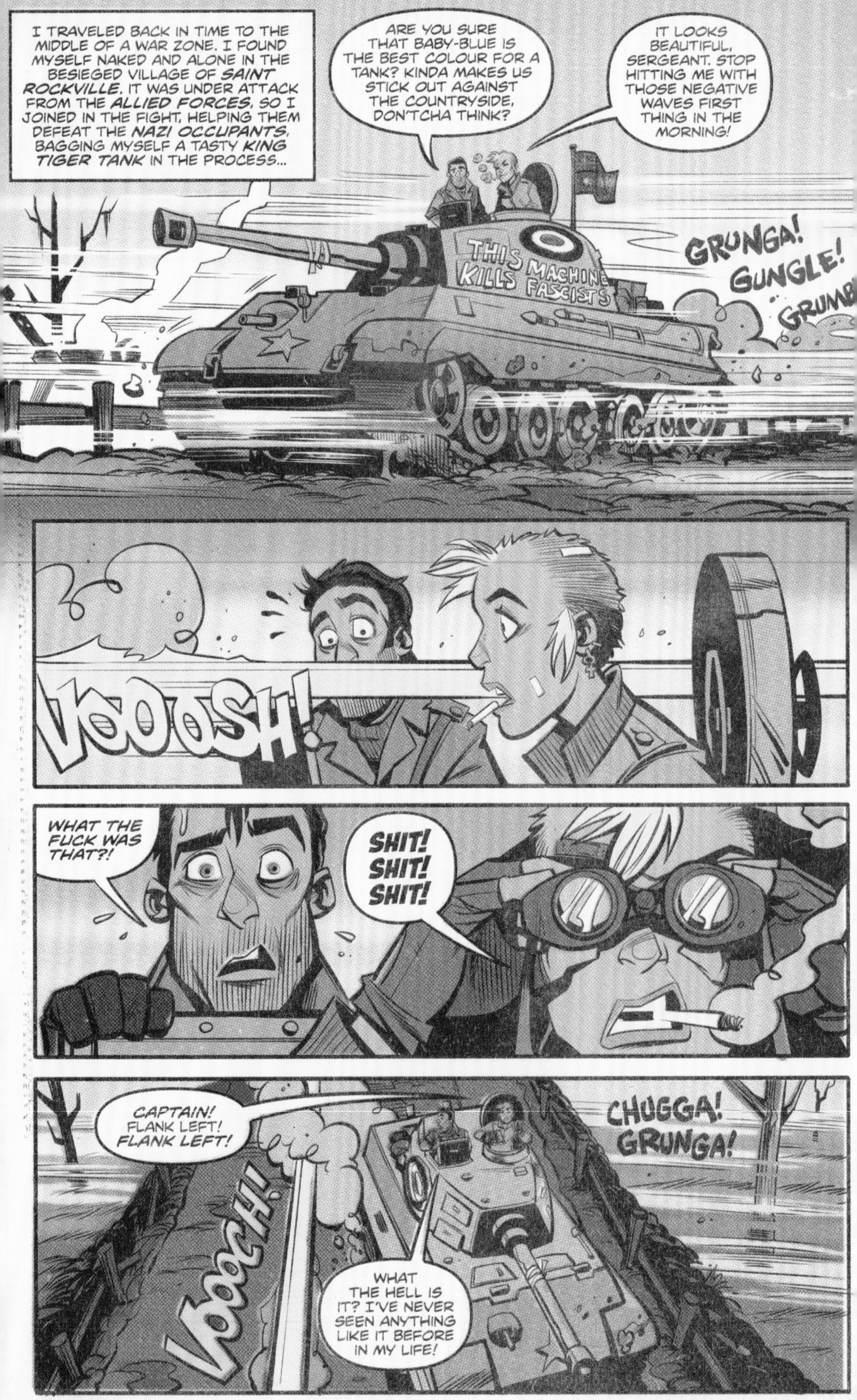
I TRAVELED BACK IN TIME TO THE MIDDLE OF A WAR ZONE. I FOUND MYSELF NAKED AND ALONE IN THE BESIEGED VILLAGE OF SAINT ROCKVILLE. IT WAS UNDER ATTACK FROM THE ALLIED FORCES, SO I JOINED IN THE FIGHT, HELPING THEM DEFEAT THE NAZI OCCUPANTS, BAGGING MYSELF A TASTY KING TIGER TANK IN THE PROCESS...
ARE YOU SURE THAT BABY-BLUE IS THE BEST COLOUR FOR A TANK? KINDA MAKES US STICK OUT AGAINST THE COUNTRYSIDE, DON'TCHA THINK?
IT LOOKS BEAUTIFUL, SERGEANT. STOP HITTING ME WITH THOSE NEGATIVE WAVES FIRST THING IN THE MORNING!
THIS MACHINE KILLS FASCISTS
GRUNGA! GUNGLE! GRUMB
VOOOSH!
WHAT THE FUCK WAS THAT?!
SHIT! SHIT! SHIT!
CAPTAIN! FLANK LEFT! FLANK LEFT!
CHUGGA! GRUNGA!
VOOOCH!
WHAT THE HELL IS IT? I'VE NEVER SEEN ANYTHING LIKE IT BEFORE IN MY LIFE!

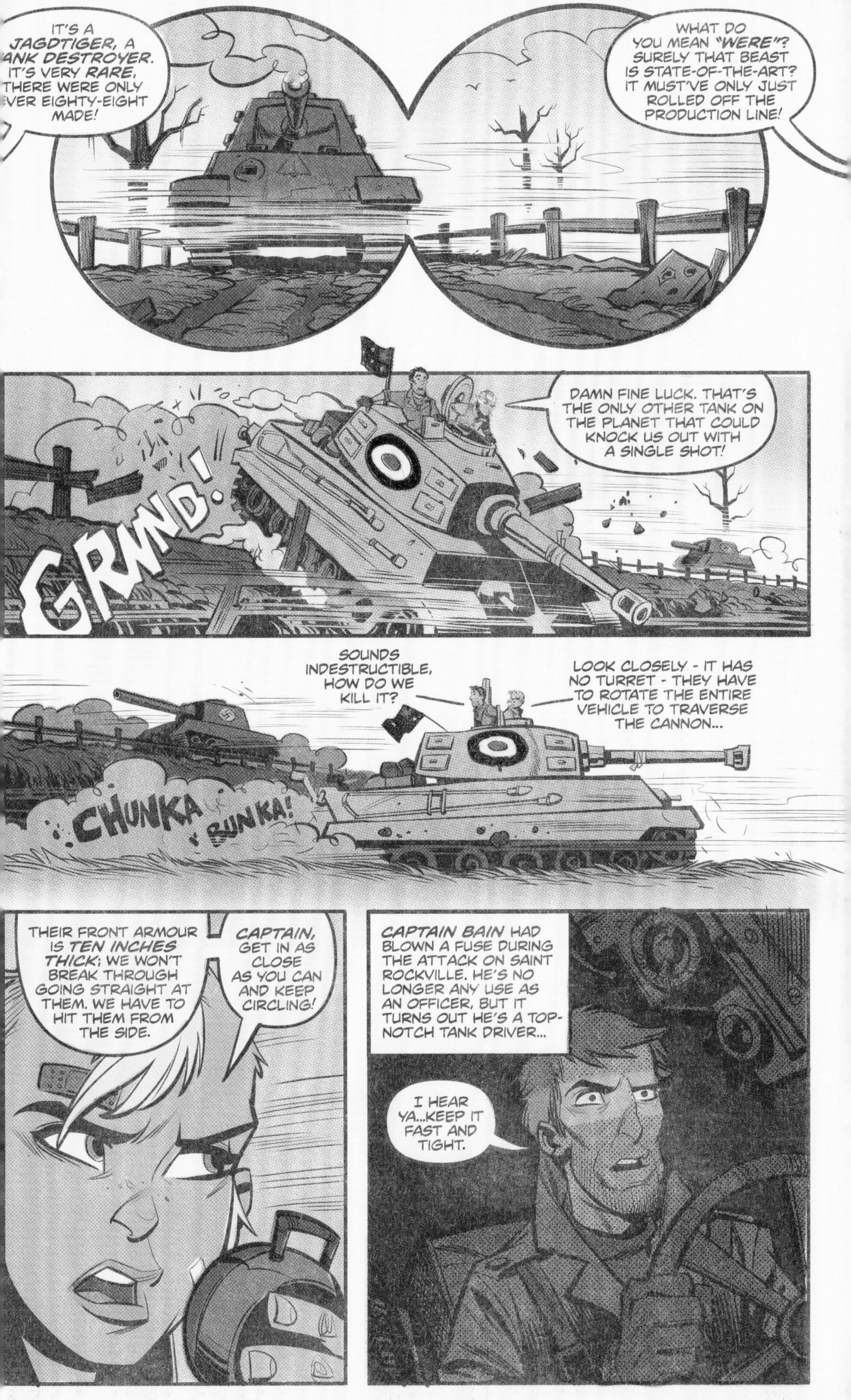
IT'S A JAGDTIGER, A TANK DESTROYER. IT'S VERY RARE, THERE WERE ONLY EVER EIGHTY-EIGHT MADE!
WHAT DO YOU MEAN "WERE"? SURELY THAT BEAST IS STATE-OF-THE-ART? IT MUST'VE ONLY JUST ROLLED OFF THE PRODUCTION LINE!
DAMN FINE LUCK. THAT'S THE ONLY OTHER TANK ON THE PLANET THAT COULD KNOCK US OUT WITH A SINGLE SHOT!
GRNND!
SOUNDS INDESTRUCTIBLE, HOW DO WE KILL IT?
LOOK CLOSELY - IT HAS NO TURRET - THEY HAVE TO ROTATE THE ENTIRE VEHICLE TO TRAVERSE THE CANNON...
CHUNKA
BUNKA!
THEIR FRONT ARMOUR IS TEN INCHES THICK; WE WON'T BREAK THROUGH GOING STRAIGHT AT THEM. WE HAVE TO HIT THEM FROM THE SIDE.
CAPTAIN, GET IN AS CLOSE AS YOU CAN AND KEEP CIRCLING!
CAPTAIN BAIN HAD BLOWN A FUSE DURING THE ATTACK ON SAINT ROCKVILLE. HE'S NO LONGER ANY USE AS AN OFFICER, BUT IT TURNS OUT HE'S A TOP-NOTCH TANK DRIVER...
I HEAR YA...KEEP IT FAST AND TIGHT.

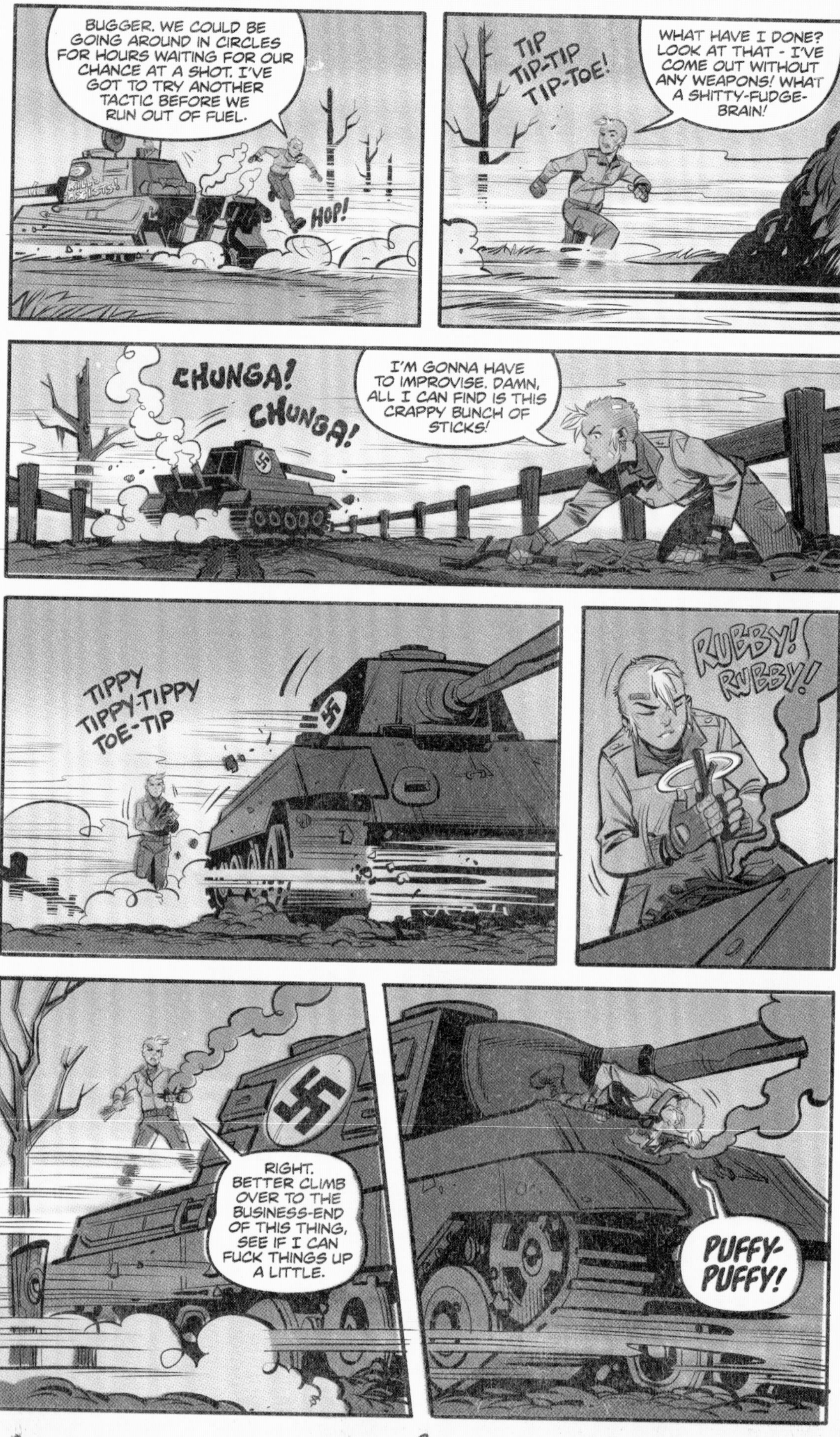
BUGGER. WE COULD BE GOING AROUND IN CIRCLES FOR HOURS WAITING FOR OUR CHANCE AT A SHOT. I'VE GOT TO TRY ANOTHER TACTIC BEFORE WE RUN OUT OF FUEL.
HOP!
TIP TIP-TIP TIP-TOE!
WHAT HAVE I DONE? LOOK AT THAT - I'VE COME OUT WITHOUT ANY WEAPONS! WHAT A SHITTY-FUDGE-BRAIN!
CHUNGA! CHUNGA!
I'M GONNA HAVE TO IMPROVISE. DAMN, ALL I CAN FIND IS THIS CRAPPY BUNCH OF STICKS!
TIPPY TIPPY-TIPPY TOE-TIP
RUBBY! RUBBY!
RIGHT. BETTER CLIMB OVER TO THE BUSINESS-END OF THIS THING, SEE IF I CAN FUCK THINGS UP A LITTLE.
PUFFY-PUFFY!

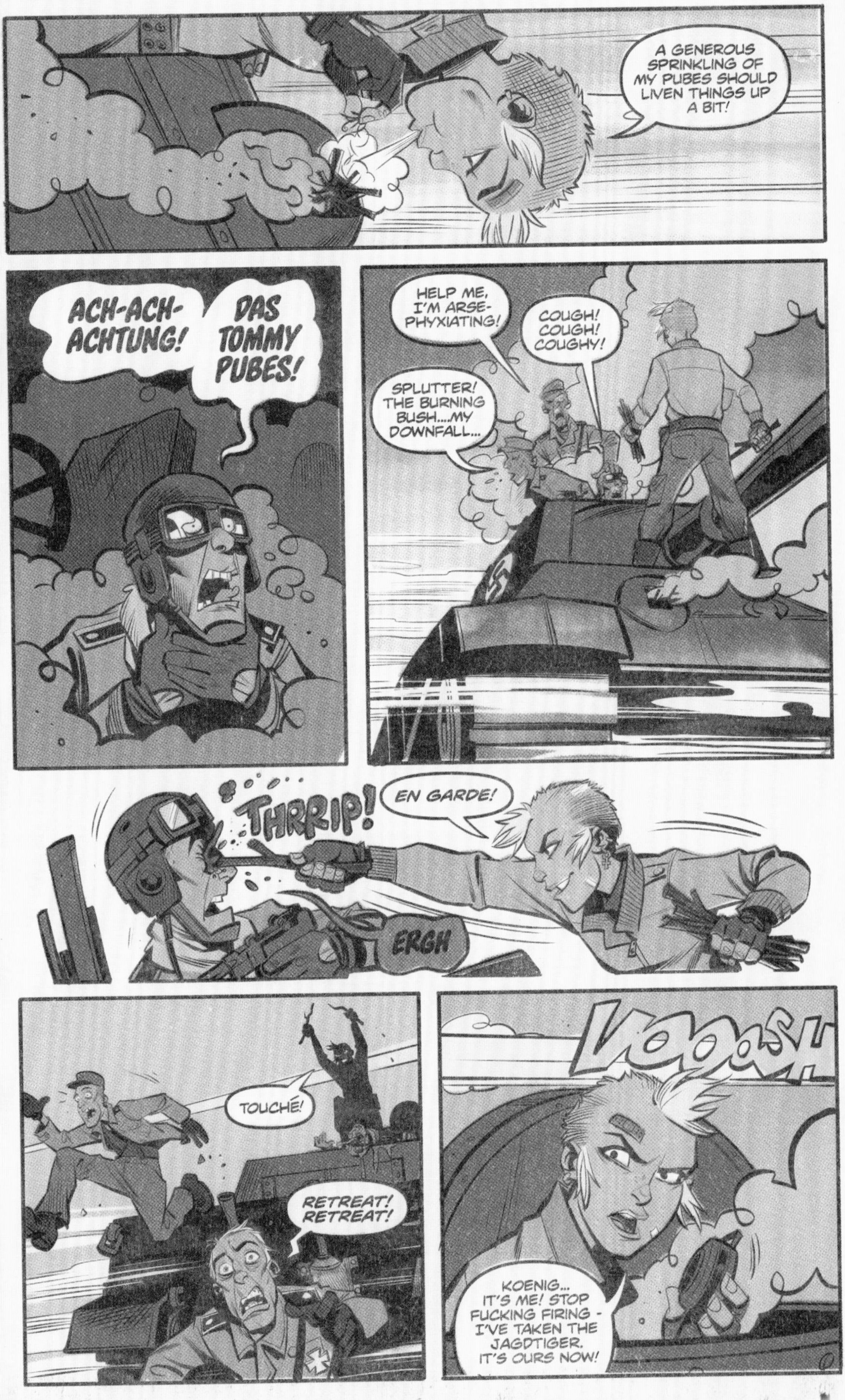
A GENEROUS SPRINKLING OF MY PUBES SHOULD LIVEN THINGS UP A BIT!
ACH-ACH-ACHTUNG!
DAS TOMMY PUBES!
HELP ME, I'M ARSE-PHYXIATING!
COUGH! COUGH! COUGHY!
SPLUTTER! THE BURNING BUSH....MY DOWNFALL...
THRRIP!
EN GARDE!
ERGH
TOUCHÉ!
RETREAT! RETREAT!
VOOSH
KOENIG... IT'S ME! STOP FUCKING FIRING - I'VE TAKEN THE JAGDTIGER. IT'S OURS NOW!

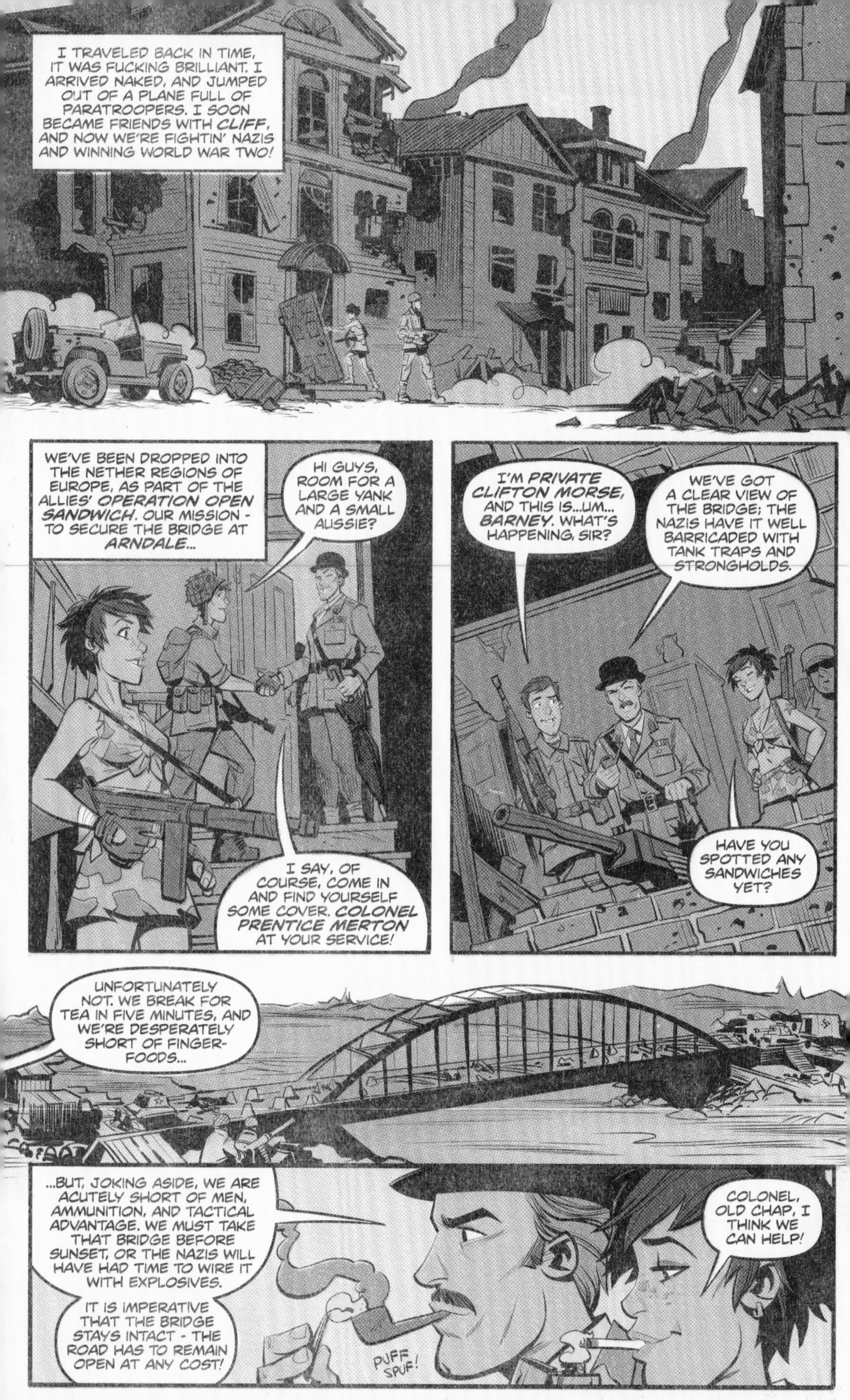

I TRAVELED BACK IN TIME, IT WAS FUCKING BRILLIANT. I ARRIVED NAKED, AND JUMPED OUT OF A PLANE FULL OF PARATROOPERS. I SOON BECAME FRIENDS WITH CLIFF, AND NOW WE'RE FIGHTIN' NAZIS AND WINNING WORLD WAR TWO!
WE'VE BEEN DROPPED INTO THE NETHER REGIONS OF EUROPE, AS PART OF THE ALLIES' OPERATION OPEN SANDWICH. OUR MISSION - TO SECURE THE BRIDGE AT ARNDALE...
HI GUYS, ROOM FOR A LARGE YANK AND A SMALL AUSSIE?
I SAY, OF COURSE, COME IN AND FIND YOURSELF SOME COVER. COLONEL PRENTICE MERTON AT YOUR SERVICE!
I'M PRIVATE CLIFTON MORSE, AND THIS IS...UM... BARNEY. WHAT'S HAPPENING, SIR?
WE'VE GOT A CLEAR VIEW OF THE BRIDGE; THE NAZIS HAVE IT WELL BARRICADED WITH TANK TRAPS AND STRONGHOLDS.
HAVE YOU SPOTTED ANY SANDWICHES YET?
UNFORTUNATELY NOT. WE BREAK FOR TEA IN FIVE MINUTES, AND WE'RE DESPERATELY SHORT OF FINGER-FOODS...
...BUT, JOKING ASIDE, WE ARE ACUTELY SHORT OF MEN, AMMUNITION, AND TACTICAL ADVANTAGE. WE MUST TAKE THAT BRIDGE BEFORE SUNSET, OR THE NAZIS WILL HAVE HAD TIME TO WIRE IT WITH EXPLOSIVES.
IT IS IMPERATIVE THAT THE BRIDGE STAYS INTACT - THE ROAD HAS TO REMAIN OPEN AT ANY COST!
PUFF SPUF!
COLONEL, OLD CHAP, I THINK WE CAN HELP!

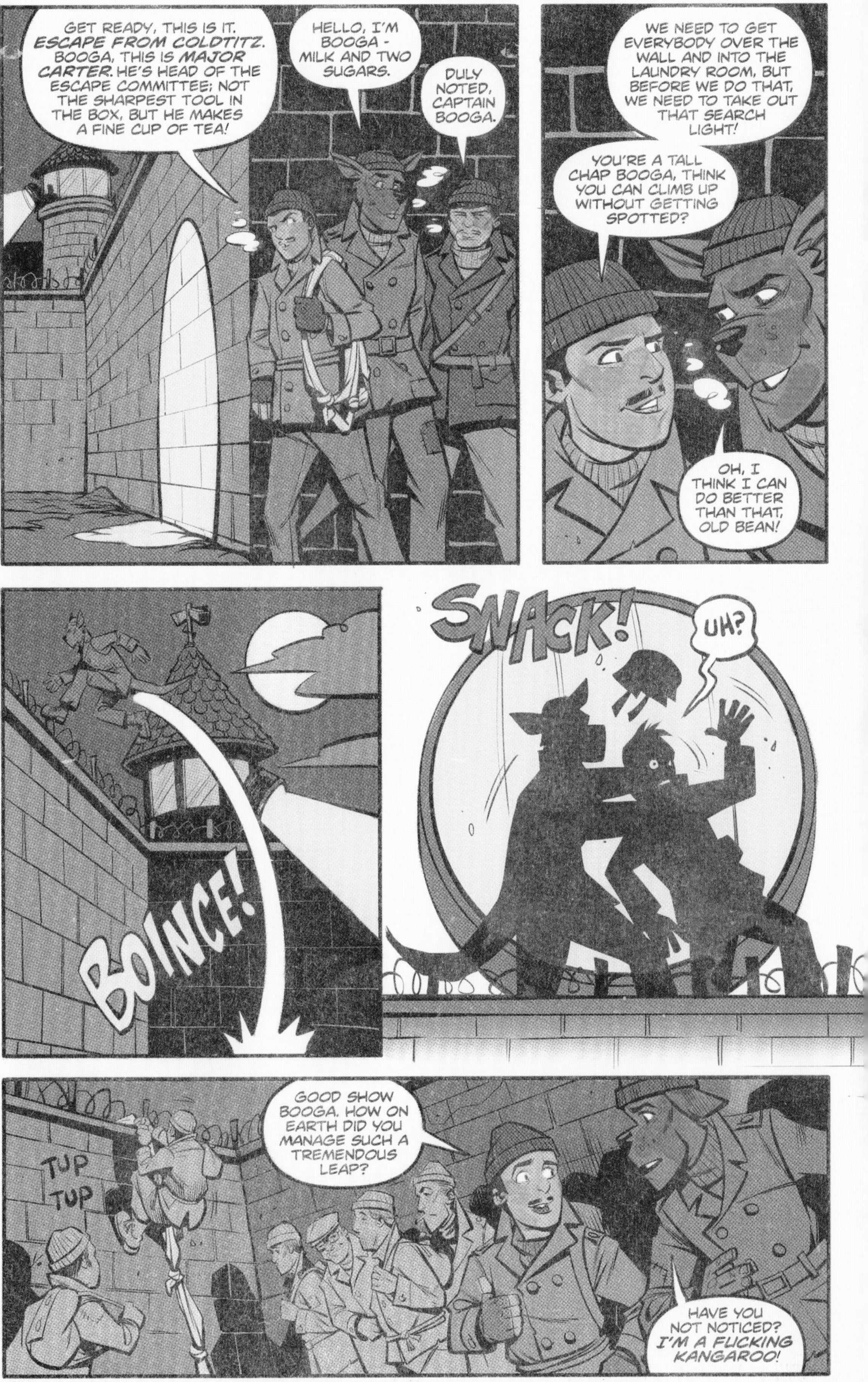
GET READY, THIS IS IT. ESCAPE FROM COLDTITZ. BOOGA, THIS IS MAJOR CARTER. HE'S HEAD OF THE ESCAPE COMMITTEE; NOT THE SHARPEST TOOL IN THE BOX, BUT HE MAKES A FINE CUP OF TEA!
HELLO, I'M BOOGA - MILK AND TWO SUGARS.
DULY NOTED, CAPTAIN BOOGA.
WE NEED TO GET EVERYBODY OVER THE WALL AND INTO THE LAUNDRY ROOM, BUT BEFORE WE DO THAT, WE NEED TO TAKE OUT THAT SEARCH LIGHT!
YOU'RE A TALL CHAP BOOGA, THINK YOU CAN CLIMB UP WITHOUT GETTING SPOTTED?
OH, I THINK I CAN DO BETTER THAN THAT, OLD BEAN!
BOINCE!
SNACK!
UH?
TUP TUP
GOOD SHOW BOOGA. HOW ON EARTH DID YOU MANAGE SUCH A TREMENDOUS LEAP?
HAVE YOU NOT NOTICED? I'M A FUCKING KANGAROO!

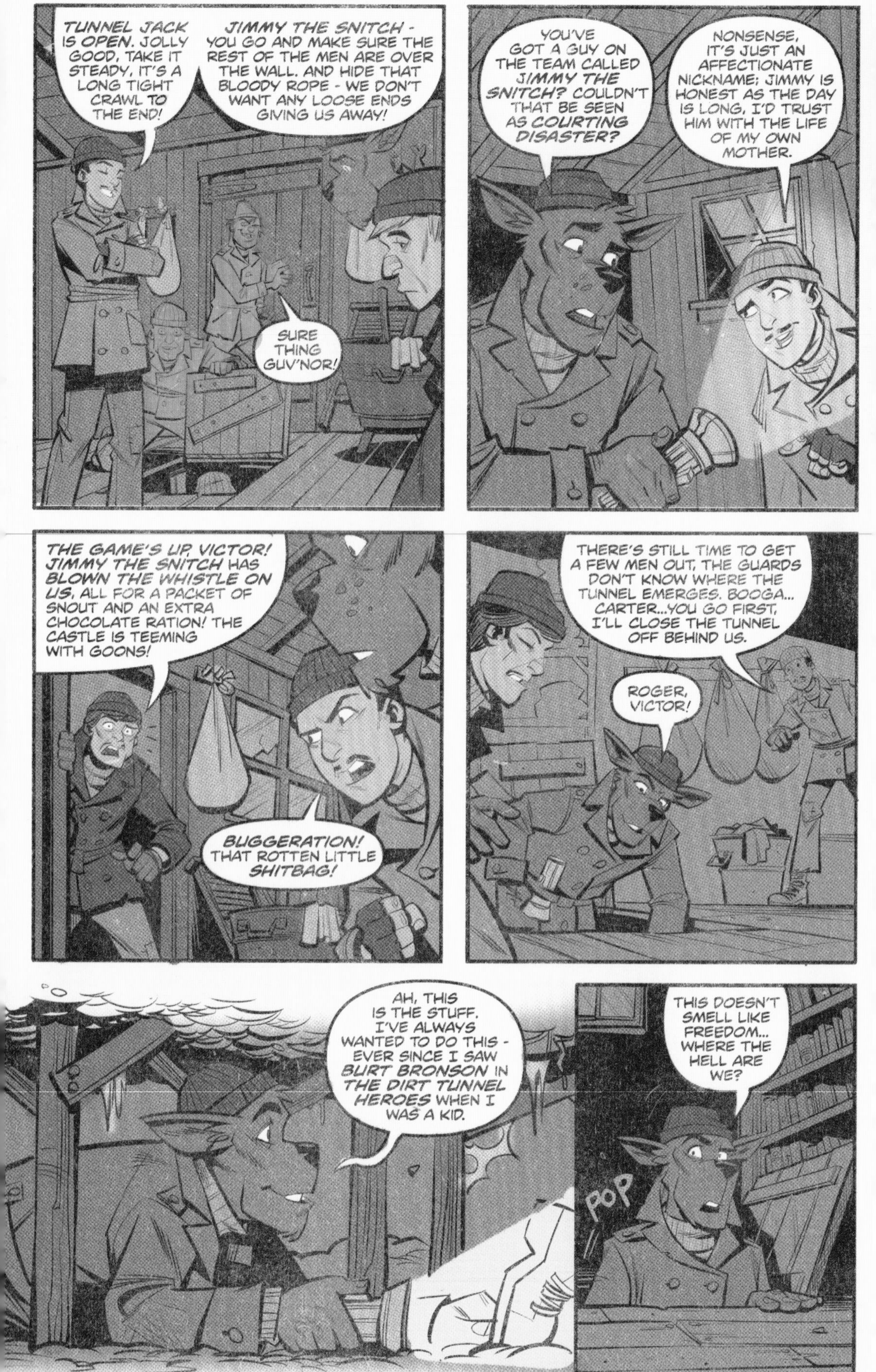
TUNNEL JACK IS OPEN. JOLLY GOOD, TAKE IT STEADY, IT'S A LONG TIGHT CRAWL TO THE END!
JIMMY THE SNITCH - YOU GO AND MAKE SURE THE REST OF THE MEN ARE OVER THE WALL. AND HIDE THAT BLOODY ROPE - WE DON'T WANT ANY LOOSE ENDS GIVING US AWAY!
SURE THING GUV'NOR!
YOU'VE GOT A GUY ON THE TEAM CALLED JIMMY THE SNITCH? COULDN'T THAT BE SEEN AS COURTING DISASTER?
NONSENSE, IT'S JUST AN AFFECTIONATE NICKNAME; JIMMY IS HONEST AS THE DAY IS LONG. I'D TRUST HIM WITH THE LIFE OF MY OWN MOTHER.
THE GAME'S UP, VICTOR! JIMMY THE SNITCH HAS BLOWN THE WHISTLE ON US, ALL FOR A PACKET OF SNOUT AND AN EXTRA CHOCOLATE RATION! THE CASTLE IS TEEMING WITH GOONS!
BUGGERATION! THAT ROTTEN LITTLE SHITBAG!
THERE'S STILL TIME TO GET A FEW MEN OUT, THE GUARDS DON'T KNOW WHERE THE TUNNEL EMERGES. BOOGA... CARTER...YOU GO FIRST, I'LL CLOSE THE TUNNEL OFF BEHIND US.
ROGER, VICTOR!
AH, THIS IS THE STUFF. I'VE ALWAYS WANTED TO DO THIS - EVER SINCE I SAW BURT BRONSON IN THE DIRT TUNNEL HEROES WHEN I WAS A KID.
POP
THIS DOESN'T SMELL LIKE FREEDOM... WHERE THE HELL ARE WE?

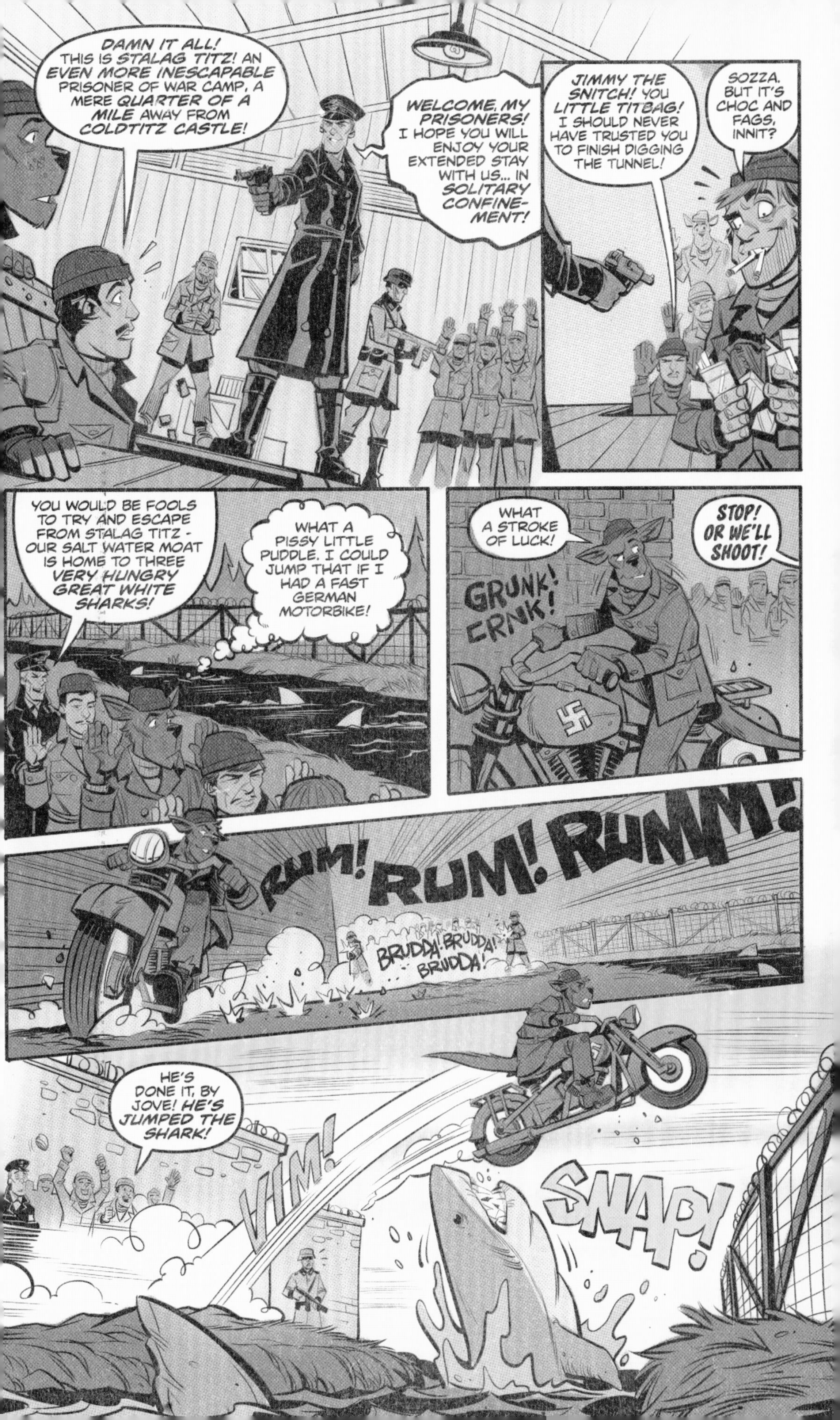
DAMN IT ALL! THIS IS STALAG TITZ! AN EVEN MORE INESCAPABLE PRISONER OF WAR CAMP, A MERE QUARTER OF A MILE AWAY FROM COLDTITZ CASTLE!
WELCOME, MY PRISONERS! I HOPE YOU WILL ENJOY YOUR EXTENDED STAY WITH US... IN SOLITARY CONFINE-MENT!
JIMMY THE SNITCH! YOU LITTLE TITBAG! I SHOULD NEVER HAVE TRUSTED YOU TO FINISH DIGGING THE TUNNEL!
SOZZA. BUT IT'S CHOC AND FAGS, INNIT?
YOU WOULD BE FOOLS TO TRY AND ESCAPE FROM STALAG TITZ - OUR SALT WATER MOAT IS HOME TO THREE VERY HUNGRY GREAT WHITE SHARKS!
WHAT A PISSY LITTLE PUDDLE. I COULD JUMP THAT IF I HAD A FAST GERMAN MOTORBIKE!
WHAT A STROKE OF LUCK!
STOP! OR WE'LL SHOOT!
GRUNK! CRNK!
RUM! RUM! RUMM!
BRUDDA! BRUDDA! BRUDDA!
HE'S DONE IT, BY JOVE! HE'S JUMPED THE SHARK!
VHM!
SNAP!

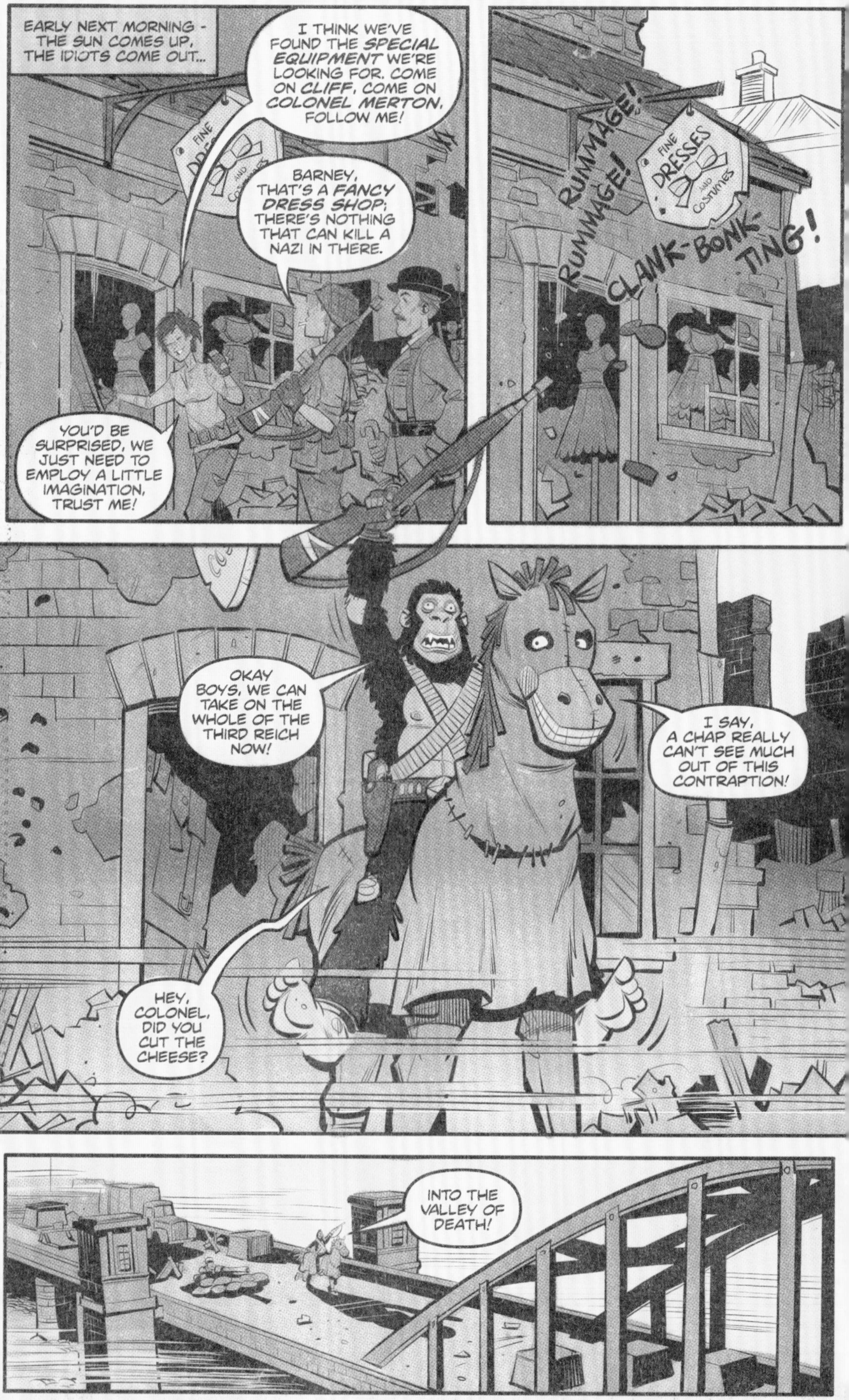
EARLY NEXT MORNING - THE SUN COMES UP, THE IDIOTS COME OUT...
I THINK WE'VE FOUND THE SPECIAL EQUIPMENT WE'RE LOOKING FOR. COME ON CLIFF, COME ON COLONEL MERTON, FOLLOW ME!
FINE DRESSES AND COSTUMES
BARNEY, THAT'S A FANCY DRESS SHOP; THERE'S NOTHING THAT CAN KILL A NAZI IN THERE.
YOU'D BE SURPRISED, WE JUST NEED TO EMPLOY A LITTLE IMAGINATION, TRUST ME!
RUMMAGE!
RUMMAGE!
CLANK-BONK-TING!
OKAY BOYS, WE CAN TAKE ON THE WHOLE OF THE THIRD REICH NOW!
I SAY, A CHAP REALLY CAN'T SEE MUCH OUT OF THIS CONTRAPTION!
HEY, COLONEL, DID YOU CUT THE CHEESE?
INTO THE VALLEY OF DEATH!

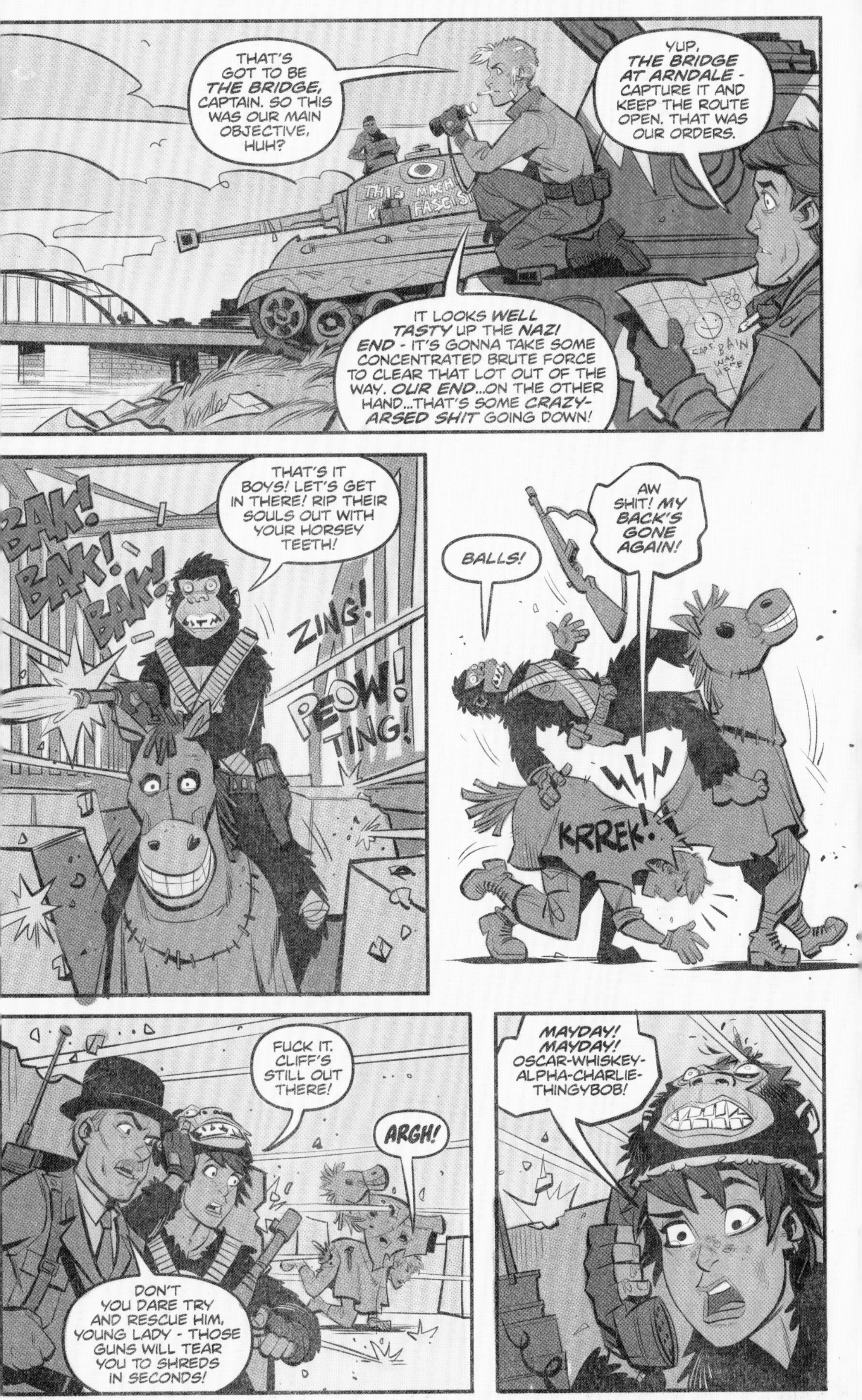
THAT'S GOT TO BE THE BRIDGE, CAPTAIN. SO THIS WAS OUR MAIN OBJECTIVE, HUH?
YUP, THE BRIDGE AT ARNDALE - CAPTURE IT AND KEEP THE ROUTE OPEN. THAT WAS OUR ORDERS.
IT LOOKS WELL TASTY UP THE NAZI END - IT'S GONNA TAKE SOME CONCENTRATED BRUTE FORCE TO CLEAR THAT LOT OUT OF THE WAY. OUR END...ON THE OTHER HAND...THAT'S SOME CRAZY-ARSED SHIT GOING DOWN!
BAK! BAK! BAK!
THAT'S IT BOYS! LET'S GET IN THERE! RIP THEIR SOULS OUT WITH YOUR HORSEY TEETH!
ZING!
PEOW!
TING!
BALLS!
AW SHIT! MY BACK'S GONE AGAIN!
KRREK!
FUCK IT. CLIFF'S STILL OUT THERE!
ARGH!
DON'T YOU DARE TRY AND RESCUE HIM, YOUNG LADY - THOSE GUNS WILL TEAR YOU TO SHREDS IN SECONDS!
MAYDAY! MAYDAY! OSCAR-WHISKEY-ALPHA-CHARLIE-THINGYBOB!

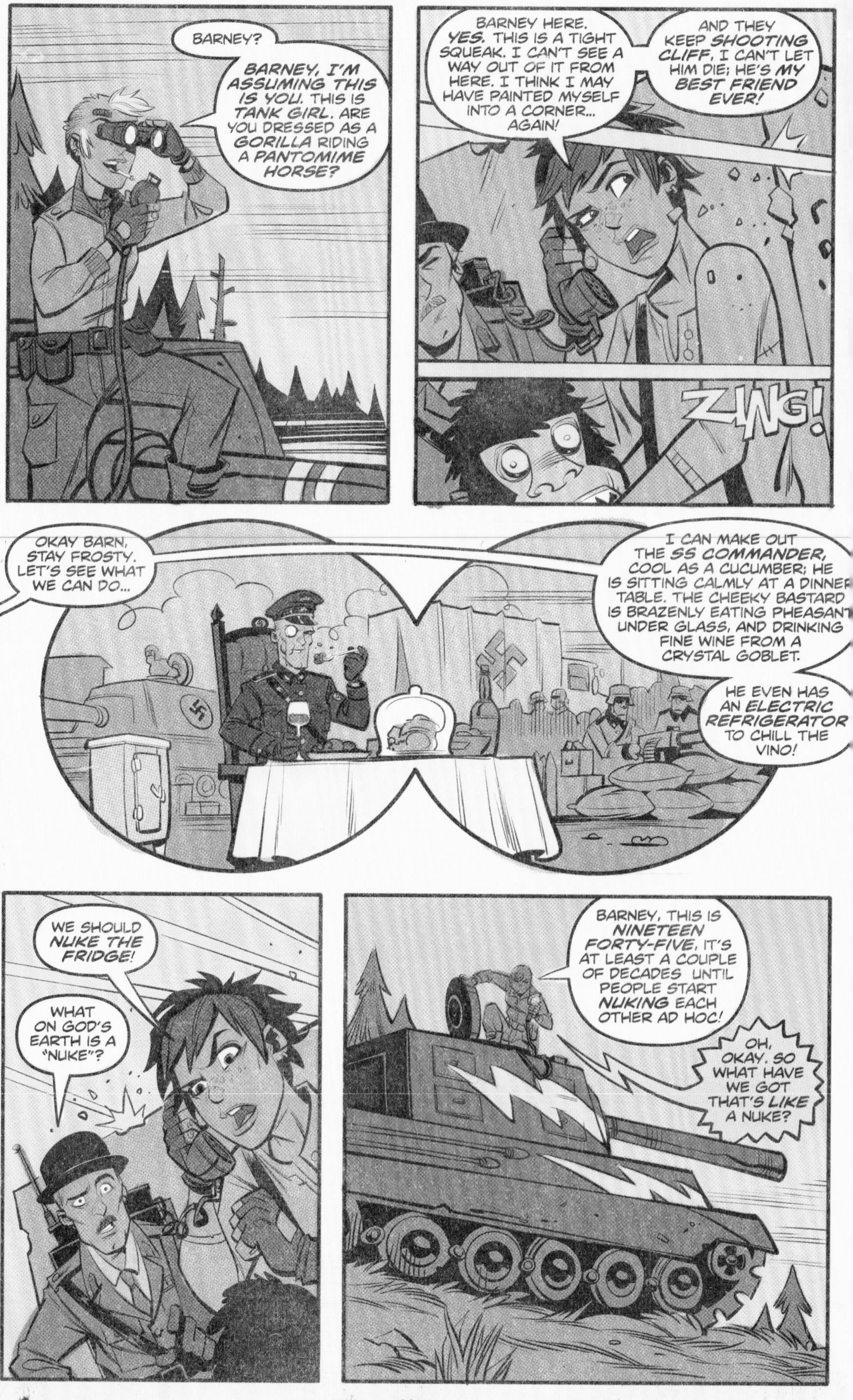

BARNEY?
BARNEY, I'M ASSUMING THIS IS YOU. THIS IS TANK GIRL. ARE YOU DRESSED AS A GORILLA RIDING A PANTOMIME HORSE?
BARNEY HERE. YES. THIS IS A TIGHT SQUEAK. I CAN'T SEE A WAY OUT OF IT FROM HERE. I THINK I MAY HAVE PAINTED MYSELF INTO A CORNER... AGAIN!
AND THEY KEEP SHOOTING CLIFF, I CAN'T LET HIM DIE; HE'S MY BEST FRIEND EVER!
ZING!
OKAY BARN, STAY FROSTY. LET'S SEE WHAT WE CAN DO...
I CAN MAKE OUT THE SS COMMANDER, COOL AS A CUCUMBER; HE IS SITTING CALMLY AT A DINNER TABLE. THE CHEEKY BASTARD IS BRAZENLY EATING PHEASANT UNDER GLASS, AND DRINKING FINE WINE FROM A CRYSTAL GOBLET.
HE EVEN HAS AN ELECTRIC REFRIGERATOR TO CHILL THE VINO!
WE SHOULD NUKE THE FRIDGE!
WHAT ON GOD'S EARTH IS A "NUKE"?
BARNEY, THIS IS NINETEEN FORTY-FIVE, IT'S AT LEAST A COUPLE OF DECADES UNTIL PEOPLE START NUKING EACH OTHER AD HOC!
OH, OKAY. SO WHAT HAVE WE GOT THAT'S LIKE A NUKE?

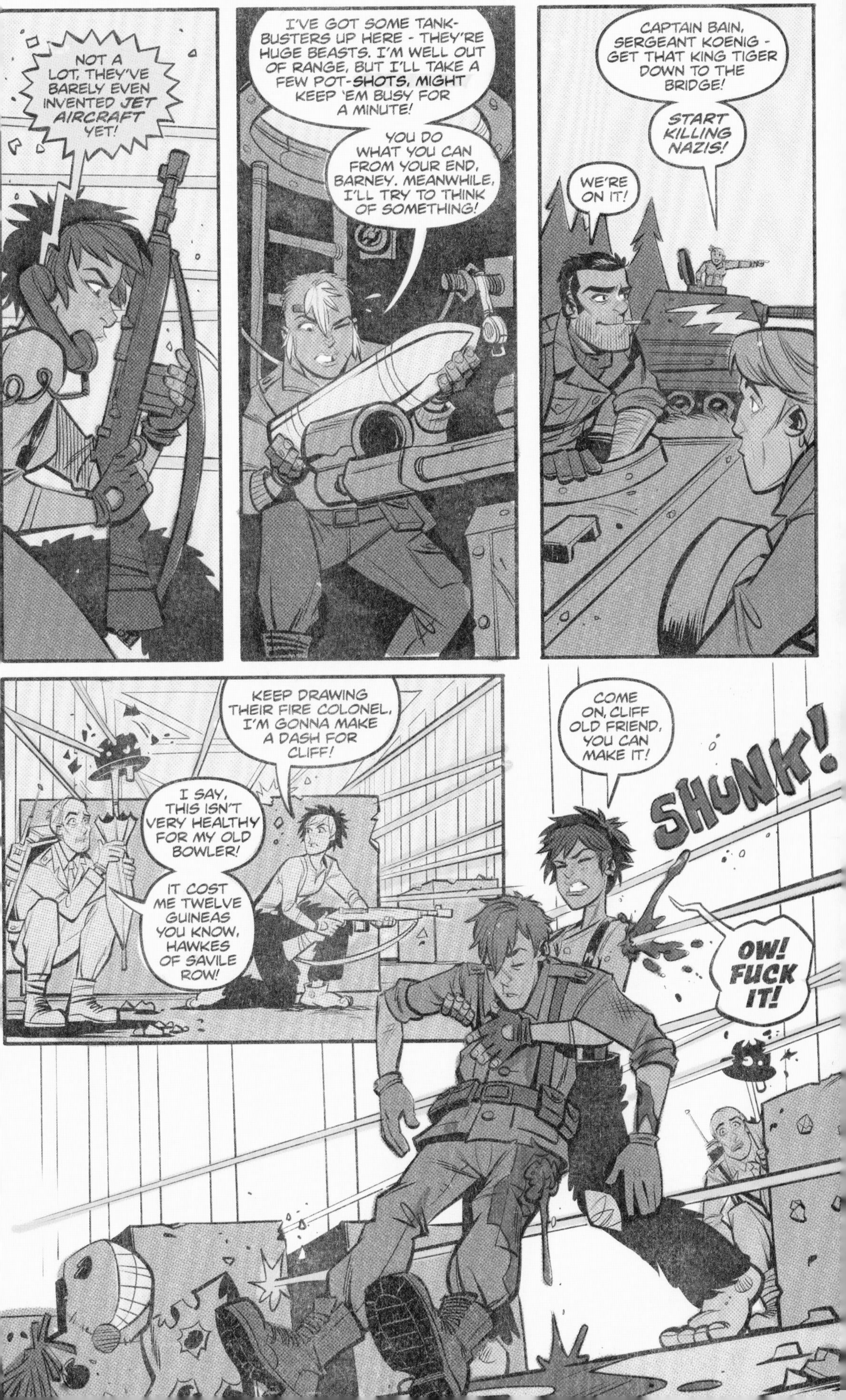
NOT A LOT, THEY'VE BARELY EVEN INVENTED JET AIRCRAFT YET!
I'VE GOT SOME TANK-BUSTERS UP HERE - THEY'RE HUGE BEASTS. I'M WELL OUT OF RANGE, BUT I'LL TAKE A FEW POT-SHOTS, MIGHT KEEP 'EM BUSY FOR A MINUTE!
YOU DO WHAT YOU CAN FROM YOUR END, BARNEY. MEANWHILE, I'LL TRY TO THINK OF SOMETHING!
CAPTAIN BAIN, SERGEANT KOENIG - GET THAT KING TIGER DOWN TO THE BRIDGE!
START KILLING NAZIS!
WE'RE ON IT!
KEEP DRAWING THEIR FIRE COLONEL, I'M GONNA MAKE A DASH FOR CLIFF!
I SAY, THIS ISN'T VERY HEALTHY FOR MY OLD BOWLER!
IT COST ME TWELVE GUINEAS YOU KNOW, HAWKES OF SAVILE ROW!
COME ON, CLIFF OLD FRIEND, YOU CAN MAKE IT!
SHUNK!
OW! FUCK IT!

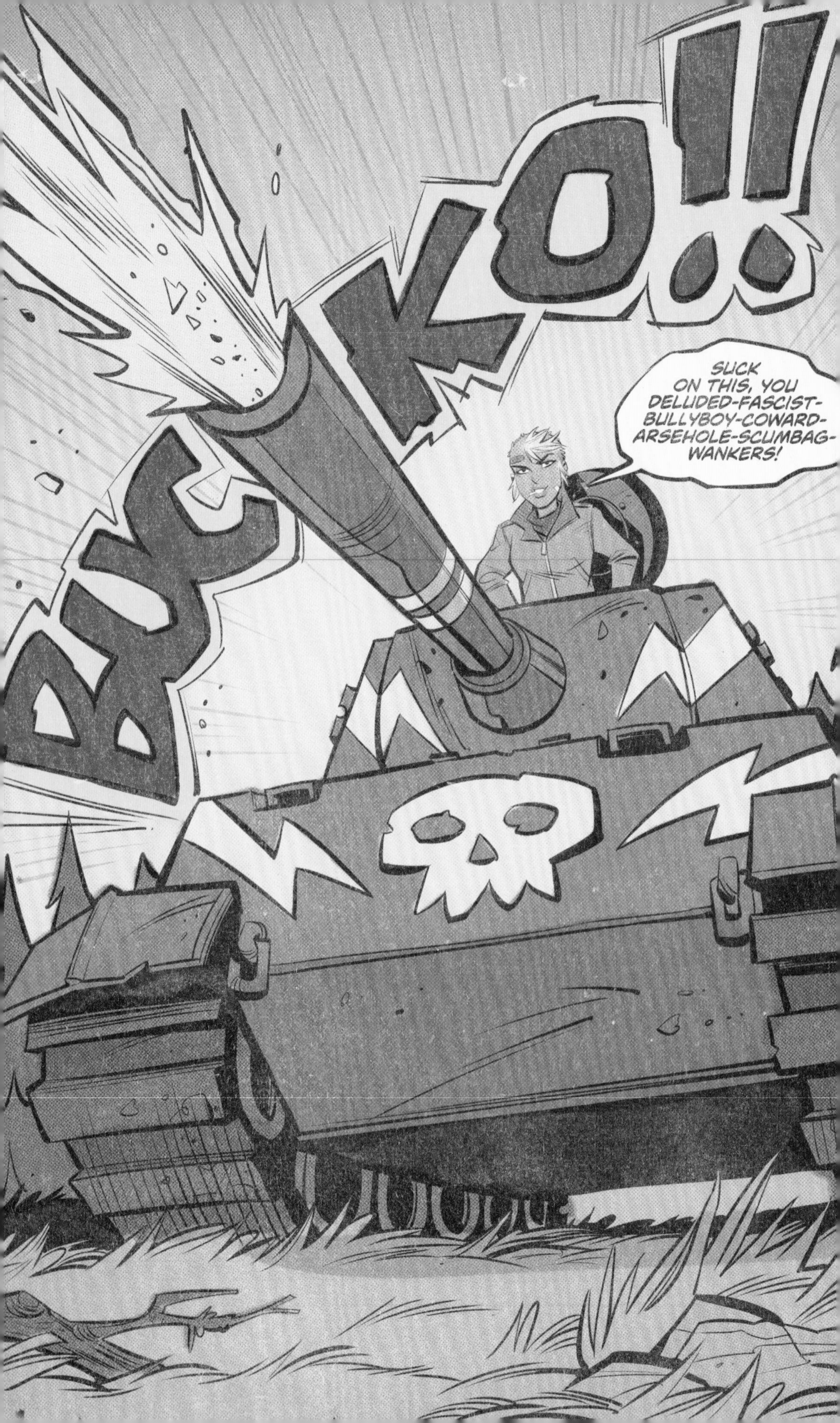
BUUCKO..!!
SUCK ON THIS, YOU DELUDED-FASCIST-BULLYBOY-COWARD-ARSEHOLE-SCUMBAG-WANKERS!

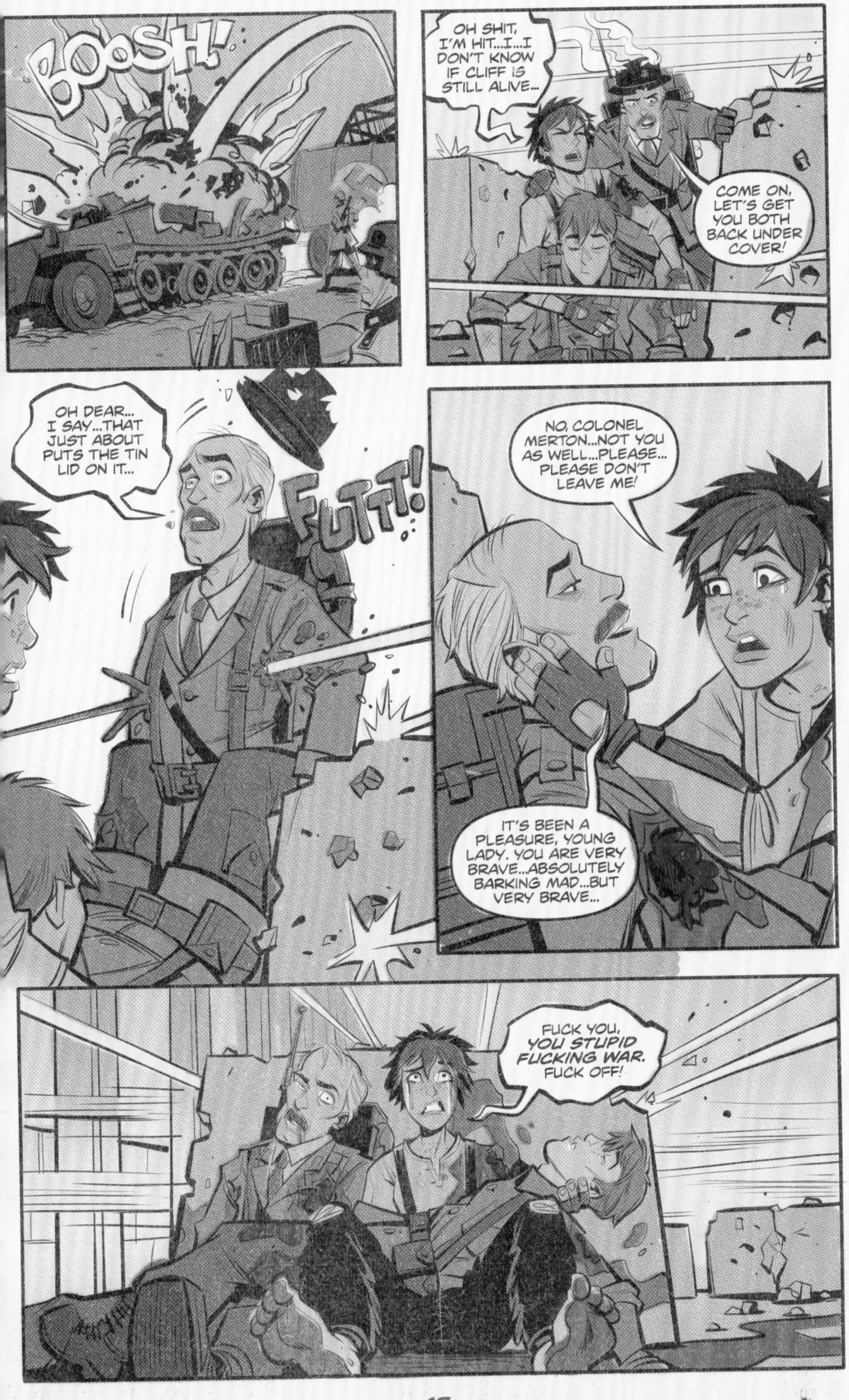
BOOSH!
OH SHIT, I'M HIT...I...I DON'T KNOW IF CLIFF IS STILL ALIVE...
COME ON, LET'S GET YOU BOTH BACK UNDER COVER!
OH DEAR... I SAY...THAT JUST ABOUT PUTS THE TIN LID ON IT...
FUTTT!
NO, COLONEL MERTON...NOT YOU AS WELL...PLEASE... PLEASE DON'T LEAVE ME!
IT'S BEEN A PLEASURE, YOUNG LADY. YOU ARE VERY BRAVE...ABSOLUTELY BARKING MAD...BUT VERY BRAVE...
FUCK YOU, YOU STUPID FUCKING WAR. FUCK OFF!

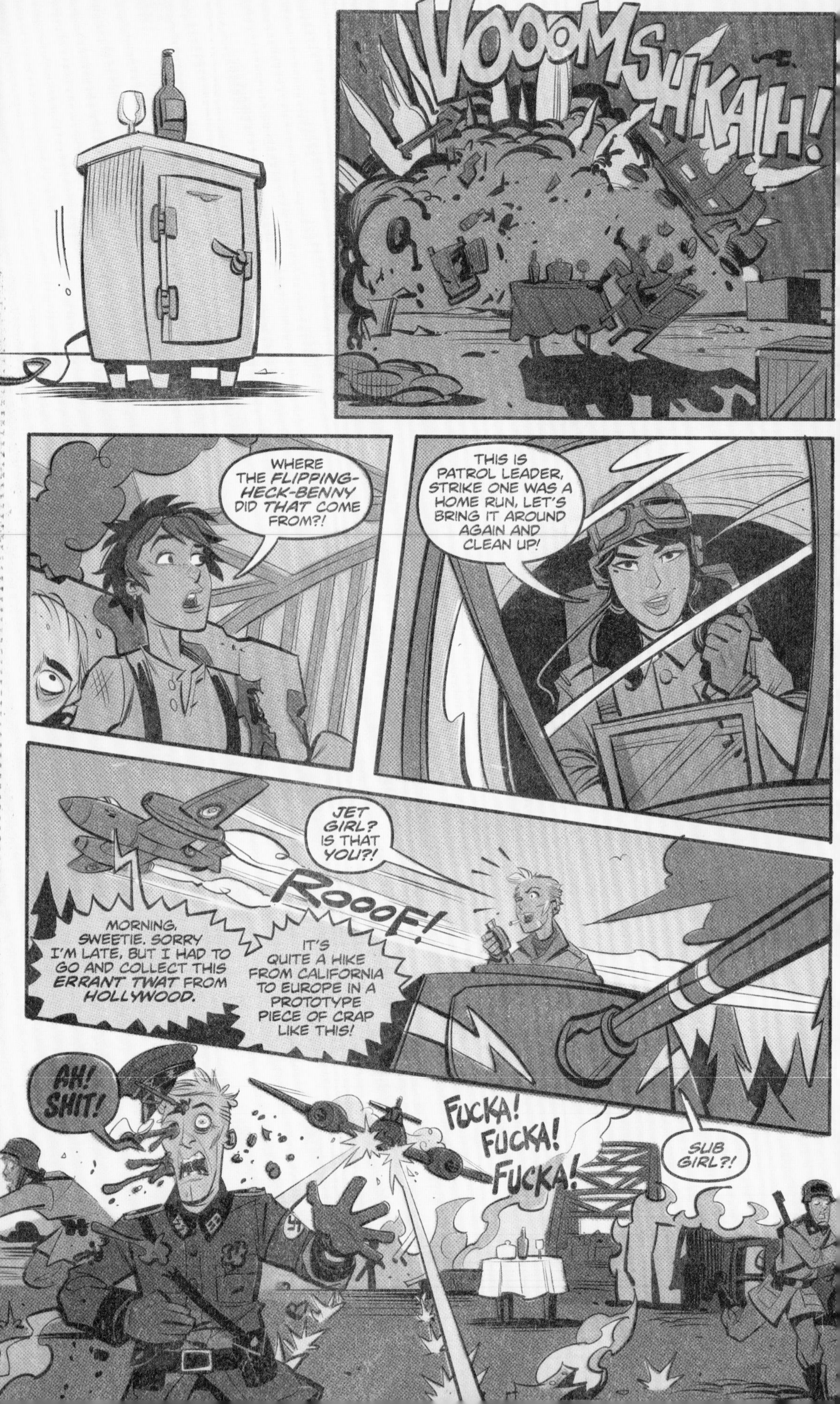
VOOOMSHKAIH!
WHERE THE FLIPPING-HECK-BENNY DID THAT COME FROM?!
THIS IS PATROL LEADER, STRIKE ONE WAS A HOME RUN, LET'S BRING IT AROUND AGAIN AND CLEAN UP!
JET GIRL? IS THAT YOU?!
ROOOF!
MORNING, SWEETIE. SORRY I'M LATE, BUT I HAD TO GO AND COLLECT THIS ERRANT TWAT FROM HOLLYWOOD.
IT'S QUITE A HIKE FROM CALIFORNIA TO EUROPE IN A PROTOTYPE PIECE OF CRAP LIKE THIS!
AH! SHIT!
FUCKA! FUCKA! FUCKA!
SUB GIRL?!

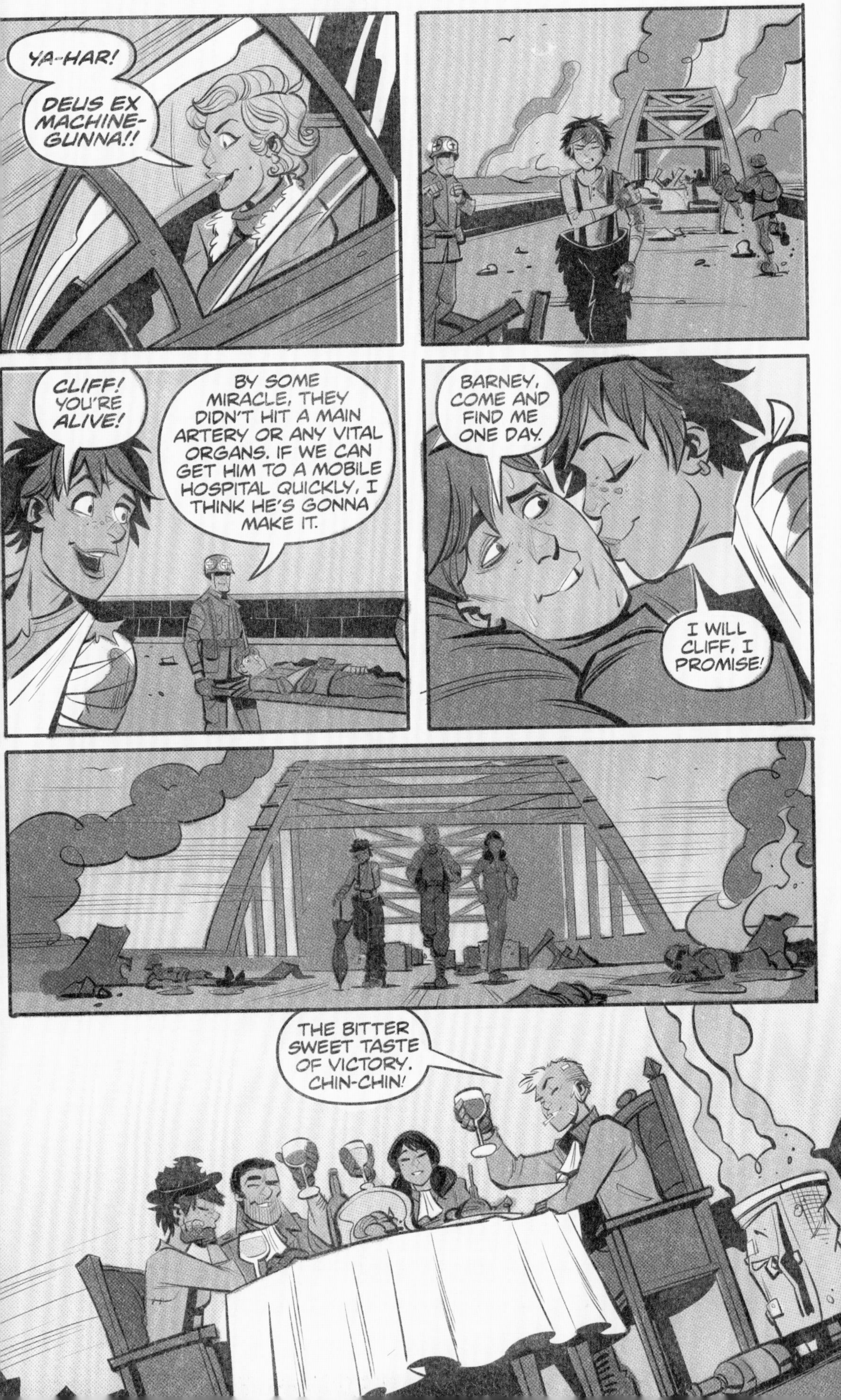
YA-HAR!
DEUS EX MACHINE-GUNNA!!
CLIFF! YOU'RE ALIVE!
BY SOME MIRACLE, THEY DIDN'T HIT A MAIN ARTERY OR ANY VITAL ORGANS. IF WE CAN GET HIM TO A MOBILE HOSPITAL QUICKLY, I THINK HE'S GONNA MAKE IT.
BARNEY, COME AND FIND ME ONE DAY.
I WILL CLIFF, I PROMISE!
THE BITTER SWEET TASTE OF VICTORY. CHIN-CHIN!

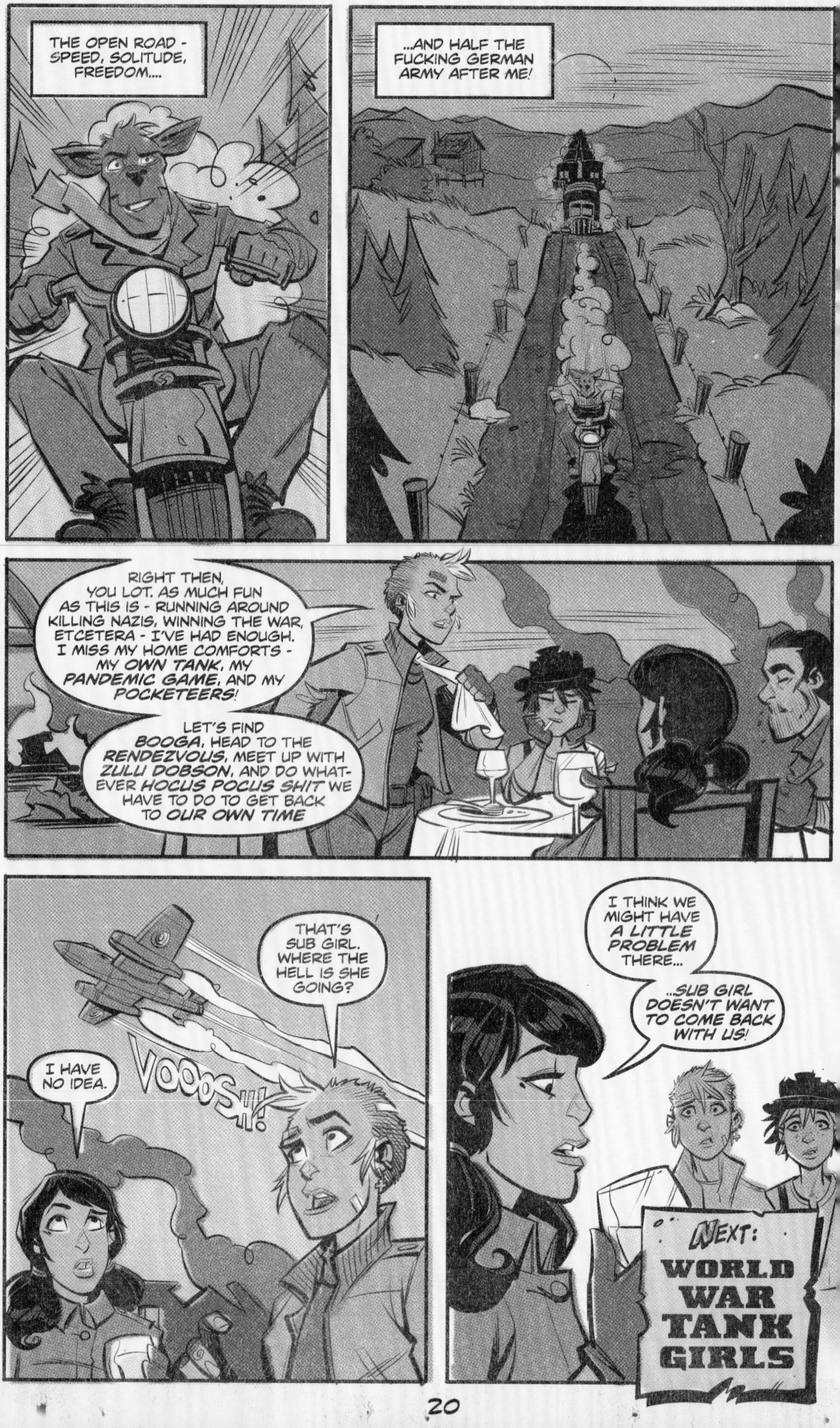
THE OPEN ROAD - SPEED, SOLITUDE, FREEDOM....
...AND HALF THE FUCKING GERMAN ARMY AFTER ME!
RIGHT THEN, YOU LOT. AS MUCH FUN AS THIS IS - RUNNING AROUND KILLING NAZIS, WINNING THE WAR, ETCETERA - I'VE HAD ENOUGH. I MISS MY HOME COMFORTS - MY OWN TANK, MY PANDEMIC GAME, AND MY POCKETEERS!
LET'S FIND BOOGA, HEAD TO THE RENDEZVOUS, MEET UP WITH ZULU DOBSON, AND DO WHAT-EVER HOCUS POCUS SHIT WE HAVE TO DO TO GET BACK TO OUR OWN TIME
THAT'S SUB GIRL. WHERE THE HELL IS SHE GOING?
VOOOSH!
I HAVE NO IDEA.
I THINK WE MIGHT HAVE A LITTLE PROBLEM THERE...
...SUB GIRL DOESN'T WANT TO COME BACK WITH US!
NEXT:
WORLD WAR TANK GIRLS

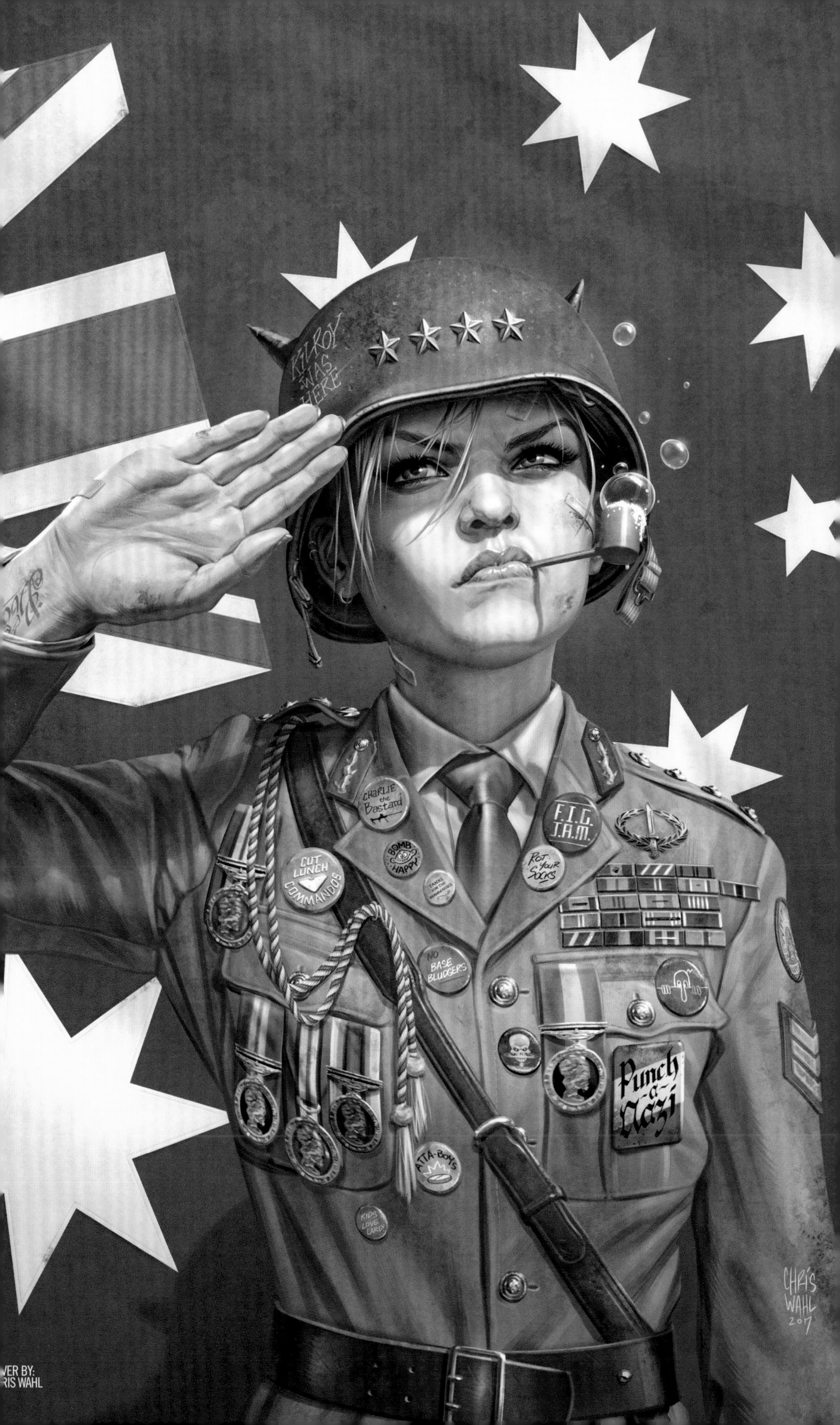
KILROY WAS HERE
CHARLIE the Bastard
F.I.G. J.A.M.
BOMB HAPPY
CUT LUNCH COMMANDOS
ROT YOUR SOCKS
NO BASE BLUDGERS
Punch a Nazi
ATTA-BOYS
CHRIS WAHL 2017

VER BY:
RIS WAHL

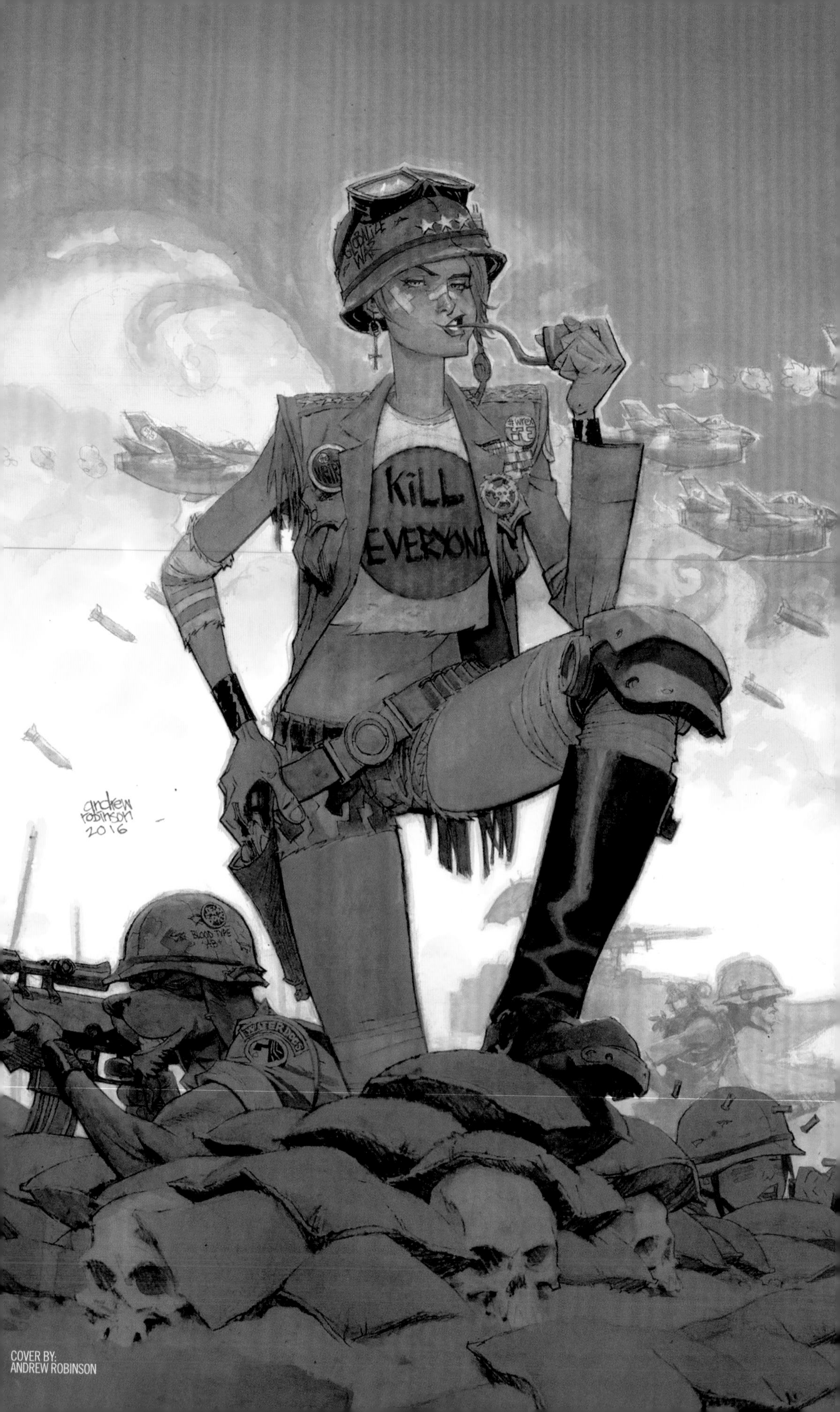
KiLL
EVERYONE
andrew robinson 2016

COVER BY:
ANDREW ROBINSON

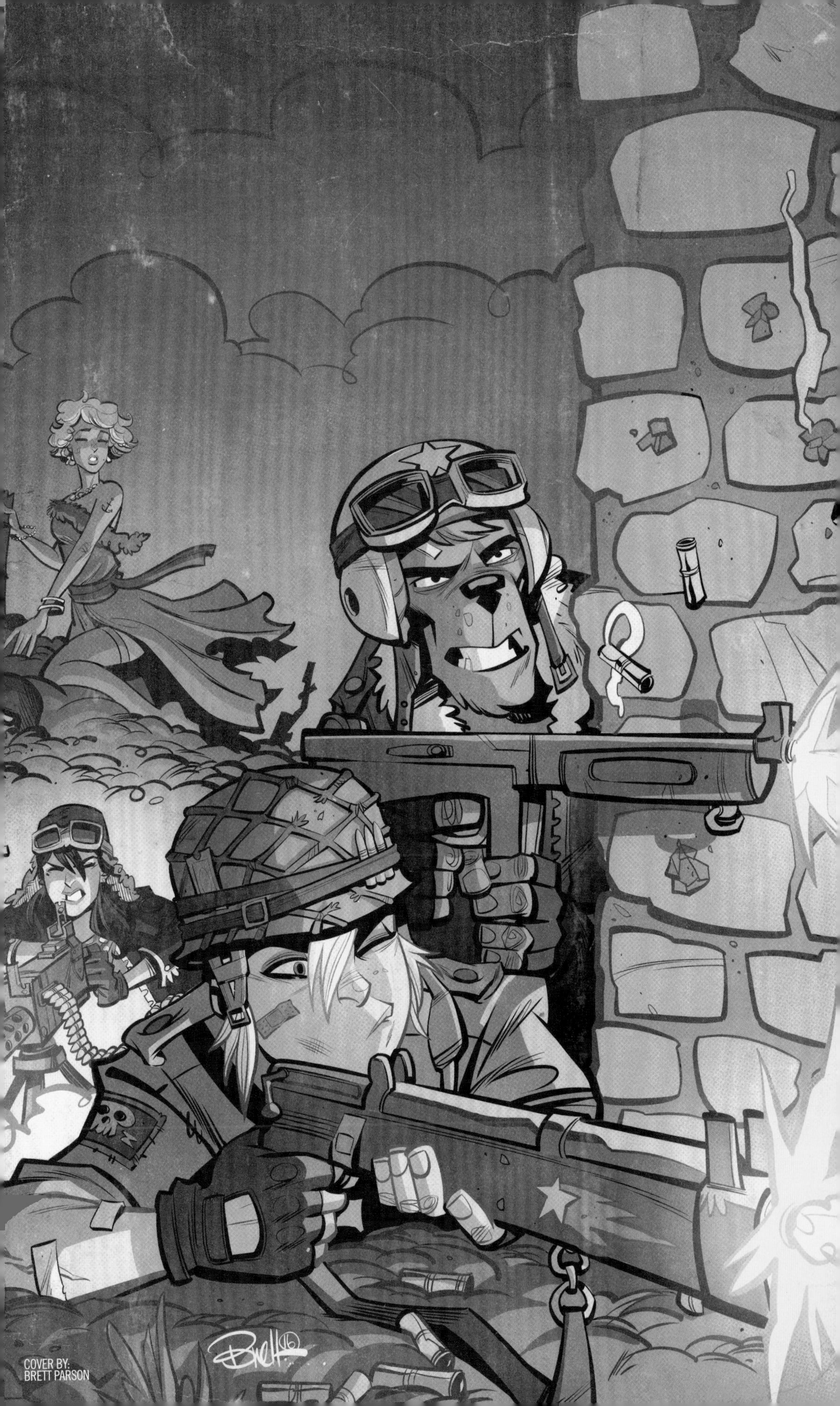

COVER BY:
BRETT PARSON

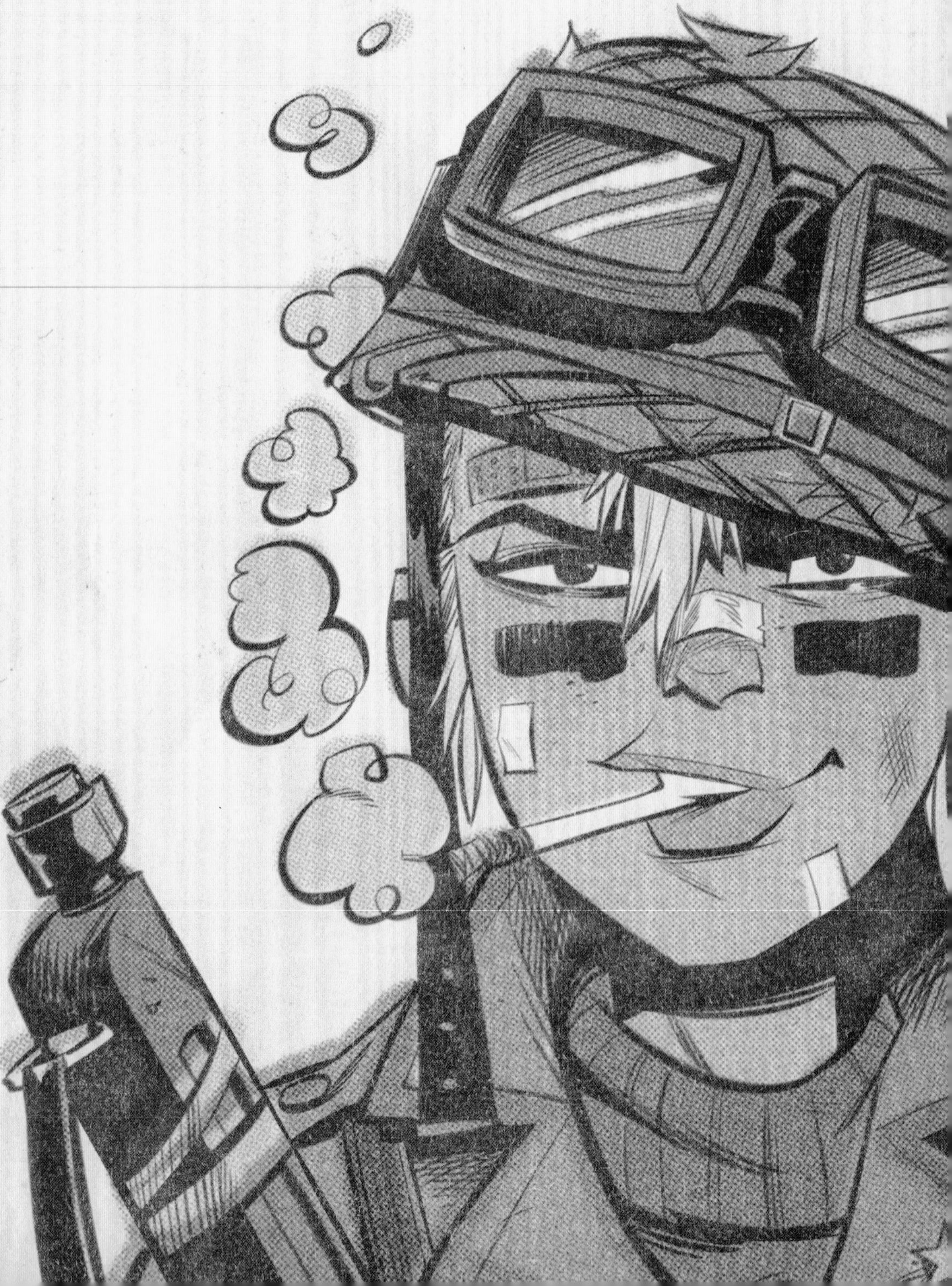

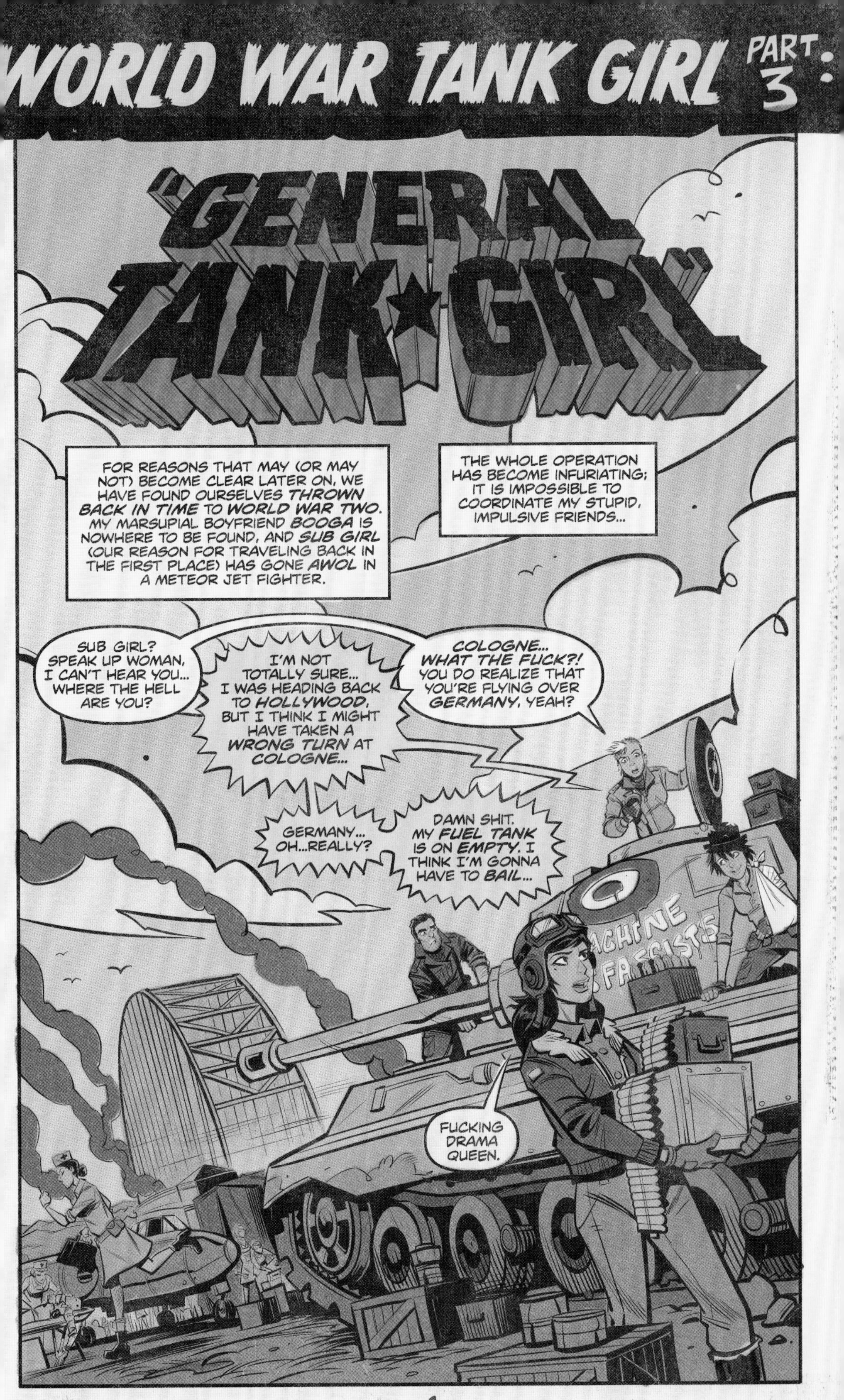
WORLD WAR TANK GIRL PART: 3:
"GENERAL TANK★GIRL"
FOR REASONS THAT MAY (OR MAY NOT) BECOME CLEAR LATER ON, WE HAVE FOUND OURSELVES THROWN BACK IN TIME TO WORLD WAR TWO. MY MARSUPIAL BOYFRIEND BOOGA IS NOWHERE TO BE FOUND, AND SUB GIRL (OUR REASON FOR TRAVELING BACK IN THE FIRST PLACE) HAS GONE AWOL IN A METEOR JET FIGHTER.
THE WHOLE OPERATION HAS BECOME INFURIATING; IT IS IMPOSSIBLE TO COORDINATE MY STUPID, IMPULSIVE FRIENDS...
SUB GIRL? SPEAK UP WOMAN, I CAN'T HEAR YOU... WHERE THE HELL ARE YOU?
I'M NOT TOTALLY SURE... I WAS HEADING BACK TO HOLLYWOOD, BUT I THINK I MIGHT HAVE TAKEN A WRONG TURN AT COLOGNE...
COLOGNE... WHAT THE FUCK?! YOU DO REALIZE THAT YOU'RE FLYING OVER GERMANY, YEAH?
GERMANY... OH...REALLY?
DAMN SHIT. MY FUEL TANK IS ON EMPTY. I THINK I'M GONNA HAVE TO BAIL...
MACHINE FASCISTS
FUCKING DRAMA QUEEN.

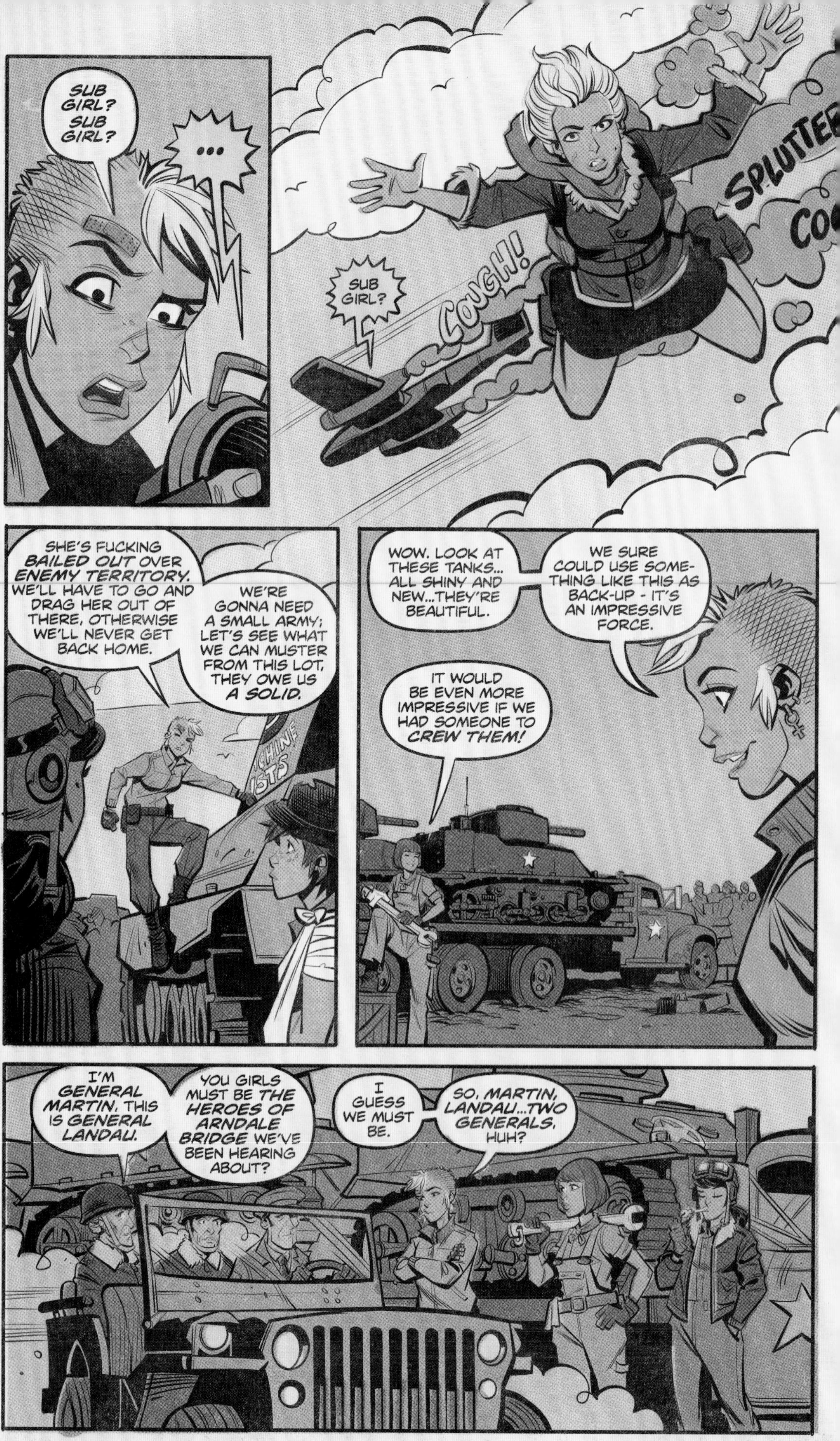
SUB GIRL? SUB GIRL?
...
SUB GIRL?
COUGH!
COUGH!
SPLUTTER
SHE'S FUCKING BAILED OUT OVER ENEMY TERRITORY. WE'LL HAVE TO GO AND DRAG HER OUT OF THERE, OTHERWISE WE'LL NEVER GET BACK HOME.
WE'RE GONNA NEED A SMALL ARMY; LET'S SEE WHAT WE CAN MUSTER FROM THIS LOT, THEY OWE US A SOLID.
WOW. LOOK AT THESE TANKS... ALL SHINY AND NEW...THEY'RE BEAUTIFUL.
WE SURE COULD USE SOMETHING LIKE THIS AS BACK-UP - IT'S AN IMPRESSIVE FORCE.
IT WOULD BE EVEN MORE IMPRESSIVE IF WE HAD SOMEONE TO CREW THEM!
I'M GENERAL MARTIN. THIS IS GENERAL LANDAU.
YOU GIRLS MUST BE THE HEROES OF ARNDALE BRIDGE WE'VE BEEN HEARING ABOUT?
I GUESS WE MUST BE.
SO, MARTIN, LANDAU...TWO GENERALS, HUH?

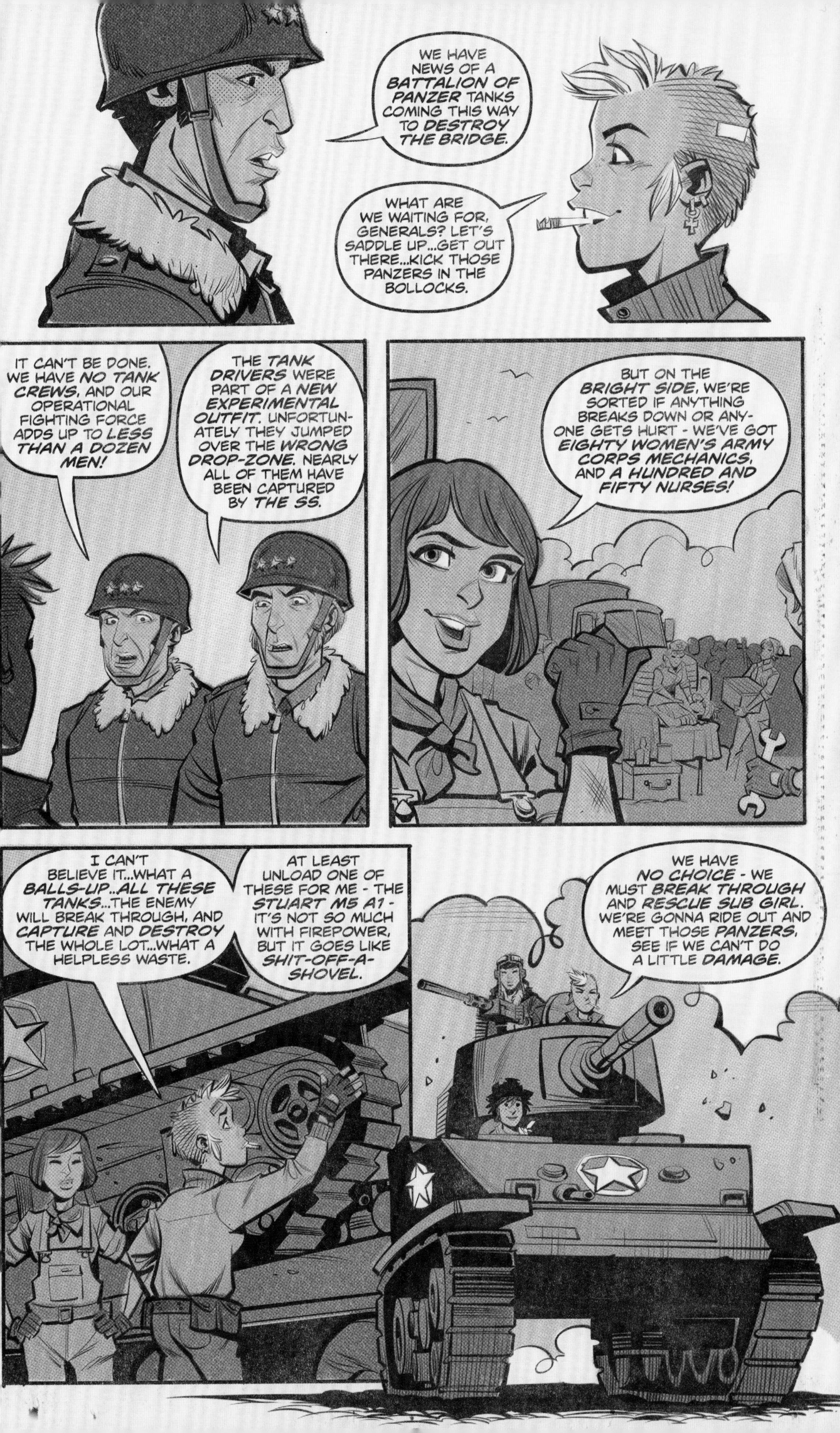
WE HAVE NEWS OF A BATTALION OF PANZER TANKS COMING THIS WAY TO DESTROY THE BRIDGE.
WHAT ARE WE WAITING FOR, GENERALS? LET'S SADDLE UP...GET OUT THERE...KICK THOSE PANZERS IN THE BOLLOCKS.
IT CAN'T BE DONE. WE HAVE NO TANK CREWS, AND OUR OPERATIONAL FIGHTING FORCE ADDS UP TO LESS THAN A DOZEN MEN!
THE TANK DRIVERS WERE PART OF A NEW EXPERIMENTAL OUTFIT. UNFORTUN-ATELY THEY JUMPED OVER THE WRONG DROP-ZONE. NEARLY ALL OF THEM HAVE BEEN CAPTURED BY THE SS.
BUT ON THE BRIGHT SIDE, WE'RE SORTED IF ANYTHING BREAKS DOWN OR ANY-ONE GETS HURT - WE'VE GOT EIGHTY WOMEN'S ARMY CORPS MECHANICS, AND A HUNDRED AND FIFTY NURSES!
I CAN'T BELIEVE IT...WHAT A BALLS-UP...ALL THESE TANKS...THE ENEMY WILL BREAK THROUGH, AND CAPTURE AND DESTROY THE WHOLE LOT...WHAT A HELPLESS WASTE.
AT LEAST UNLOAD ONE OF THESE FOR ME - THE STUART M5 A1 - IT'S NOT SO MUCH WITH FIREPOWER, BUT IT GOES LIKE SHIT-OFF-A-SHOVEL.
WE HAVE NO CHOICE - WE MUST BREAK THROUGH AND RESCUE SUB GIRL. WE'RE GONNA RIDE OUT AND MEET THOSE PANZERS, SEE IF WE CAN'T DO A LITTLE DAMAGE.

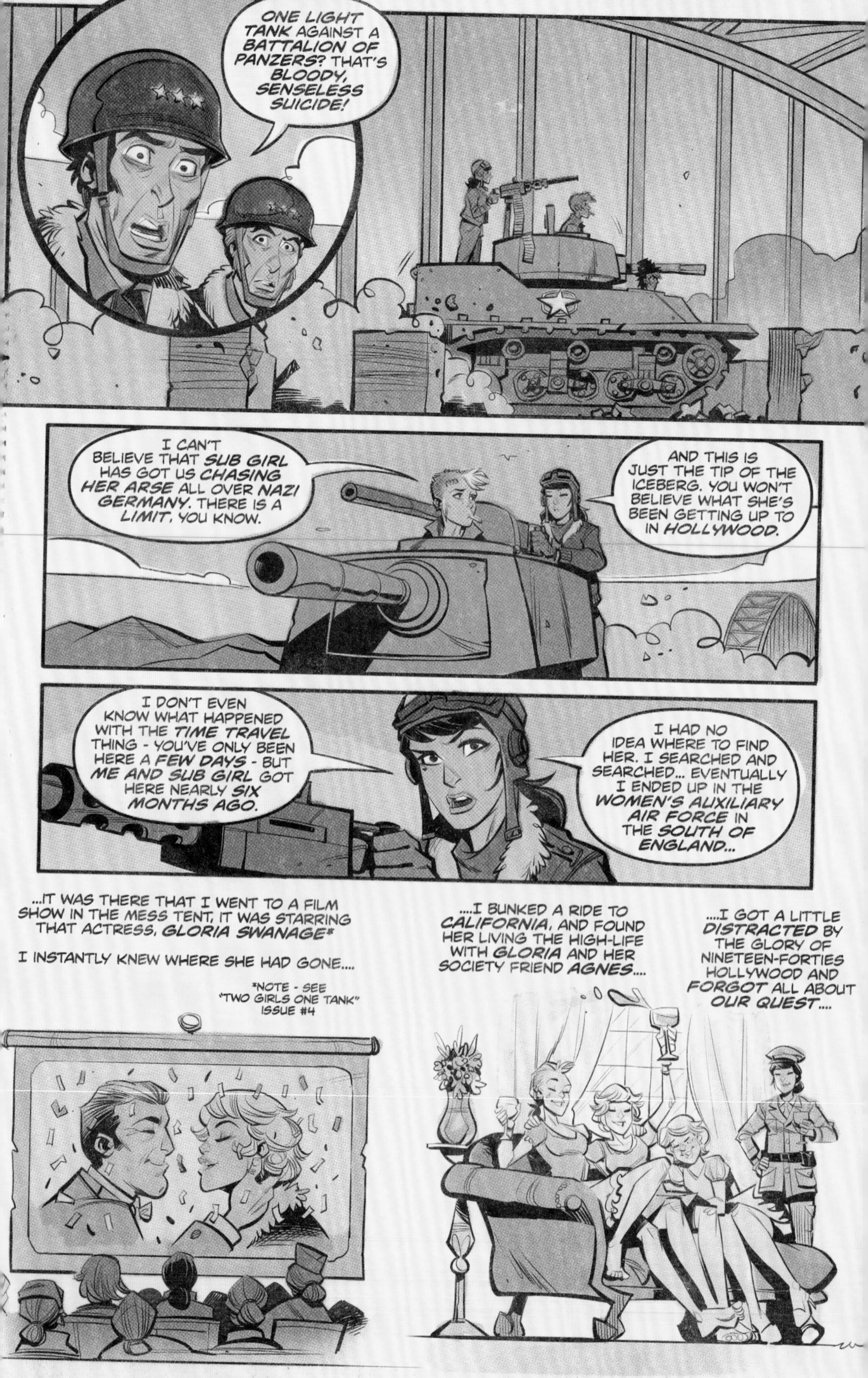

ONE LIGHT TANK AGAINST A BATTALION OF PANZERS? THAT'S BLOODY, SENSELESS SUICIDE!
I CAN'T BELIEVE THAT SUB GIRL HAS GOT US CHASING HER ARSE ALL OVER NAZI GERMANY. THERE IS A LIMIT, YOU KNOW.
AND THIS IS JUST THE TIP OF THE ICEBERG. YOU WON'T BELIEVE WHAT SHE'S BEEN GETTING UP TO IN HOLLYWOOD.
I DON'T EVEN KNOW WHAT HAPPENED WITH THE TIME TRAVEL THING - YOU'VE ONLY BEEN HERE A FEW DAYS - BUT ME AND SUB GIRL GOT HERE NEARLY SIX MONTHS AGO.
I HAD NO IDEA WHERE TO FIND HER. I SEARCHED AND SEARCHED... EVENTUALLY I ENDED UP IN THE WOMEN'S AUXILIARY AIR FORCE IN THE SOUTH OF ENGLAND...
...IT WAS THERE THAT I WENT TO A FILM SHOW IN THE MESS TENT, IT WAS STARRING THAT ACTRESS, GLORIA SWANAGE*
I INSTANTLY KNEW WHERE SHE HAD GONE....
*NOTE - SEE "TWO GIRLS ONE TANK" ISSUE #4
....I BUNKED A RIDE TO CALIFORNIA, AND FOUND HER LIVING THE HIGH-LIFE WITH GLORIA AND HER SOCIETY FRIEND AGNES....
....I GOT A LITTLE DISTRACTED BY THE GLORY OF NINETEEN-FORTIES HOLLYWOOD AND FORGOT ALL ABOUT OUR QUEST....

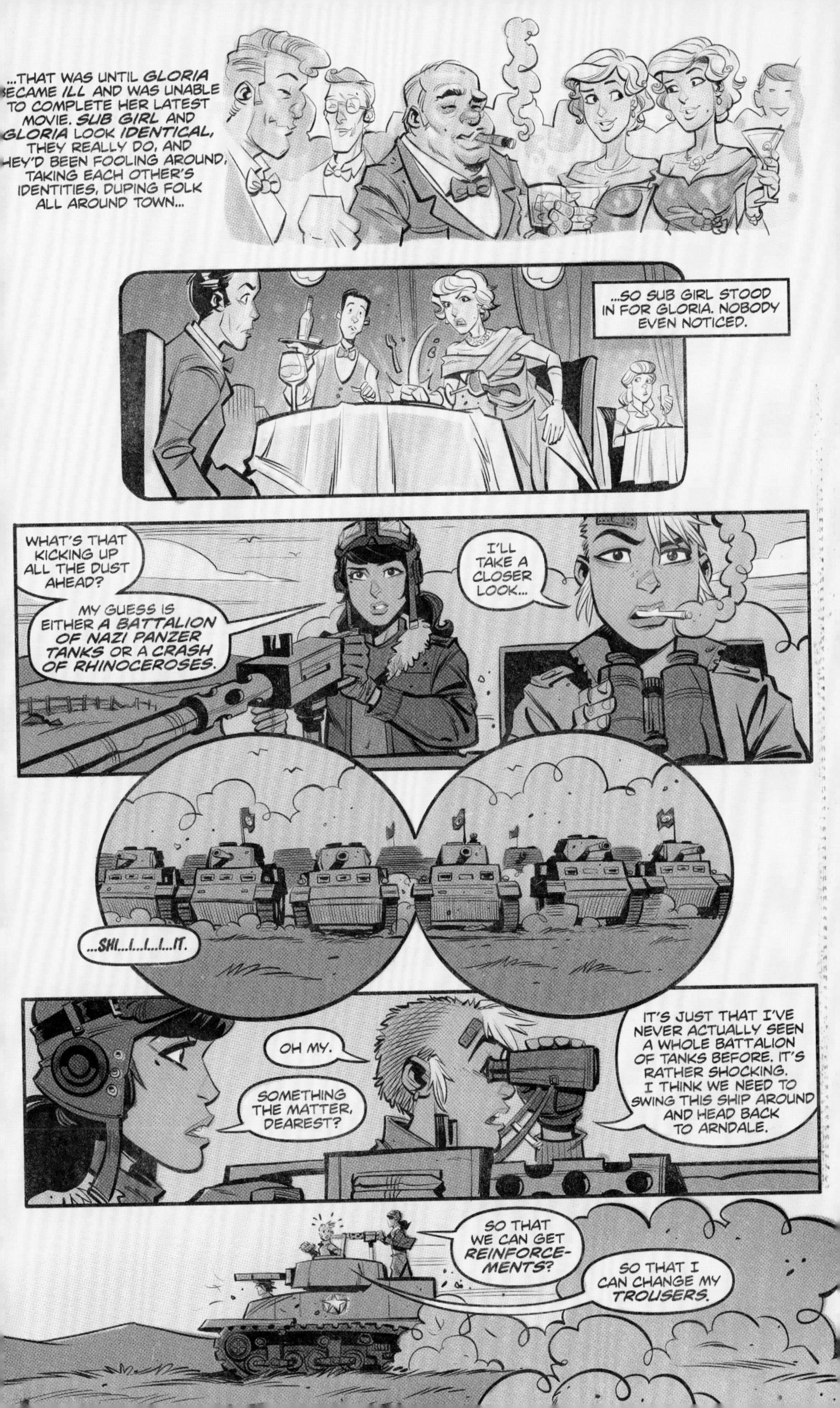
...THAT WAS UNTIL GLORIA BECAME ILL AND WAS UNABLE TO COMPLETE HER LATEST MOVIE. SUB GIRL AND GLORIA LOOK IDENTICAL, THEY REALLY DO, AND THEY'D BEEN FOOLING AROUND, TAKING EACH OTHER'S IDENTITIES, DUPING FOLK ALL AROUND TOWN...
...SO SUB GIRL STOOD IN FOR GLORIA. NOBODY EVEN NOTICED.
WHAT'S THAT KICKING UP ALL THE DUST AHEAD?
MY GUESS IS EITHER A BATTALION OF NAZI PANZER TANKS OR A CRASH OF RHINOCEROSES.
I'LL TAKE A CLOSER LOOK...
...SHI...I...I...I...IT.
OH MY.
SOMETHING THE MATTER, DEAREST?
IT'S JUST THAT I'VE NEVER ACTUALLY SEEN A WHOLE BATTALION OF TANKS BEFORE. IT'S RATHER SHOCKING. I THINK WE NEED TO SWING THIS SHIP AROUND AND HEAD BACK TO ARNDALE.
SO THAT WE CAN GET REINFORCEMENTS?
SO THAT I CAN CHANGE MY TROUSERS.

BONUS CUT-OUT MASK

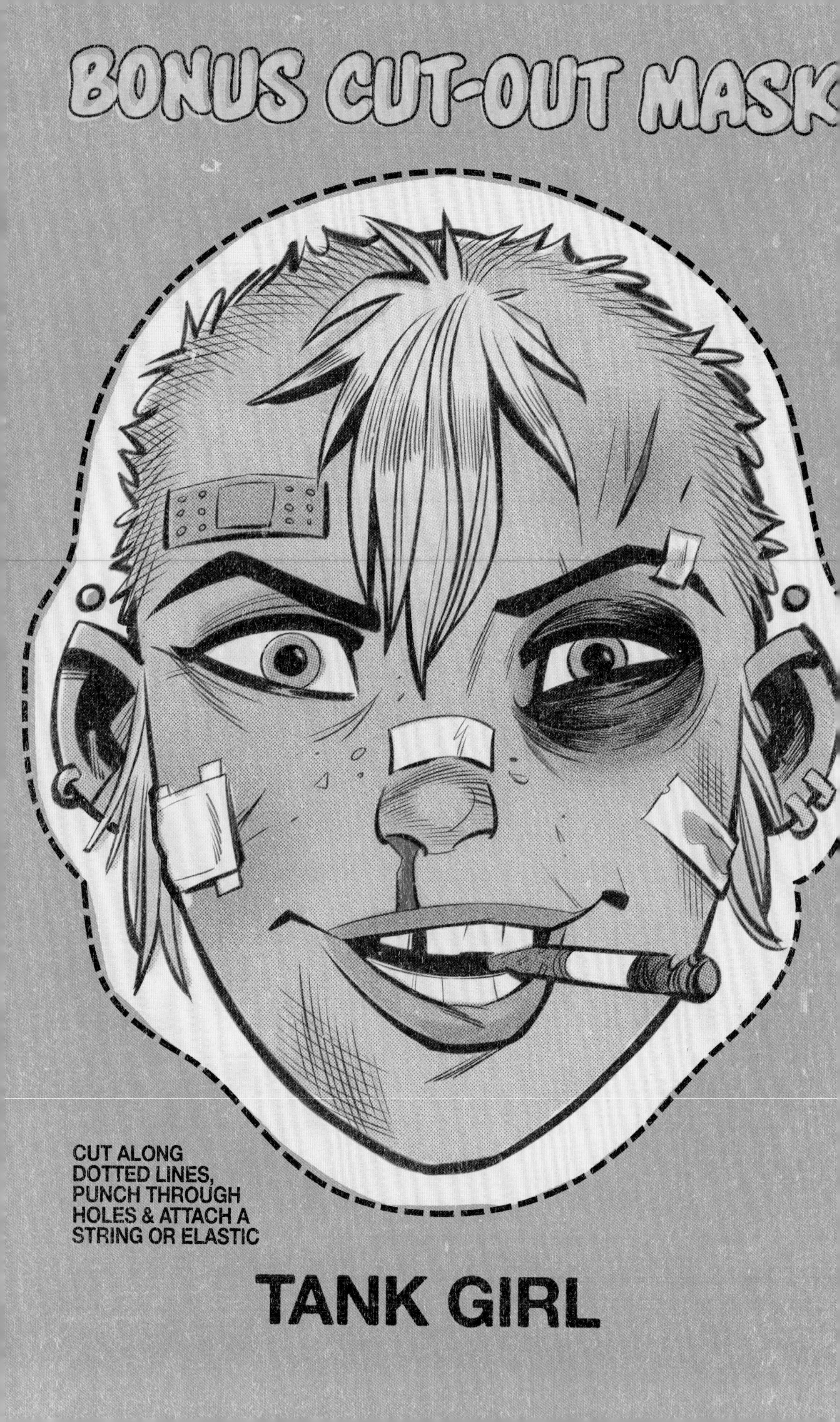

CUT ALONG DOTTED LINES, PUNCH THROUGH HOLES & ATTACH A STRING OR ELASTIC

TANK GIRL

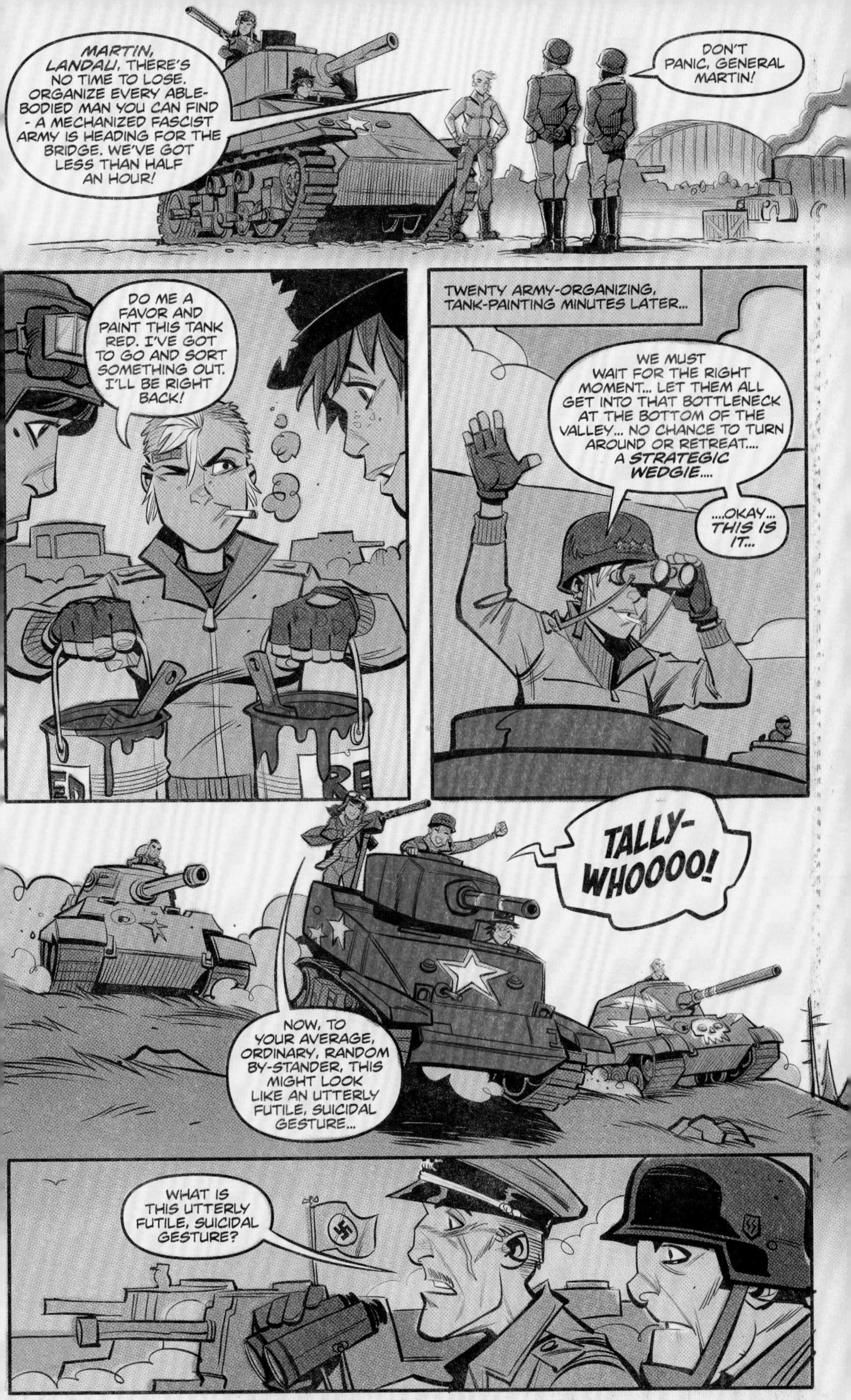

MARTIN, LANDAU, THERE'S NO TIME TO LOSE. ORGANIZE EVERY ABLE-BODIED MAN YOU CAN FIND - A MECHANIZED FASCIST ARMY IS HEADING FOR THE BRIDGE. WE'VE GOT LESS THAN HALF AN HOUR!
DON'T PANIC, GENERAL MARTIN!
DO ME A FAVOR AND PAINT THIS TANK RED. I'VE GOT TO GO AND SORT SOMETHING OUT. I'LL BE RIGHT BACK!
TWENTY ARMY-ORGANIZING, TANK-PAINTING MINUTES LATER...
WE MUST WAIT FOR THE RIGHT MOMENT... LET THEM ALL GET INTO THAT BOTTLENECK AT THE BOTTOM OF THE VALLEY... NO CHANCE TO TURN AROUND OR RETREAT.... A STRATEGIC WEDGIE....
...OKAY... THIS IS IT...
TALLY-WHOOOO!
NOW, TO YOUR AVERAGE, ORDINARY, RANDOM BY-STANDER, THIS MIGHT LOOK LIKE AN UTTERLY FUTILE, SUICIDAL GESTURE...
WHAT IS THIS UTTERLY FUTILE, SUICIDAL GESTURE?

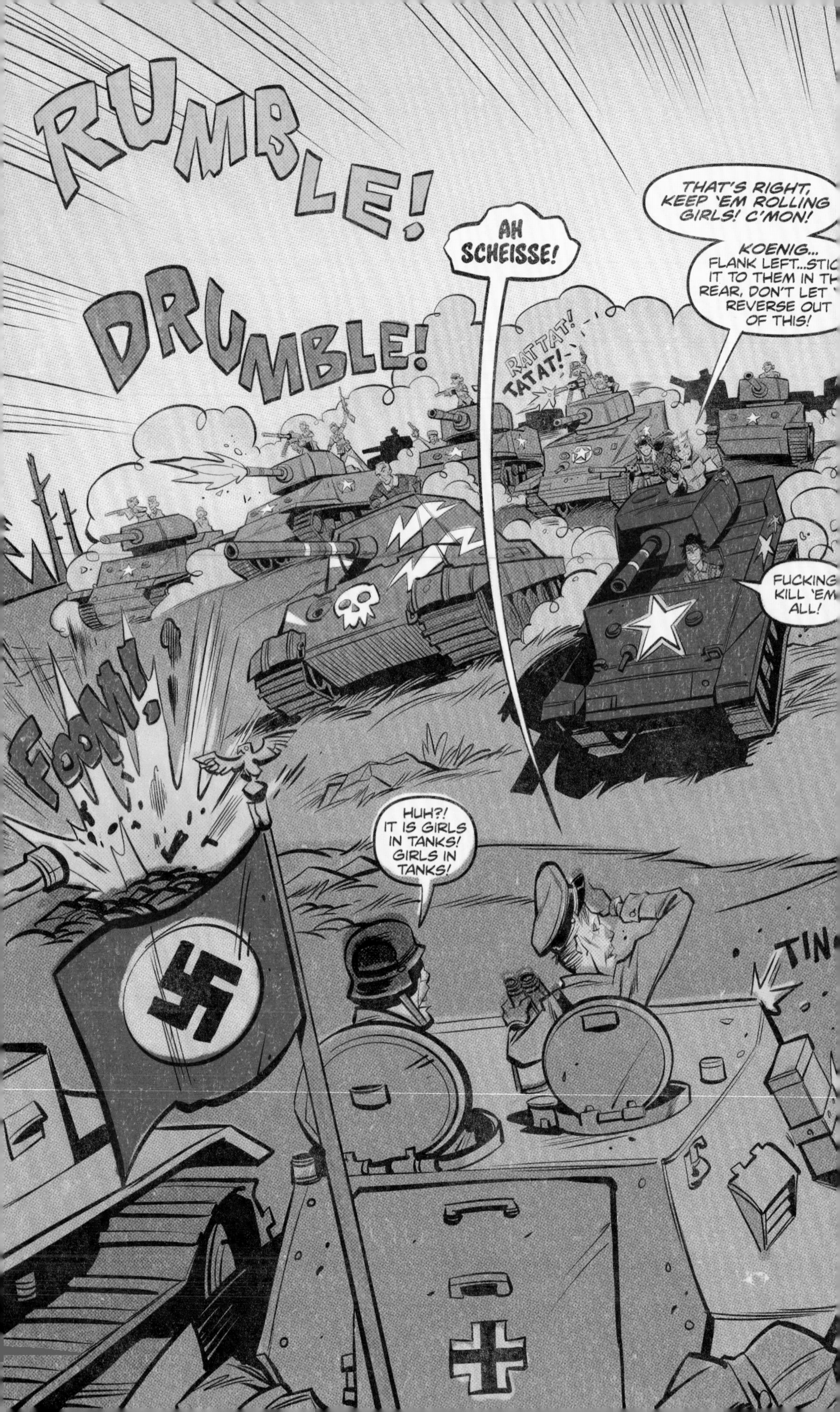
RUMBLE!
DRUMBLE!
AH SCHEISSE!
THAT'S RIGHT, KEEP 'EM ROLLING GIRLS! C'MON!
KOENIG... FLANK LEFT...STIC IT TO THEM IN TH REAR, DON'T LET REVERSE OUT OF THIS!
RATTAT! TATAT!
FUCKING KILL 'EM ALL!
FOOM!
HUH?! IT IS GIRLS IN TANKS! GIRLS IN TANKS!
TIN

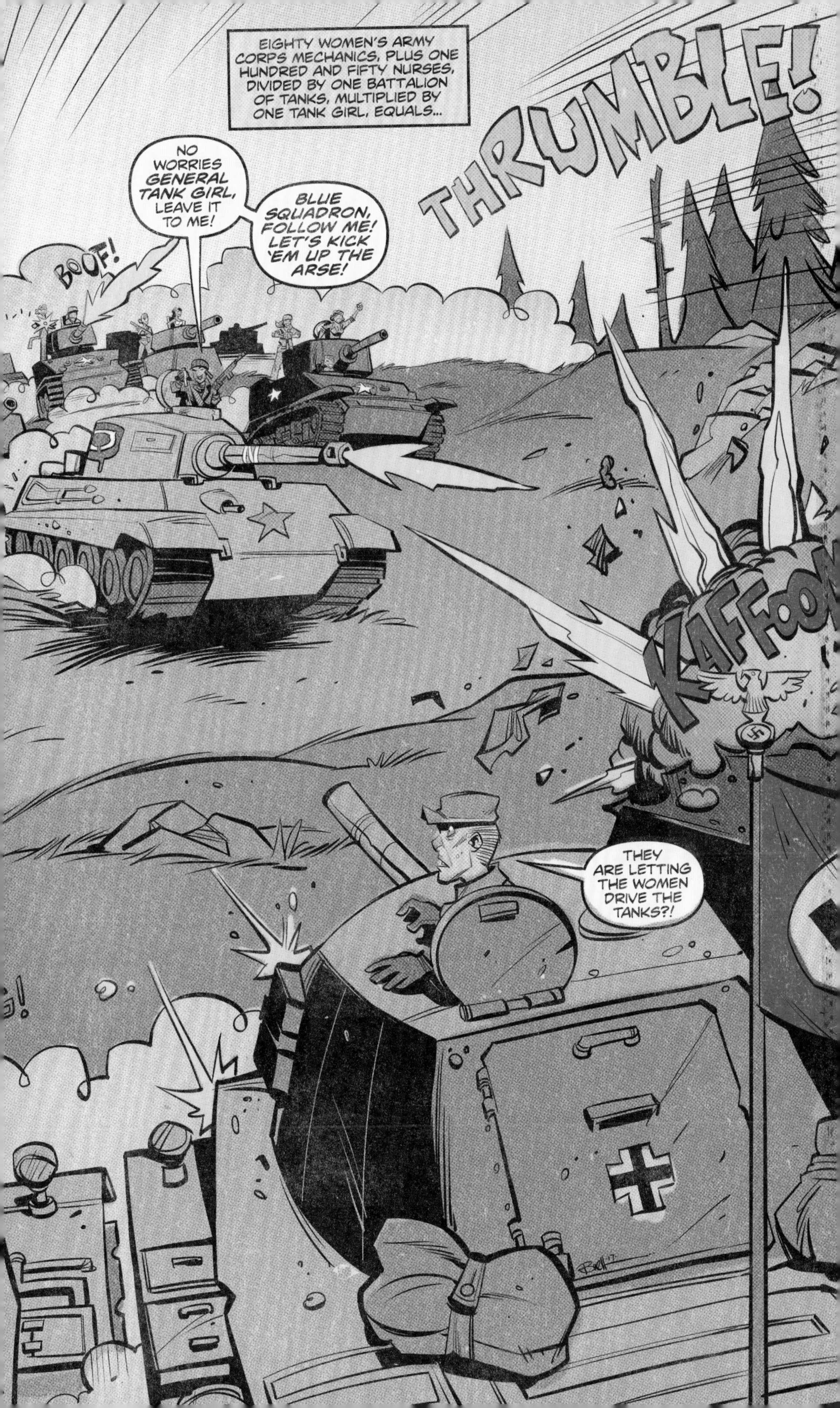

EIGHTY WOMEN'S ARMY CORPS MECHANICS, PLUS ONE HUNDRED AND FIFTY NURSES, DIVIDED BY ONE BATTALION OF TANKS, MULTIPLIED BY ONE TANK GIRL, EQUALS...
THRUMBLE!
NO WORRIES GENERAL TANK GIRL, LEAVE IT TO ME!
BLUE SQUADRON, FOLLOW ME! LET'S KICK 'EM UP THE ARSE!
BOOF!
KAFFOOM
THEY ARE LETTING THE WOMEN DRIVE THE TANKS?!

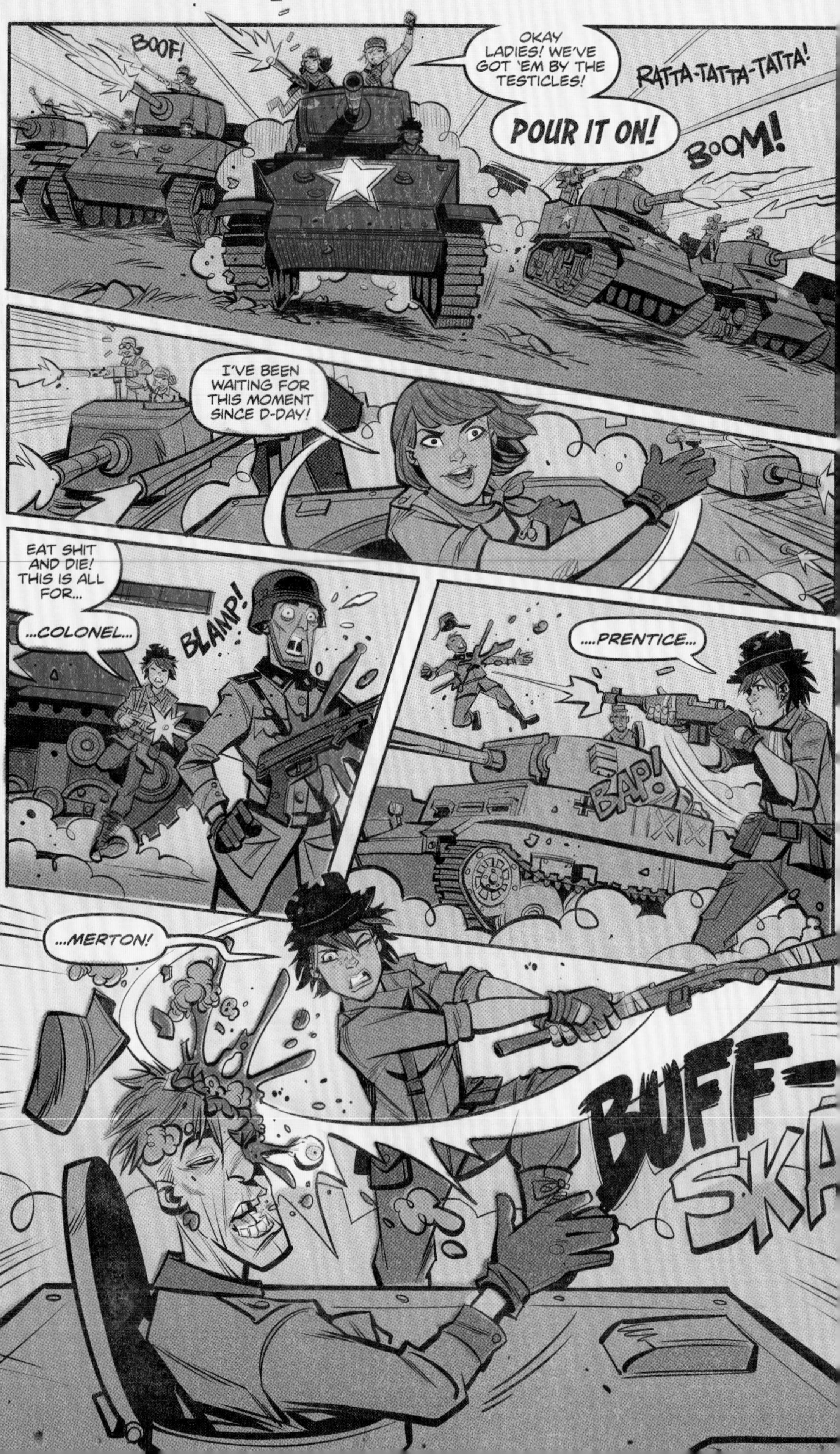
BOOF!
OKAY LADIES! WE'VE GOT 'EM BY THE TESTICLES!
POUR IT ON!
RATTA-TATTA-TATTA!
BOOM!
I'VE BEEN WAITING FOR THIS MOMENT SINCE D-DAY!
EAT SHIT AND DIE! THIS IS ALL FOR...
...COLONEL...
BLAMP!
....PRENTICE...
BAP!
...MERTON!
BUFF-
SKA

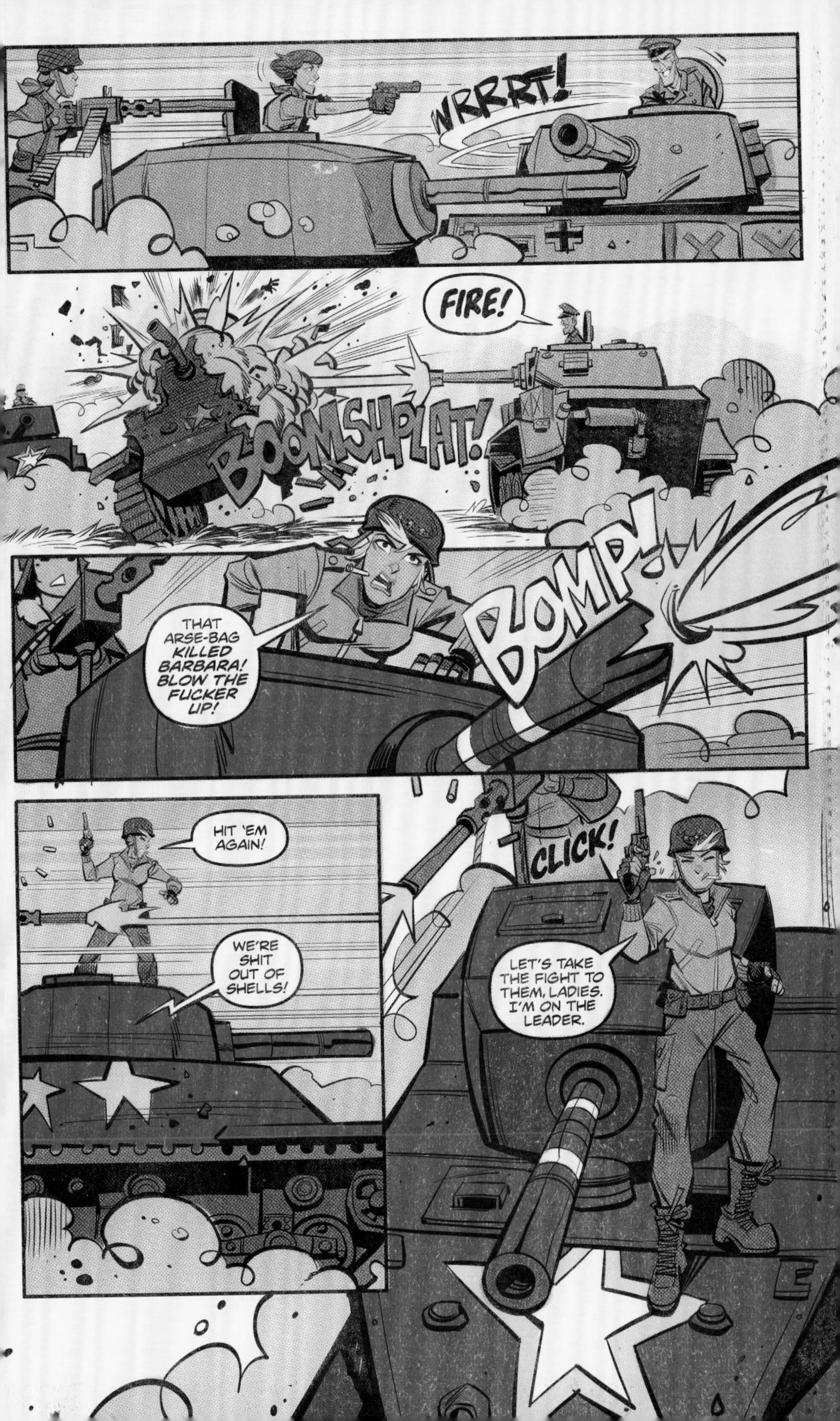
WRRRT!
FIRE!
BOOMSHPLAT!
THAT ARSE-BAG KILLED BARBARA! BLOW THE FUCKER UP!
BOMP!
HIT 'EM AGAIN!
WE'RE SHIT OUT OF SHELLS!
CLICK!
LET'S TAKE THE FIGHT TO THEM, LADIES. I'M ON THE LEADER.

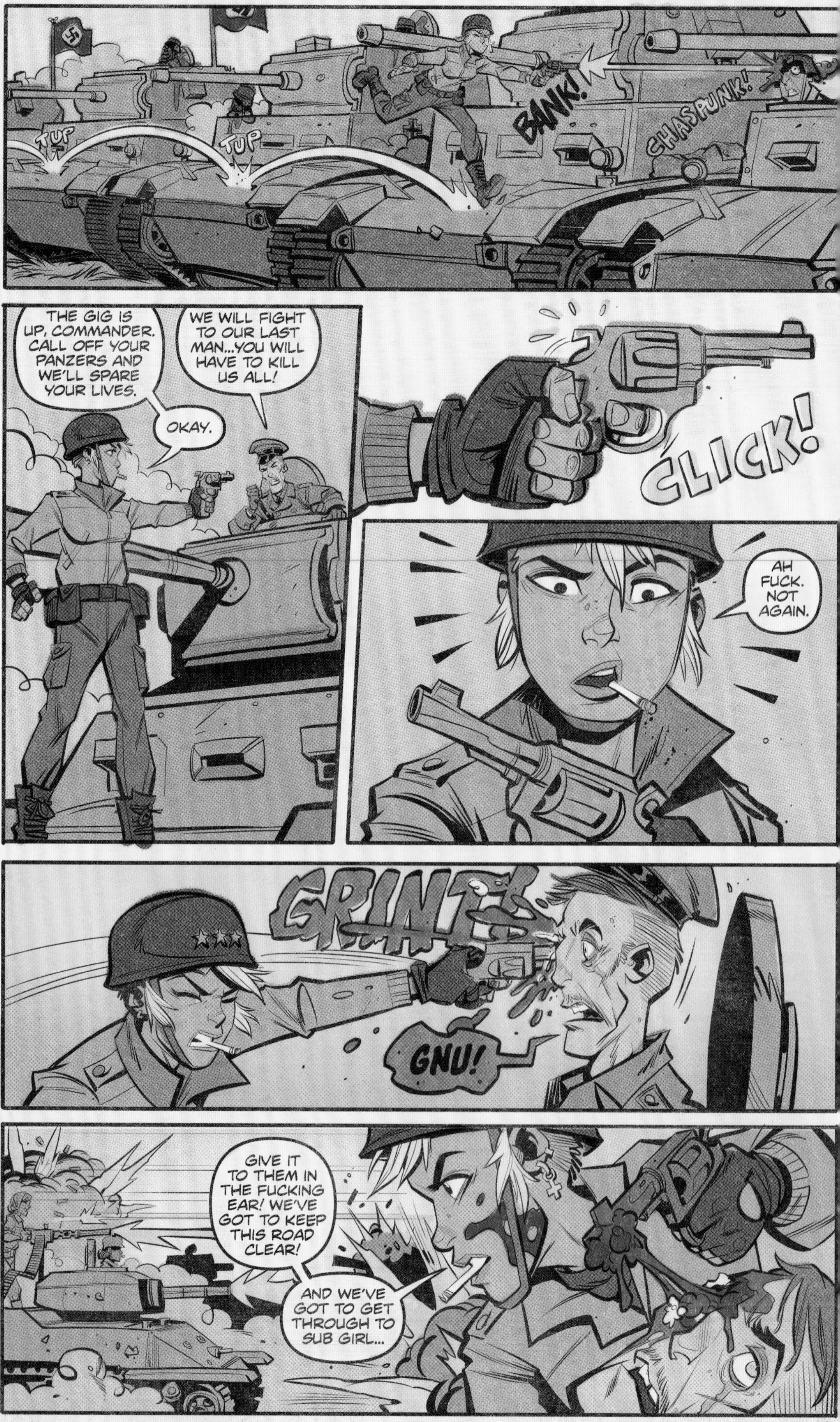
TUP
TUP
BANK!
CHASPUNK!
THE GIG IS UP, COMMANDER. CALL OFF YOUR PANZERS AND WE'LL SPARE YOUR LIVES.
WE WILL FIGHT TO OUR LAST MAN...YOU WILL HAVE TO KILL US ALL!
OKAY.
CLICK!
AH FUCK. NOT AGAIN.
GRINT!
GNU!
GIVE IT TO THEM IN THE FUCKING EAR! WE'VE GOT TO KEEP THIS ROAD CLEAR!
AND WE'VE GOT TO GET THROUGH TO SUB GIRL...

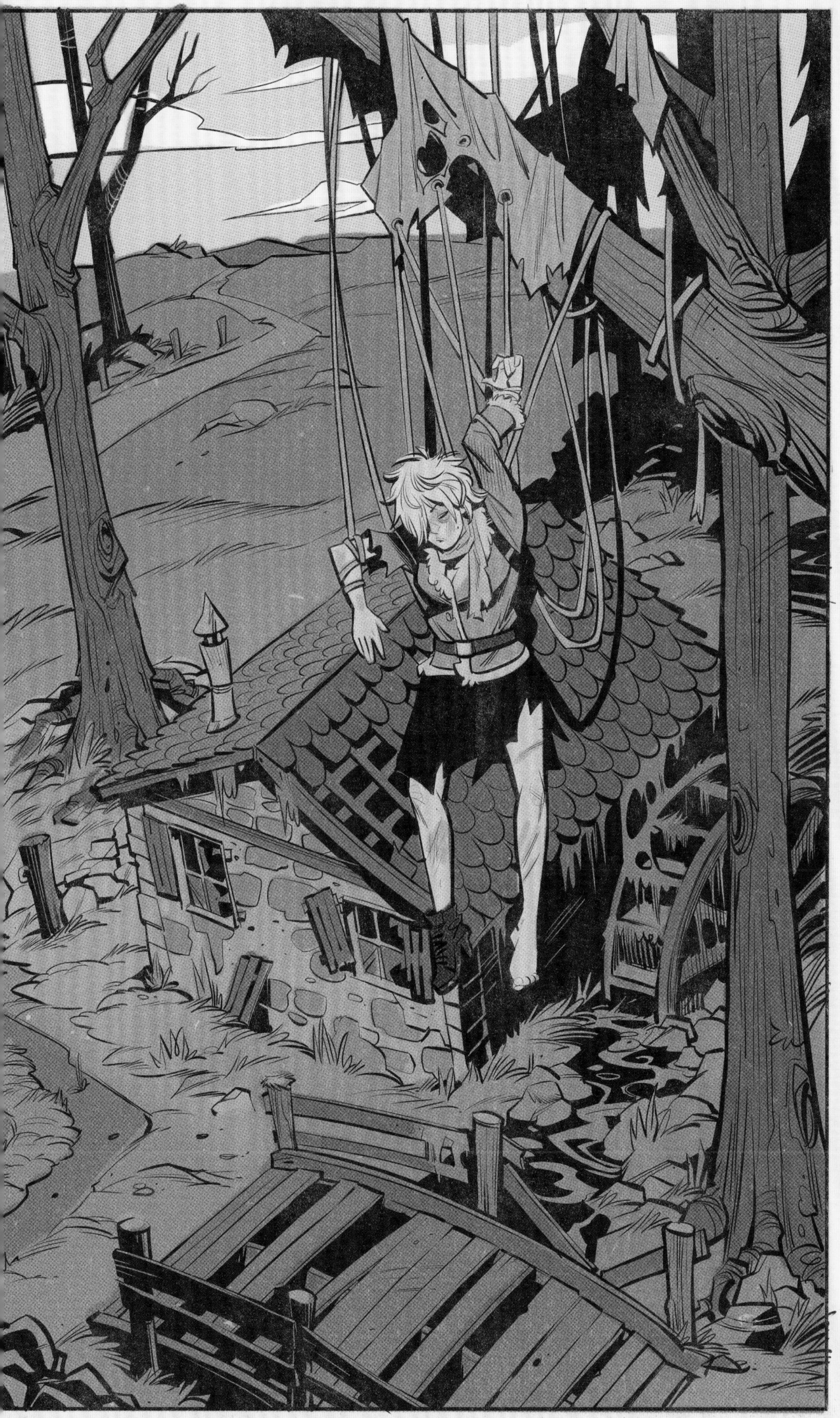

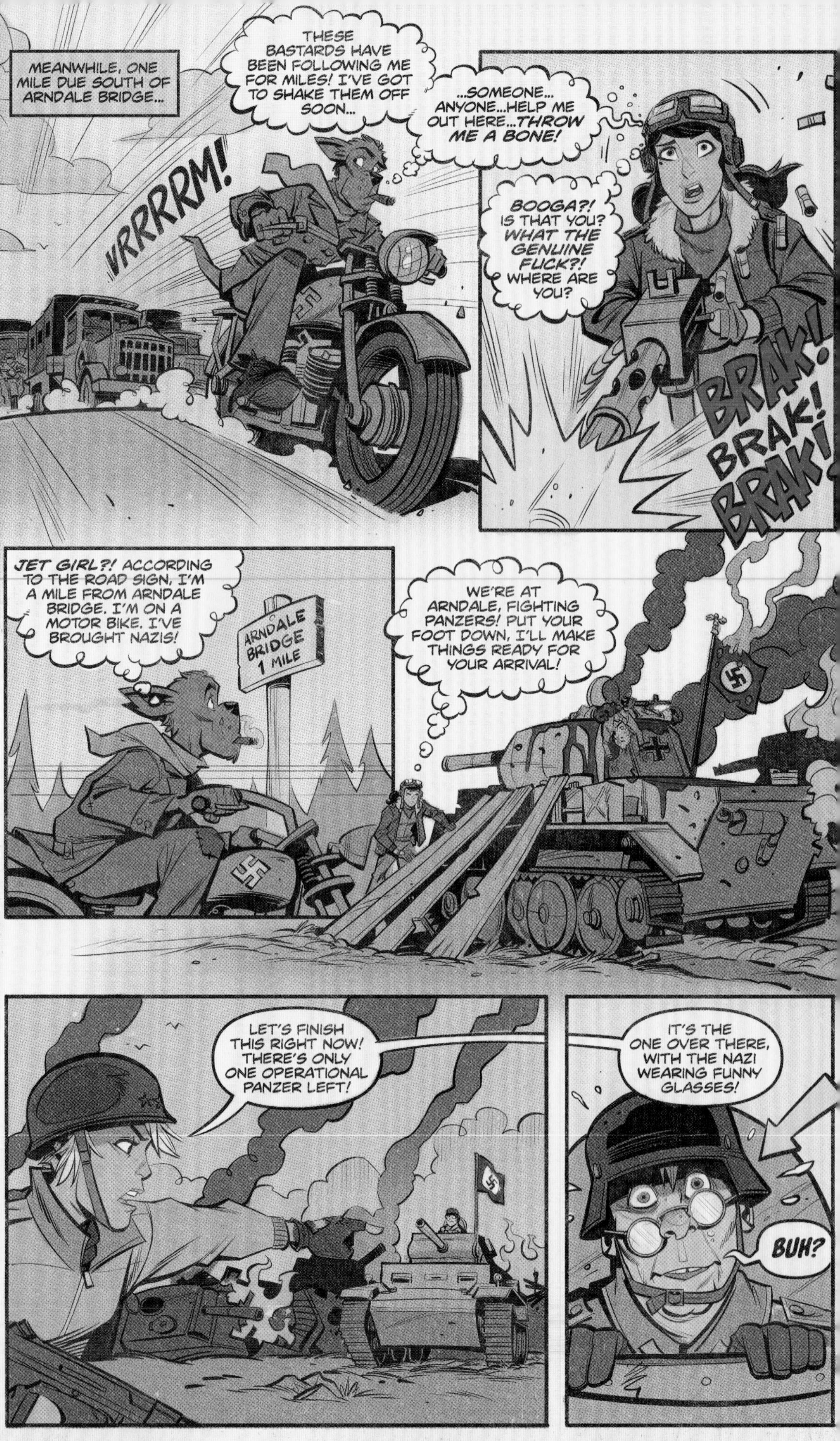

MEANWHILE, ONE MILE DUE SOUTH OF ARNDALE BRIDGE...
THESE BASTARDS HAVE BEEN FOLLOWING ME FOR MILES! I'VE GOT TO SHAKE THEM OFF SOON...
...SOMEONE... ANYONE...HELP ME OUT HERE...THROW ME A BONE!
VRRRRM!
BOOGA?! IS THAT YOU? WHAT THE GENUINE FUCK?! WHERE ARE YOU?
BRAK! BRAK! BRAK!
JET GIRL?! ACCORDING TO THE ROAD SIGN, I'M A MILE FROM ARNDALE BRIDGE. I'M ON A MOTOR BIKE. I'VE BROUGHT NAZIS!
ARNDALE BRIDGE 1 MILE
WE'RE AT ARNDALE, FIGHTING PANZERS! PUT YOUR FOOT DOWN, I'LL MAKE THINGS READY FOR YOUR ARRIVAL!
LET'S FINISH THIS RIGHT NOW! THERE'S ONLY ONE OPERATIONAL PANZER LEFT!
IT'S THE ONE OVER THERE, WITH THE NAZI WEARING FUNNY GLASSES!
BUH?

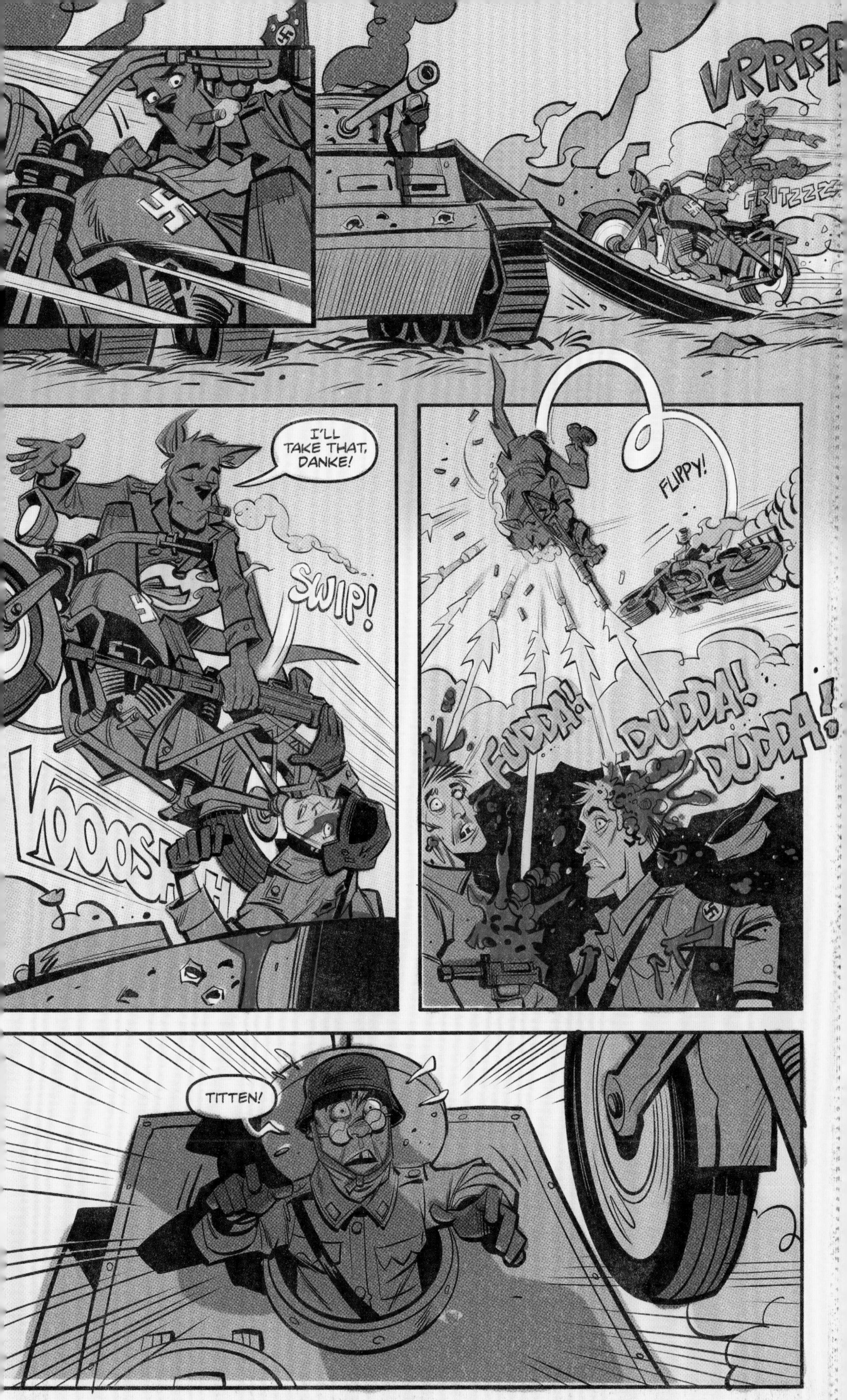
VRRRR
FRITZZZ
I'LL TAKE THAT, DANKE!
SWIP!
VOOOSH
FLIPPY!
FUDDA!
DUDDA!
DUDDA!
TITTEN!

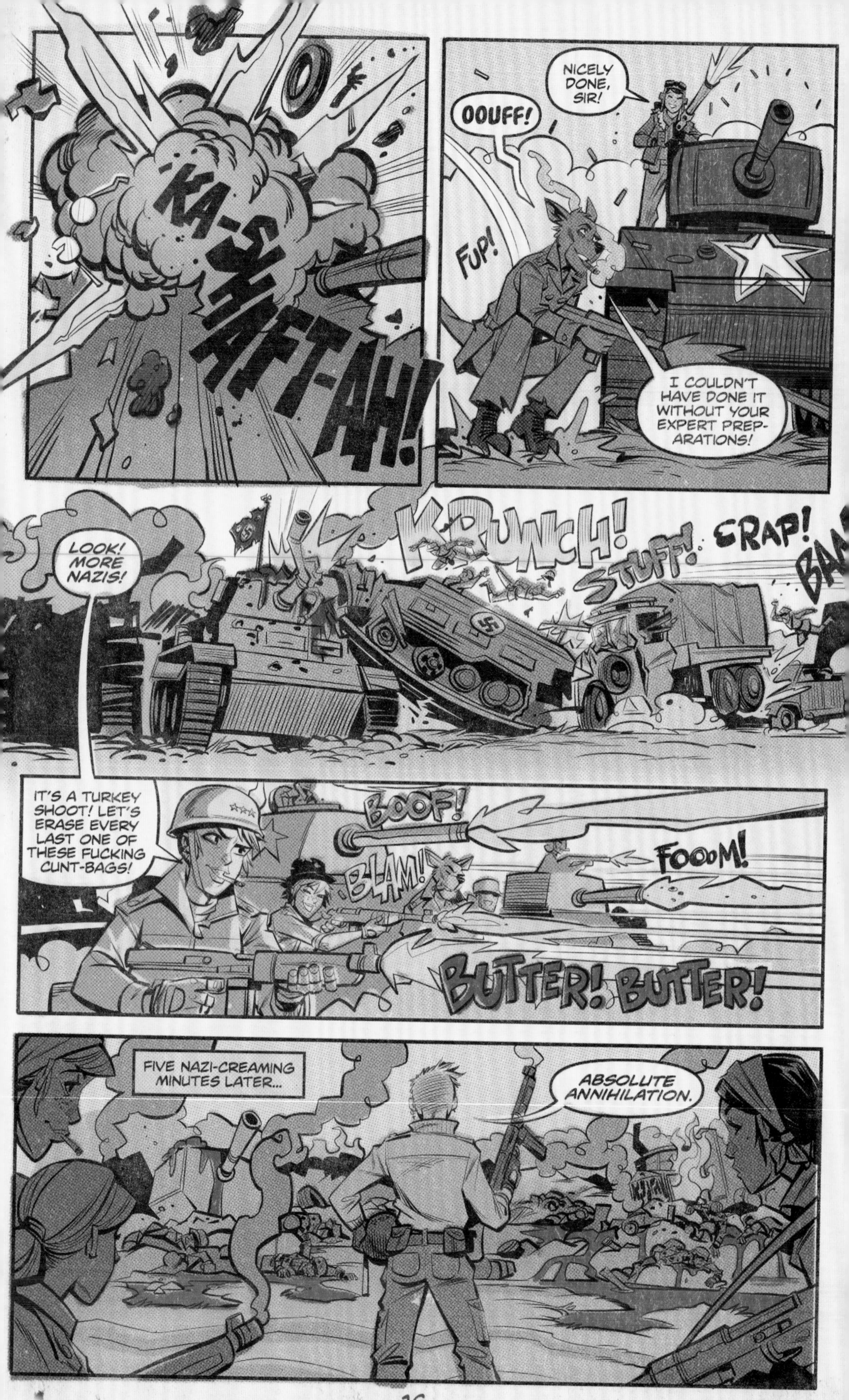
KA-SHAFT-AH!
NICELY DONE, SIR!
OOUFF!
FUP!
I COULDN'T HAVE DONE IT WITHOUT YOUR EXPERT PREP-ARATIONS!
LOOK! MORE NAZIS!
KRUNCH!
STUFF!
CRAP!
IT'S A TURKEY SHOOT! LET'S ERASE EVERY LAST ONE OF THESE FUCKING CUNT-BAGS!
BOOF!
BLAM!
FOOOM!
BUTTER! BUTTER!
FIVE NAZI-CREAMING MINUTES LATER...
ABSOLUTE ANNIHILATION.

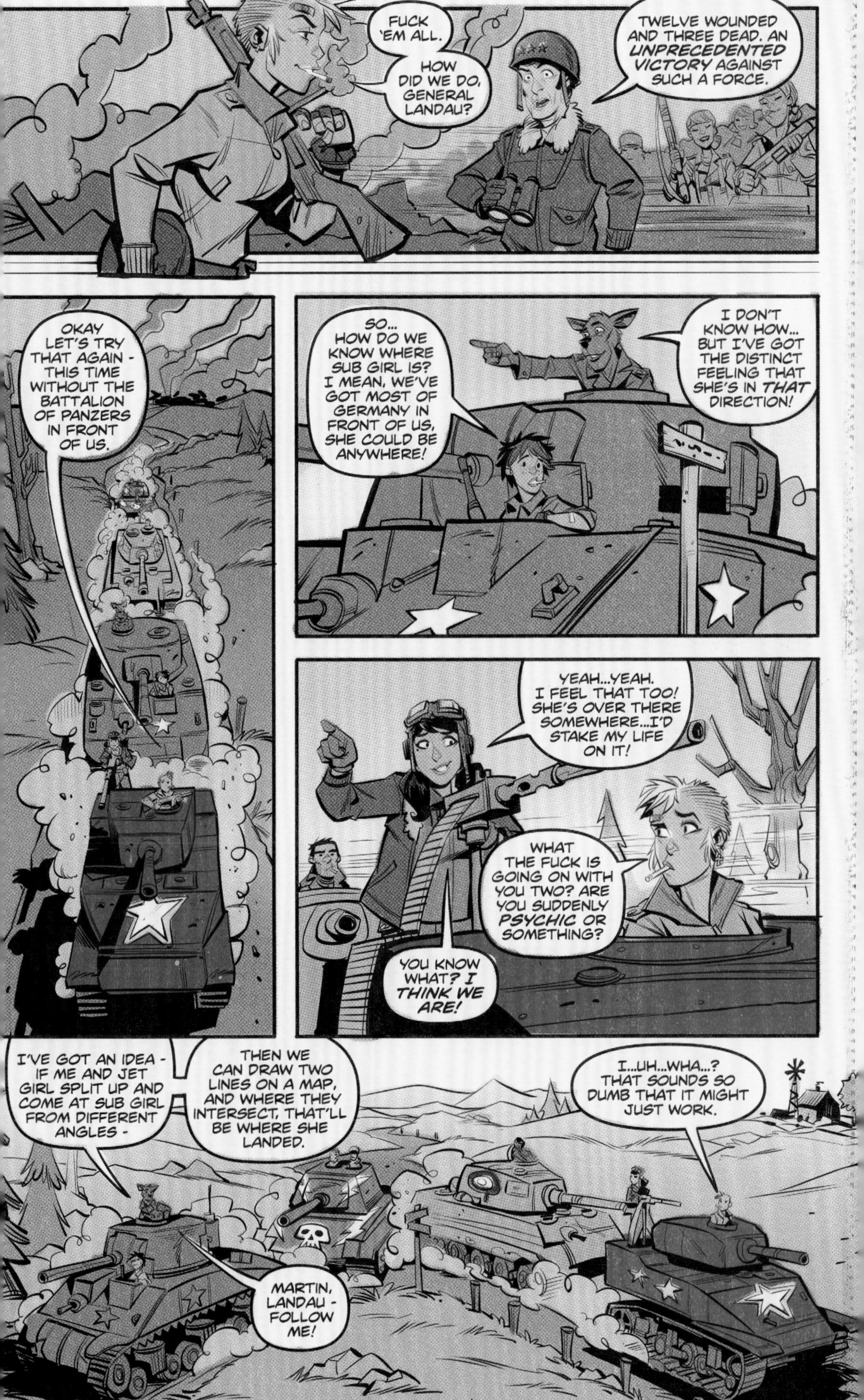

FUCK 'EM ALL.
HOW DID WE DO, GENERAL LANDAU?
TWELVE WOUNDED AND THREE DEAD. AN UNPRECEDENTED VICTORY AGAINST SUCH A FORCE.
OKAY LET'S TRY THAT AGAIN - THIS TIME WITHOUT THE BATTALION OF PANZERS IN FRONT OF US.
SO... HOW DO WE KNOW WHERE SUB GIRL IS? I MEAN, WE'VE GOT MOST OF GERMANY IN FRONT OF US, SHE COULD BE ANYWHERE!
I DON'T KNOW HOW... BUT I'VE GOT THE DISTINCT FEELING THAT SHE'S IN THAT DIRECTION!
YEAH...YEAH. I FEEL THAT TOO! SHE'S OVER THERE SOMEWHERE...I'D STAKE MY LIFE ON IT!
WHAT THE FUCK IS GOING ON WITH YOU TWO? ARE YOU SUDDENLY PSYCHIC OR SOMETHING?
YOU KNOW WHAT? I THINK WE ARE!
I'VE GOT AN IDEA - IF ME AND JET GIRL SPLIT UP AND COME AT SUB GIRL FROM DIFFERENT ANGLES -
THEN WE CAN DRAW TWO LINES ON A MAP, AND WHERE THEY INTERSECT, THAT'LL BE WHERE SHE LANDED.
I...UH...WHA...? THAT SOUNDS SO DUMB THAT IT MIGHT JUST WORK.
MARTIN, LANDAU - FOLLOW ME!

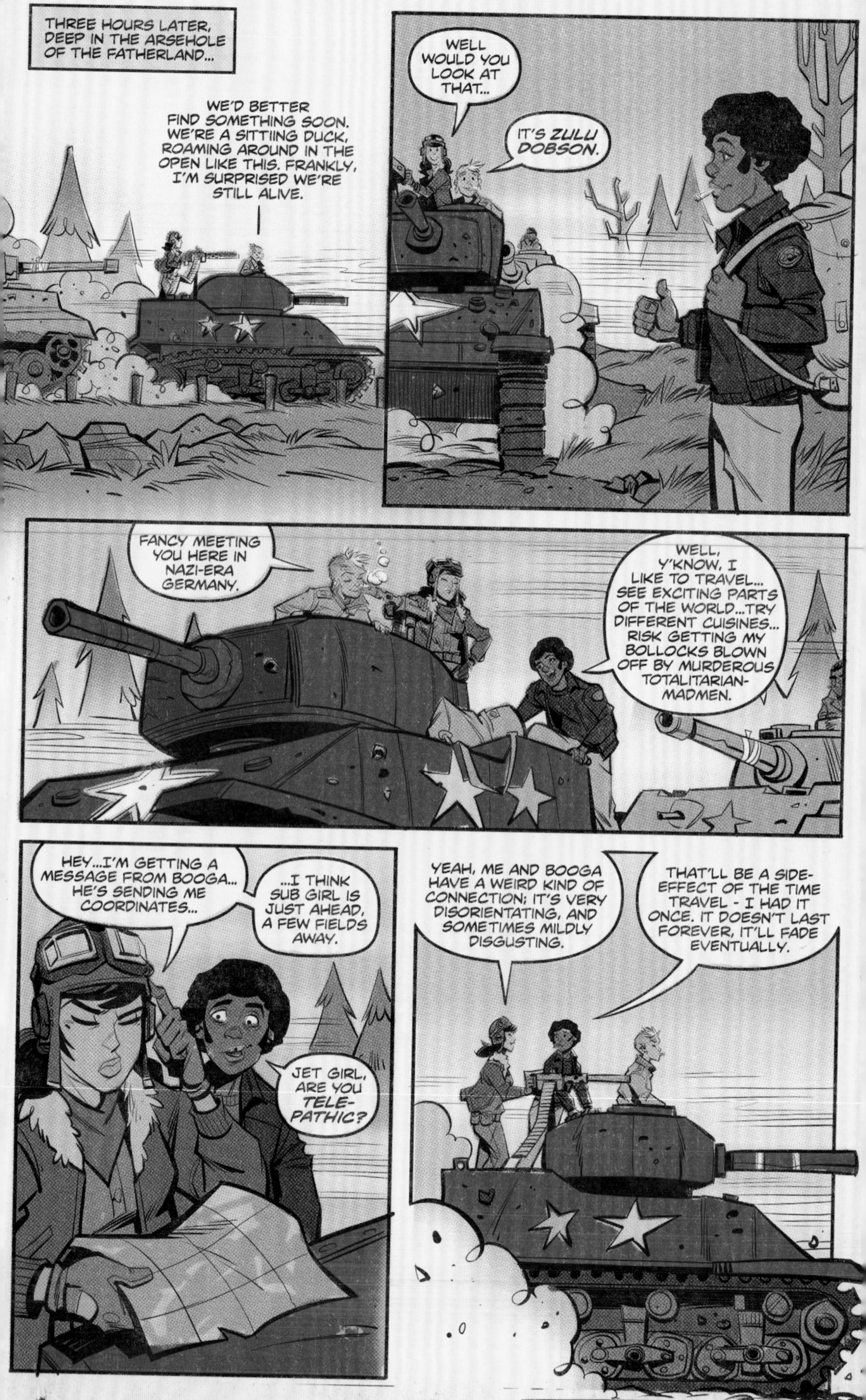
THREE HOURS LATER, DEEP IN THE ARSEHOLE OF THE FATHERLAND...
WE'D BETTER FIND SOMETHING SOON. WE'RE A SITTIING DUCK, ROAMING AROUND IN THE OPEN LIKE THIS. FRANKLY, I'M SURPRISED WE'RE STILL ALIVE.
WELL WOULD YOU LOOK AT THAT...
IT'S ZULU DOBSON.
FANCY MEETING YOU HERE IN NAZI-ERA GERMANY.
WELL, Y'KNOW, I LIKE TO TRAVEL... SEE EXCITING PARTS OF THE WORLD...TRY DIFFERENT CUISINES... RISK GETTING MY BOLLOCKS BLOWN OFF BY MURDEROUS TOTALITARIAN-MADMEN.
HEY...I'M GETTING A MESSAGE FROM BOOGA... HE'S SENDING ME COORDINATES...
...I THINK SUB GIRL IS JUST AHEAD, A FEW FIELDS AWAY.
JET GIRL, ARE YOU TELE-PATHIC?
YEAH, ME AND BOOGA HAVE A WEIRD KIND OF CONNECTION; IT'S VERY DISORIENTATING, AND SOMETIMES MILDLY DISGUSTING.
THAT'LL BE A SIDE-EFFECT OF THE TIME TRAVEL - I HAD IT ONCE. IT DOESN'T LAST FOREVER, IT'LL FADE EVENTUALLY.

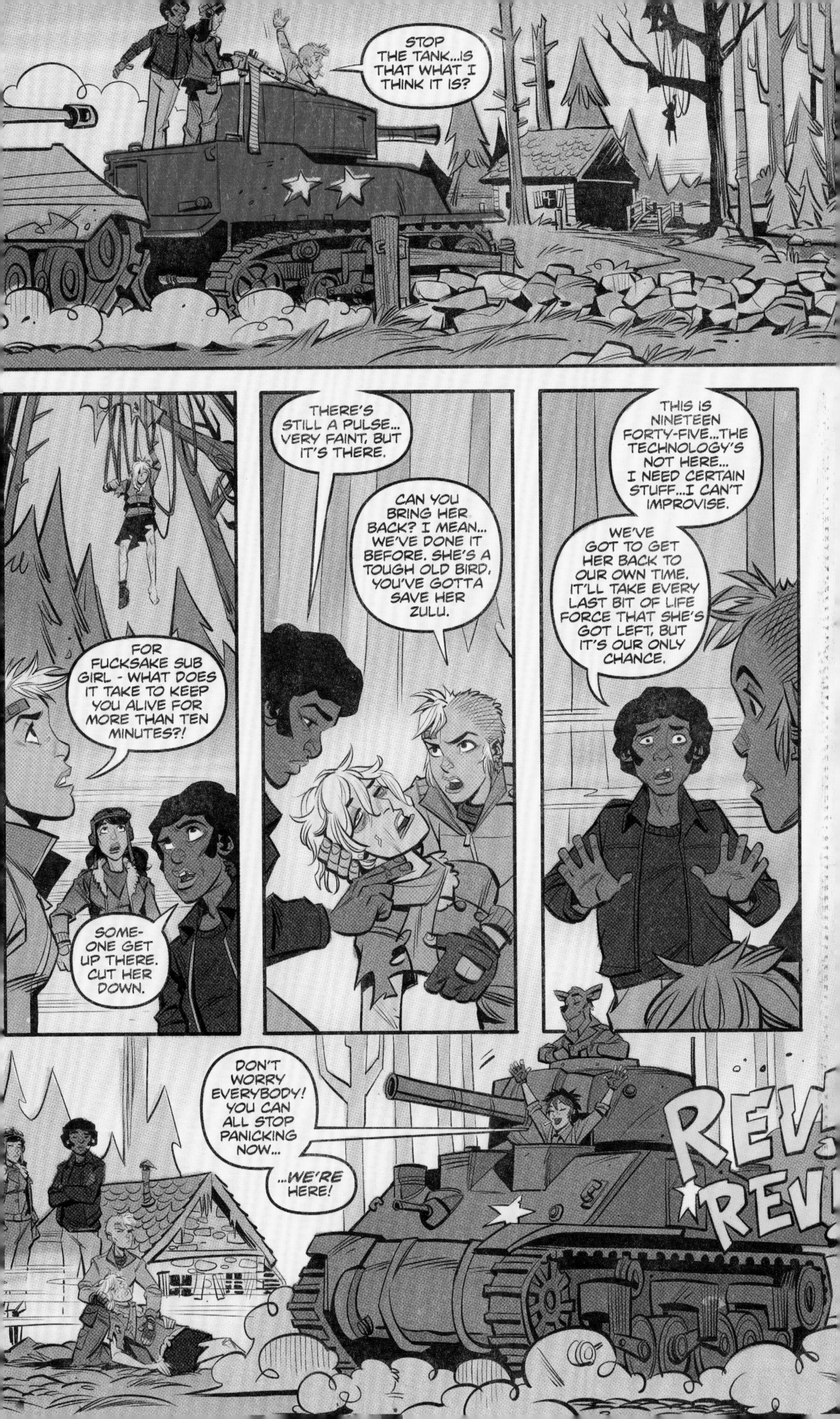

STOP THE TANK...IS THAT WHAT I THINK IT IS?
FOR FUCKSAKE SUB GIRL - WHAT DOES IT TAKE TO KEEP YOU ALIVE FOR MORE THAN TEN MINUTES?!
SOME-ONE GET UP THERE. CUT HER DOWN.
THERE'S STILL A PULSE... VERY FAINT, BUT IT'S THERE.
CAN YOU BRING HER BACK? I MEAN... WE'VE DONE IT BEFORE. SHE'S A TOUGH OLD BIRD, YOU'VE GOTTA SAVE HER ZULU.
THIS IS NINETEEN FORTY-FIVE...THE TECHNOLOGY'S NOT HERE... I NEED CERTAIN STUFF...I CAN'T IMPROVISE.
WE'VE GOT TO GET HER BACK TO OUR OWN TIME. IT'LL TAKE EVERY LAST BIT OF LIFE FORCE THAT SHE'S GOT LEFT, BUT IT'S OUR ONLY CHANCE.
DON'T WORRY EVERYBODY! YOU CAN ALL STOP PANICKING NOW...
...WE'RE HERE!
REV
REV

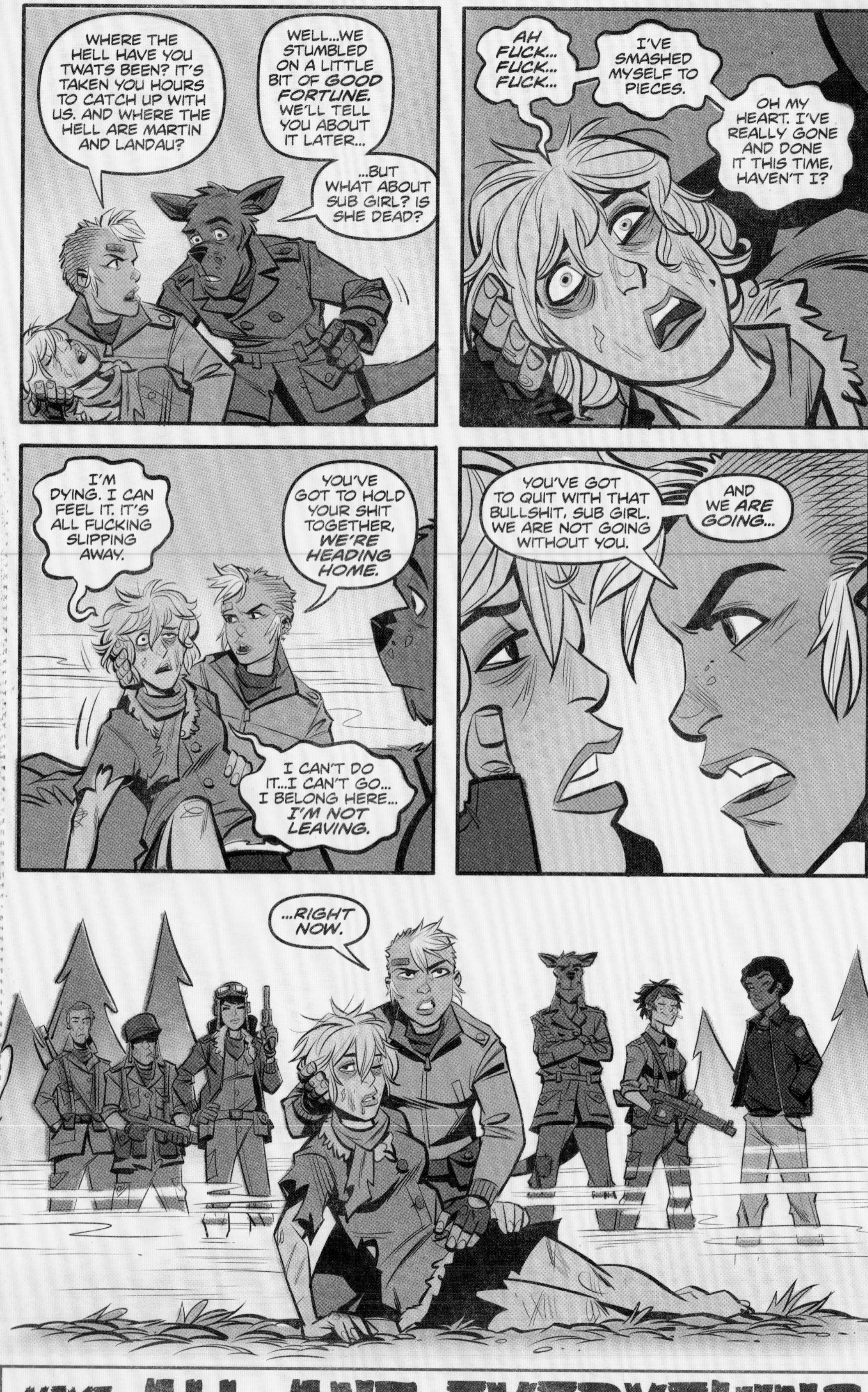
WHERE THE HELL HAVE YOU TWATS BEEN? IT'S TAKEN YOU HOURS TO CATCH UP WITH US. AND WHERE THE HELL ARE MARTIN AND LANDAU?
WELL...WE STUMBLED ON A LITTLE BIT OF GOOD FORTUNE. WE'LL TELL YOU ABOUT IT LATER...
...BUT WHAT ABOUT SUB GIRL? IS SHE DEAD?
AH FUCK... FUCK... FUCK...
I'VE SMASHED MYSELF TO PIECES.
OH MY HEART. I'VE REALLY GONE AND DONE IT THIS TIME, HAVEN'T I?
I'M DYING. I CAN FEEL IT. IT'S ALL FUCKING SLIPPING AWAY.
YOU'VE GOT TO HOLD YOUR SHIT TOGETHER, WE'RE HEADING HOME.
I CAN'T DO IT...I CAN'T GO... I BELONG HERE... I'M NOT LEAVING.
YOU'VE GOT TO QUIT WITH THAT BULLSHIT, SUB GIRL. WE ARE NOT GOING WITHOUT YOU.
AND WE ARE GOING...
...RIGHT NOW.

NEXT: ALL AND EVERYTHING

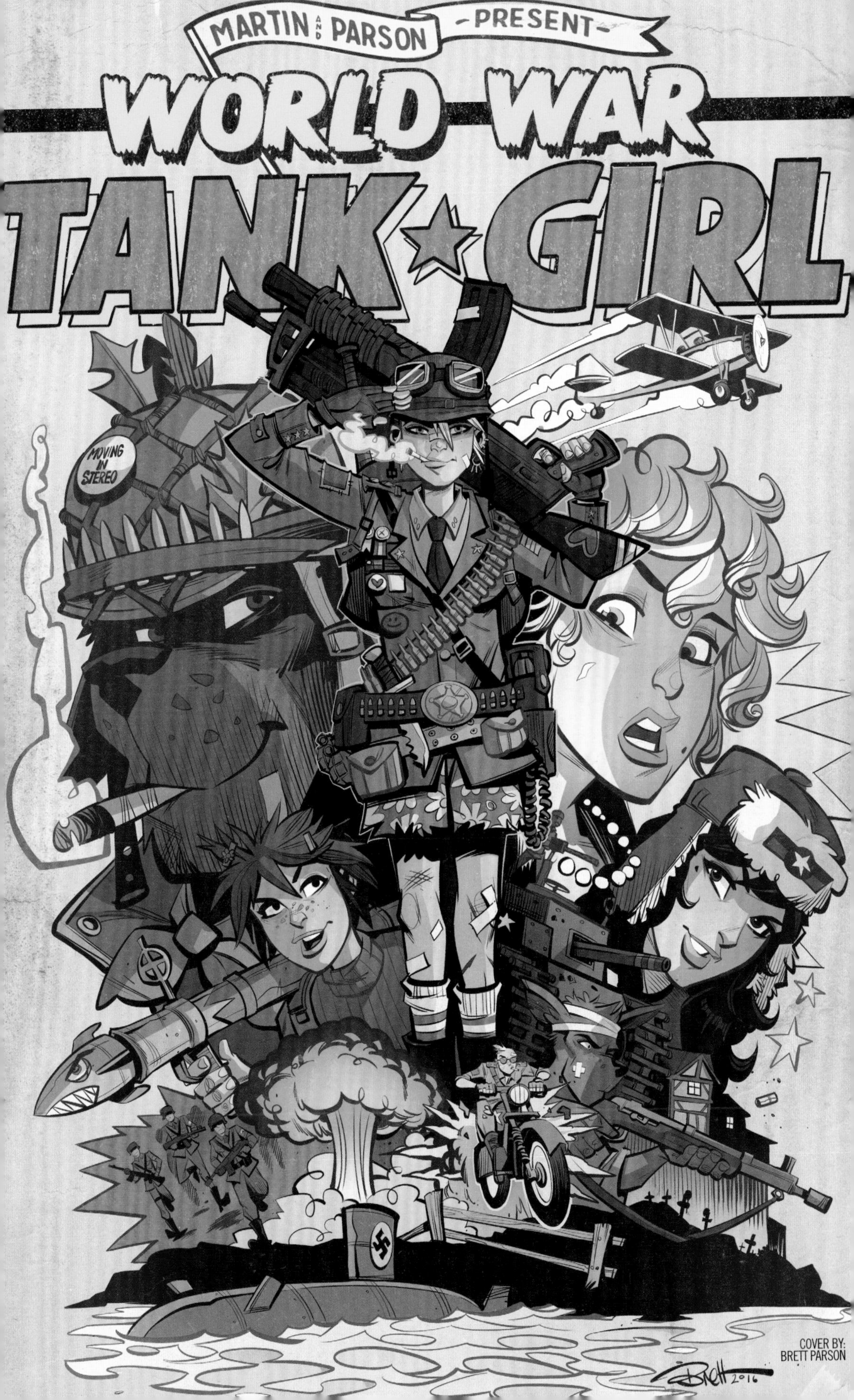
MARTIN AND PARSON
-PRESENT-
WORLD WAR
TANK GIRL
MOVING IN STEREO
BRETT 2016
COVER BY:
BRETT PARSON

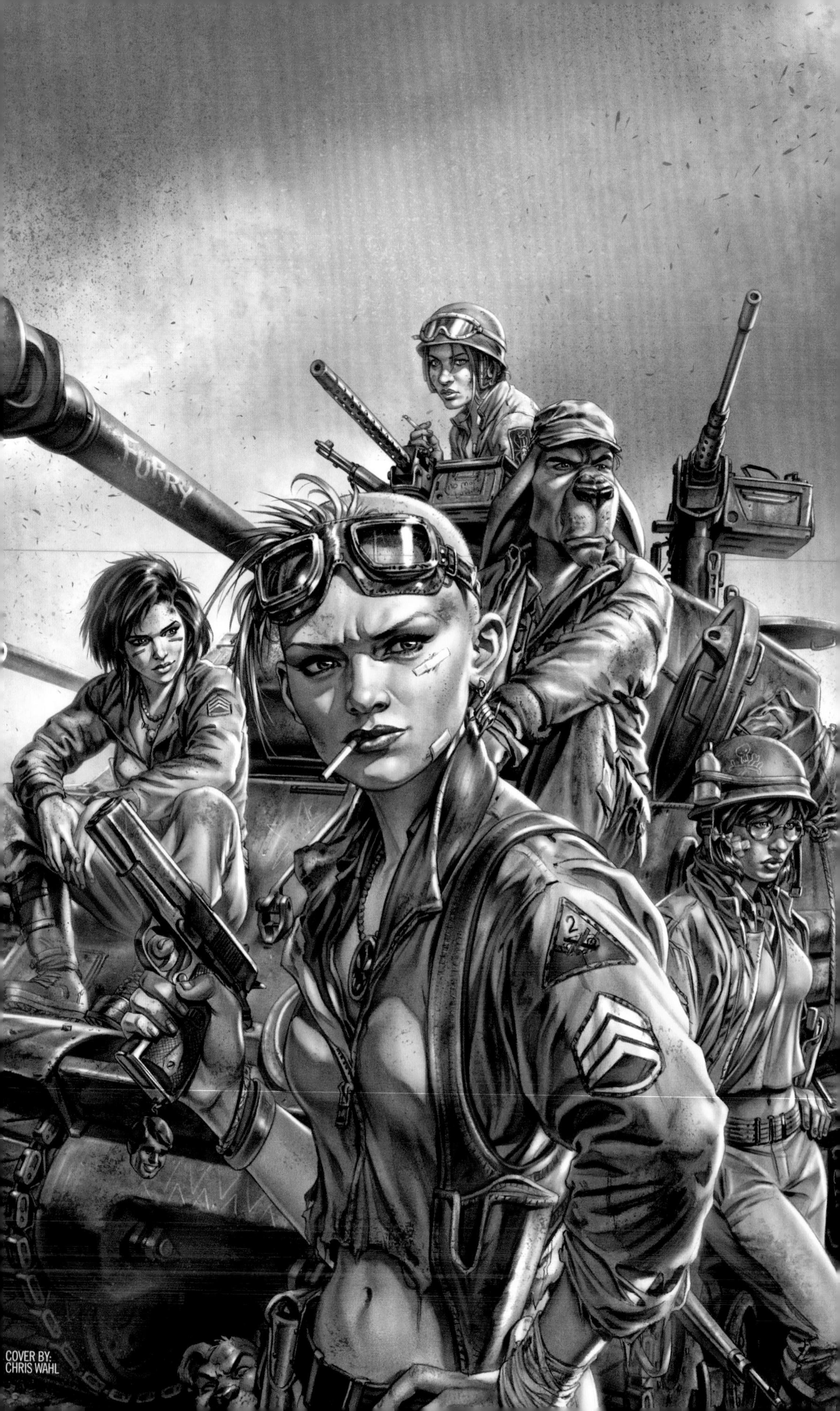
FURRY

COVER BY:
CHRIS WAHL

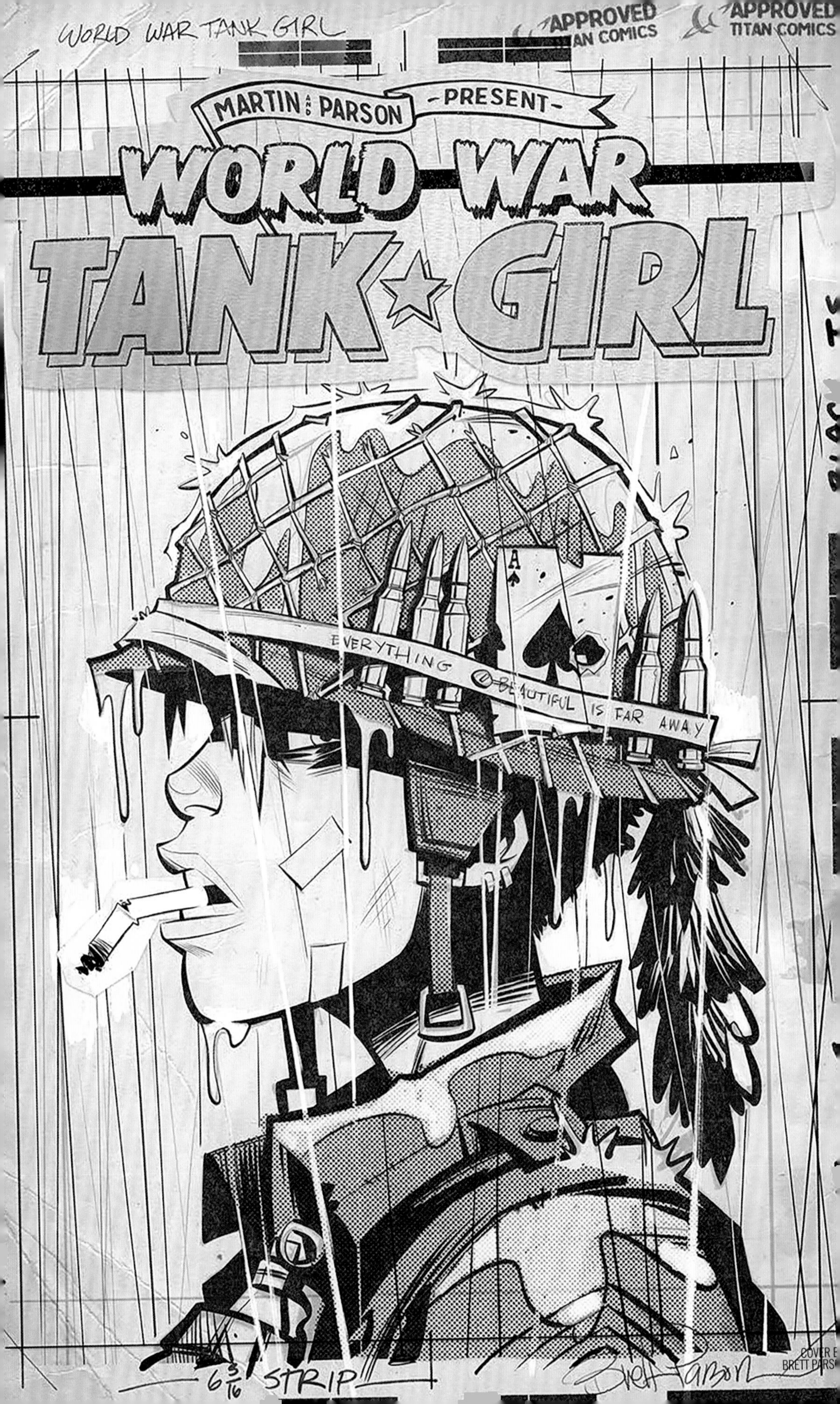
WORLD WAR TANK GIRL
APPROVED
TITAN COMICS
MARTIN AND PARSON
-PRESENT-
WORLD WAR
TANK GIRL
EVERYTHING BEAUTIFUL IS FAR AWAY
6 3/16 STRIP

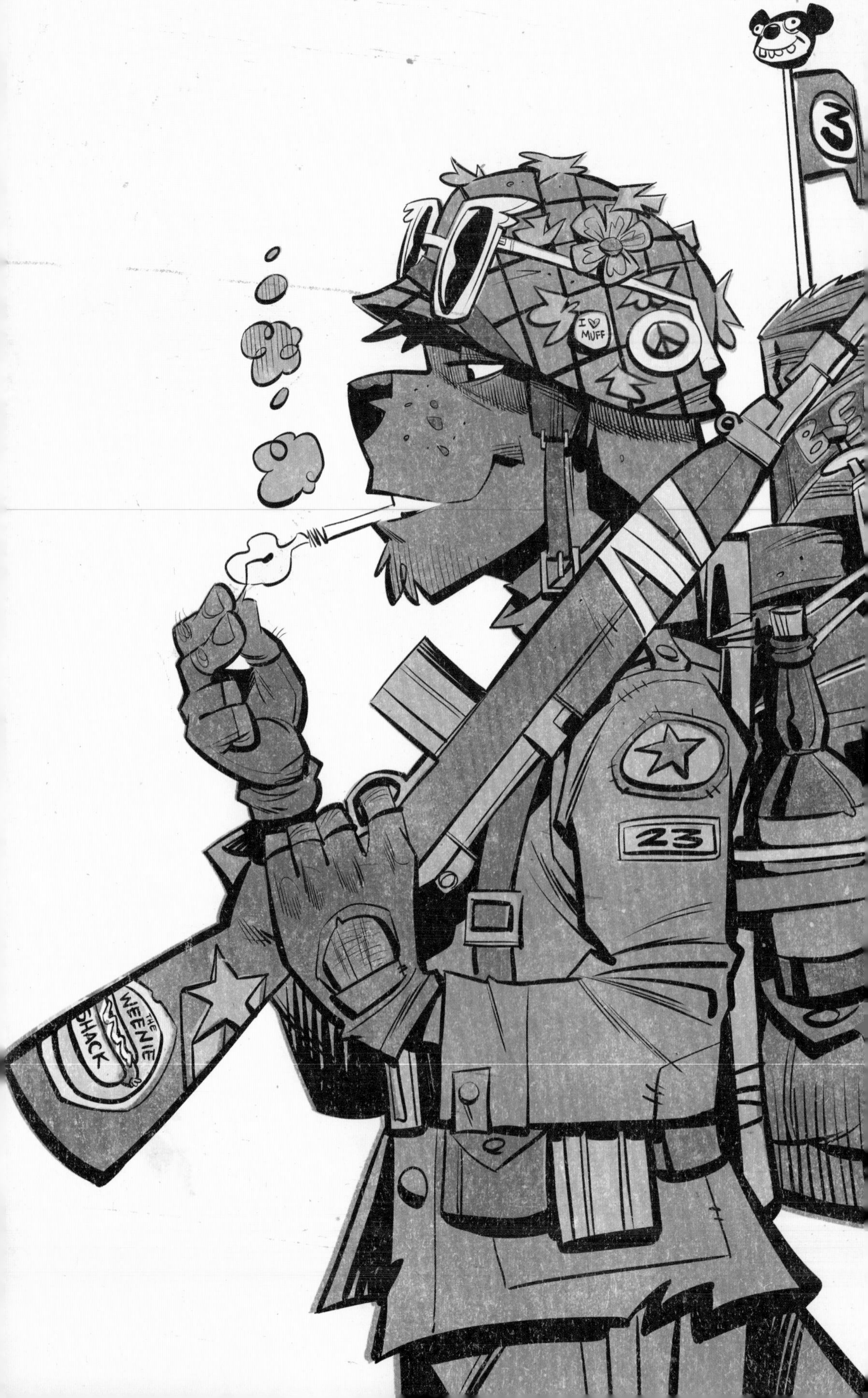
I ♥ MUFF
23
THE WEENIE SHACK

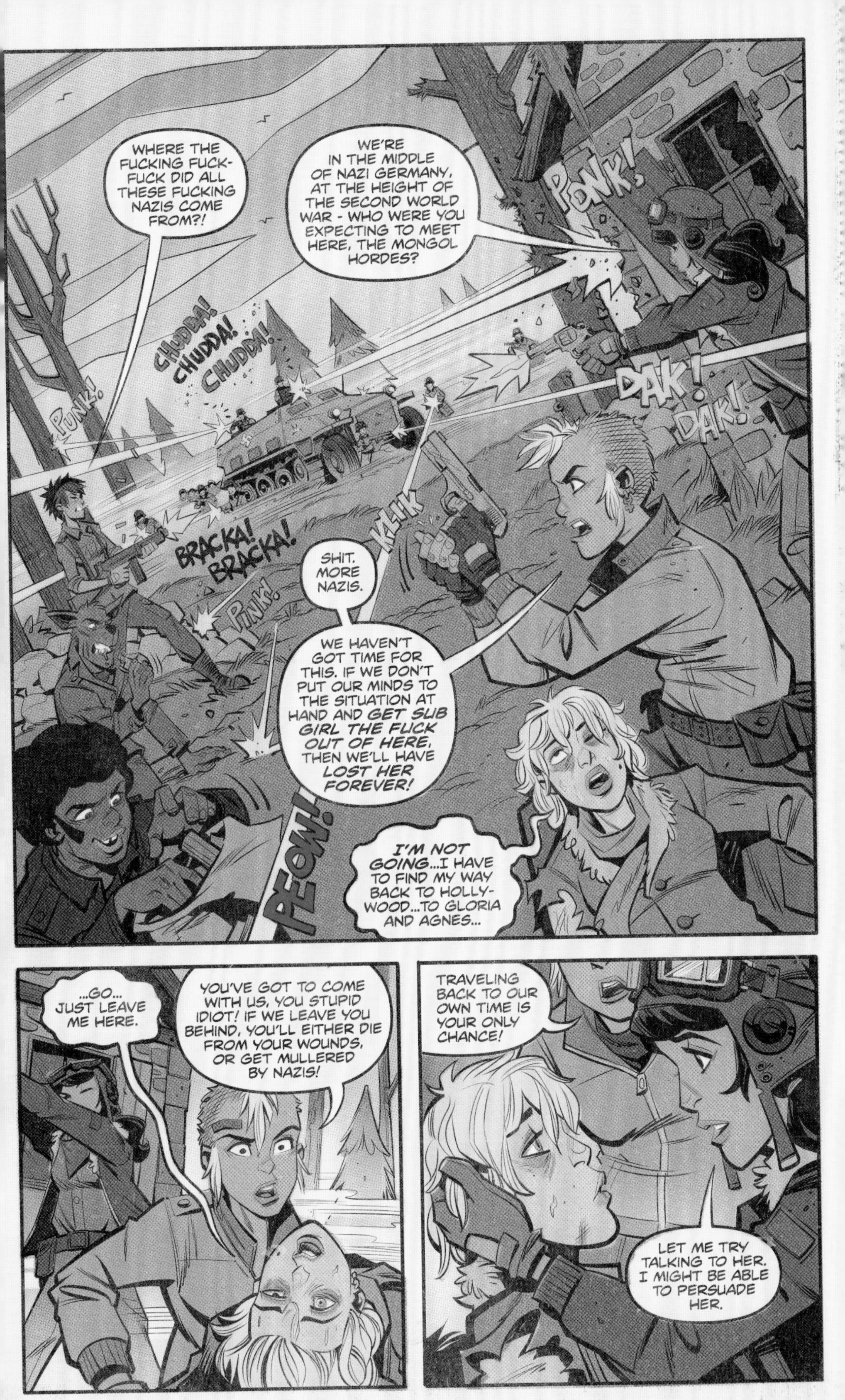

WHERE THE FUCKING FUCK-FUCK DID ALL THESE FUCKING NAZIS COME FROM?!
WE'RE IN THE MIDDLE OF NAZI GERMANY, AT THE HEIGHT OF THE SECOND WORLD WAR - WHO WERE YOU EXPECTING TO MEET HERE, THE MONGOL HORDES?
PONK!
CHUDDA! CHUDDA! CHUDDA!
PUNK!
DAK! DAK!
KLIK
BRACKA! BRACKA!
PINK!
SHIT. MORE NAZIS.
WE HAVEN'T GOT TIME FOR THIS. IF WE DON'T PUT OUR MINDS TO THE SITUATION AT HAND AND GET SUB GIRL THE FUCK OUT OF HERE, THEN WE'LL HAVE LOST HER FOREVER!
PEOW!
I'M NOT GOING...I HAVE TO FIND MY WAY BACK TO HOLLY-WOOD...TO GLORIA AND AGNES...
...GO... JUST LEAVE ME HERE.
YOU'VE GOT TO COME WITH US, YOU STUPID IDIOT! IF WE LEAVE YOU BEHIND, YOU'LL EITHER DIE FROM YOUR WOUNDS, OR GET MULLERED BY NAZIS!
TRAVELING BACK TO OUR OWN TIME IS YOUR ONLY CHANCE!
LET ME TRY TALKING TO HER. I MIGHT BE ABLE TO PERSUADE HER.

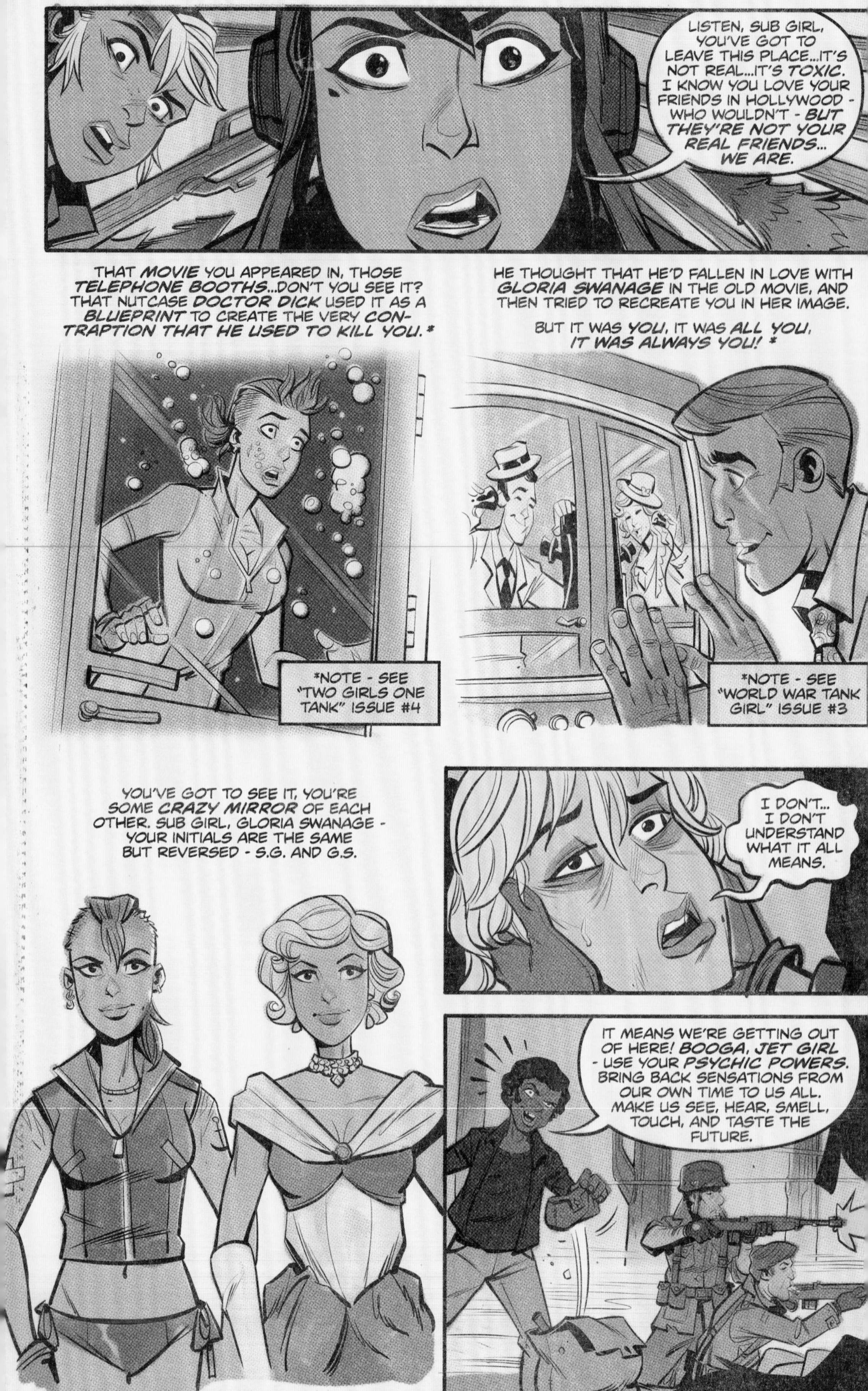
LISTEN, SUB GIRL, YOU'VE GOT TO LEAVE THIS PLACE...IT'S NOT REAL...IT'S TOXIC. I KNOW YOU LOVE YOUR FRIENDS IN HOLLYWOOD - WHO WOULDN'T - BUT THEY'RE NOT YOUR REAL FRIENDS... WE ARE.
THAT MOVIE YOU APPEARED IN, THOSE TELEPHONE BOOTHS...DON'T YOU SEE IT? THAT NUTCASE DOCTOR DICK USED IT AS A BLUEPRINT TO CREATE THE VERY CONTRAPTION THAT HE USED TO KILL YOU.*
*NOTE - SEE "TWO GIRLS ONE TANK" ISSUE #4
HE THOUGHT THAT HE'D FALLEN IN LOVE WITH GLORIA SWANAGE IN THE OLD MOVIE, AND THEN TRIED TO RECREATE YOU IN HER IMAGE.
BUT IT WAS YOU, IT WAS ALL YOU, IT WAS ALWAYS YOU! *
*NOTE - SEE "WORLD WAR TANK GIRL" ISSUE #3
YOU'VE GOT TO SEE IT, YOU'RE SOME CRAZY MIRROR OF EACH OTHER. SUB GIRL, GLORIA SWANAGE - YOUR INITIALS ARE THE SAME BUT REVERSED - S.G. AND G.S.
I DON'T... I DON'T UNDERSTAND WHAT IT ALL MEANS.
IT MEANS WE'RE GETTING OUT OF HERE! BOOGA, JET GIRL - USE YOUR PSYCHIC POWERS. BRING BACK SENSATIONS FROM OUR OWN TIME TO US ALL. MAKE US SEE, HEAR, SMELL, TOUCH, AND TASTE THE FUTURE.

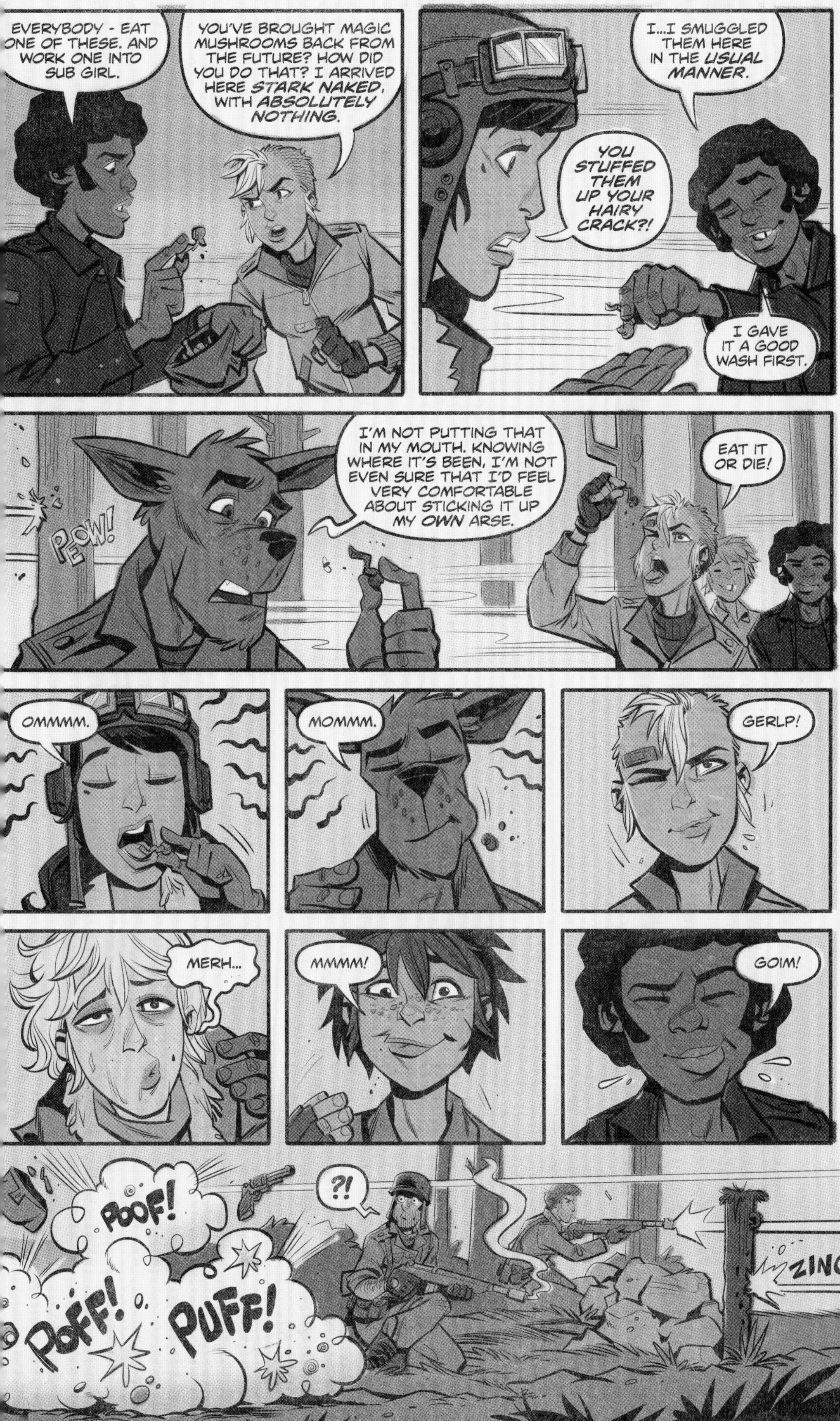
EVERYBODY - EAT ONE OF THESE. AND WORK ONE INTO SUB GIRL.
YOU'VE BROUGHT MAGIC MUSHROOMS BACK FROM THE FUTURE? HOW DID YOU DO THAT? I ARRIVED HERE STARK NAKED, WITH ABSOLUTELY NOTHING.
I...I SMUGGLED THEM HERE IN THE USUAL MANNER.
YOU STUFFED THEM UP YOUR HAIRY CRACK?!
I GAVE IT A GOOD WASH FIRST.
PEOW!
I'M NOT PUTTING THAT IN MY MOUTH. KNOWING WHERE IT'S BEEN, I'M NOT EVEN SURE THAT I'D FEEL VERY COMFORTABLE ABOUT STICKING IT UP MY OWN ARSE.
EAT IT OR DIE!
OMMMM.
MOMMM.
GERLP!
MERH...
MMMM!
GOIM!
POOF!
POFF!
PUFF!
?!
ZING!

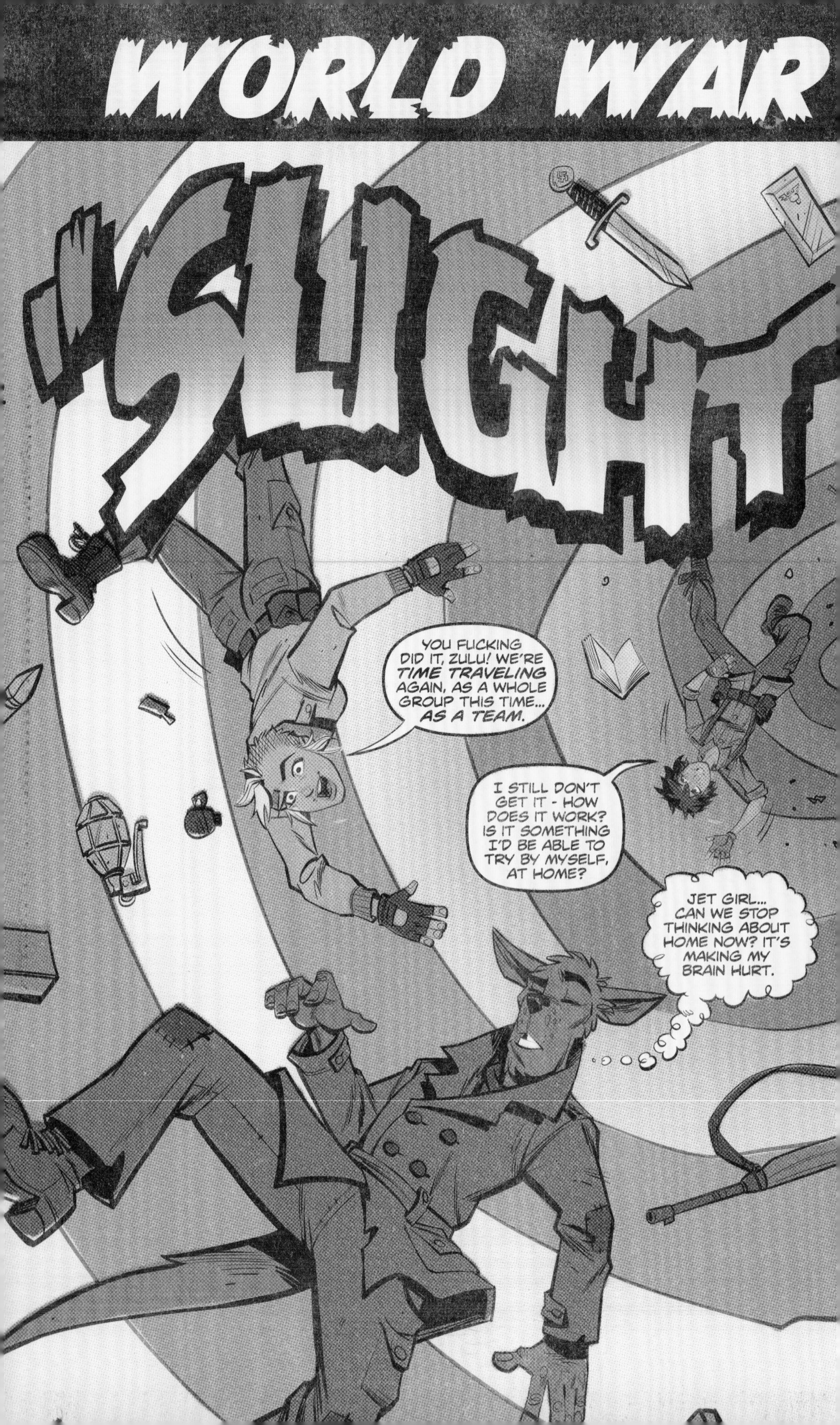
WORLD WAR
SLIGHT
YOU FUCKING DID IT, ZULU! WE'RE TIME TRAVELING AGAIN, AS A WHOLE GROUP THIS TIME... AS A TEAM.
I STILL DON'T GET IT - HOW DOES IT WORK? IS IT SOMETHING I'D BE ABLE TO TRY BY MYSELF, AT HOME?
JET GIRL... CAN WE STOP THINKING ABOUT HOME NOW? IT'S MAKING MY BRAIN HURT.

TANK GIRL PART FOUR

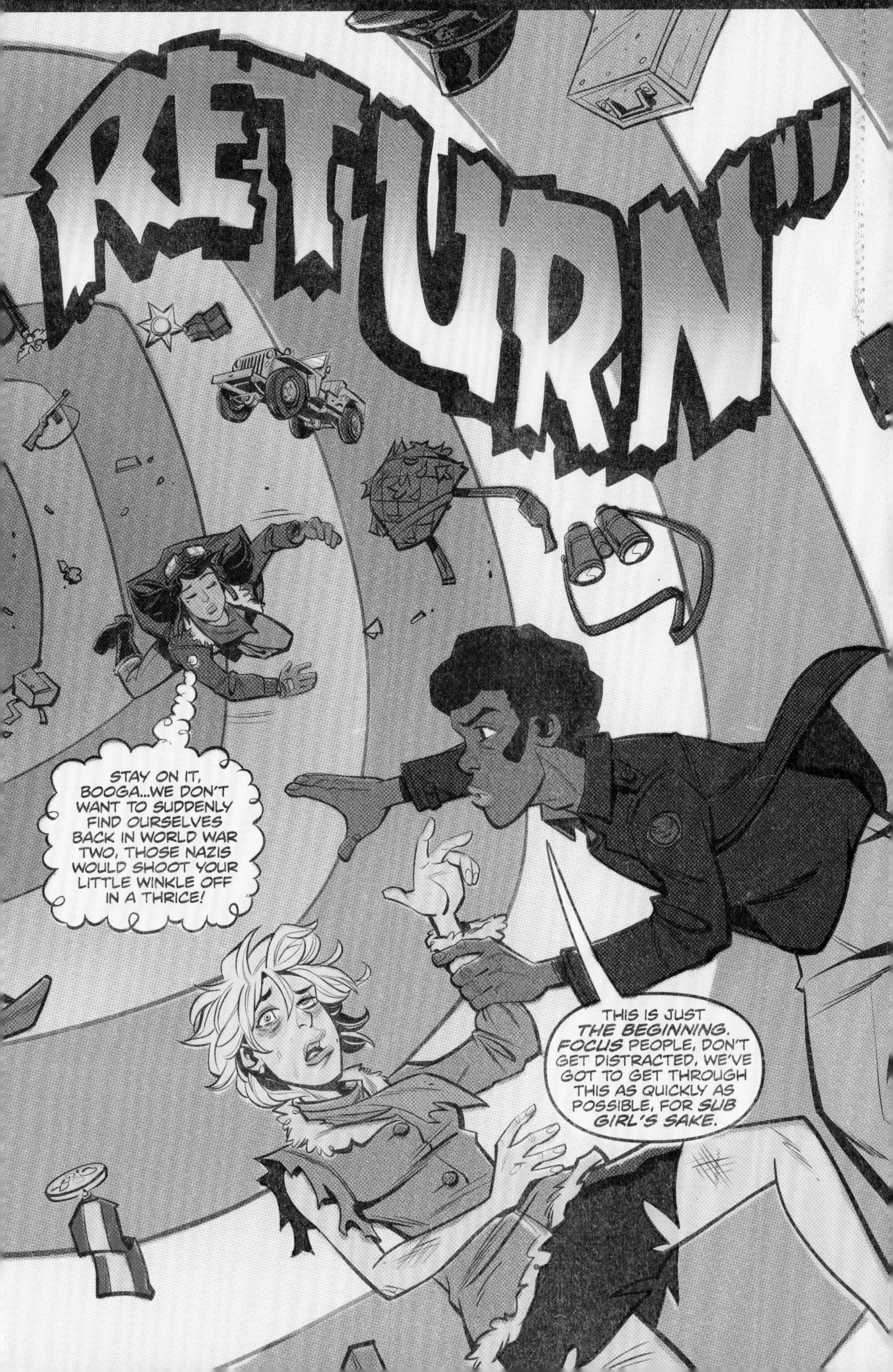
RETURN
STAY ON IT, BOOGA...WE DON'T WANT TO SUDDENLY FIND OURSELVES BACK IN WORLD WAR TWO, THOSE NAZIS WOULD SHOOT YOUR LITTLE WINKLE OFF IN A THRICE!
THIS IS JUST *THE BEGINNING. FOCUS* PEOPLE, DON'T GET DISTRACTED. WE'VE GOT TO GET THROUGH THIS AS QUICKLY AS POSSIBLE, FOR *SUB GIRL'S SAKE.*

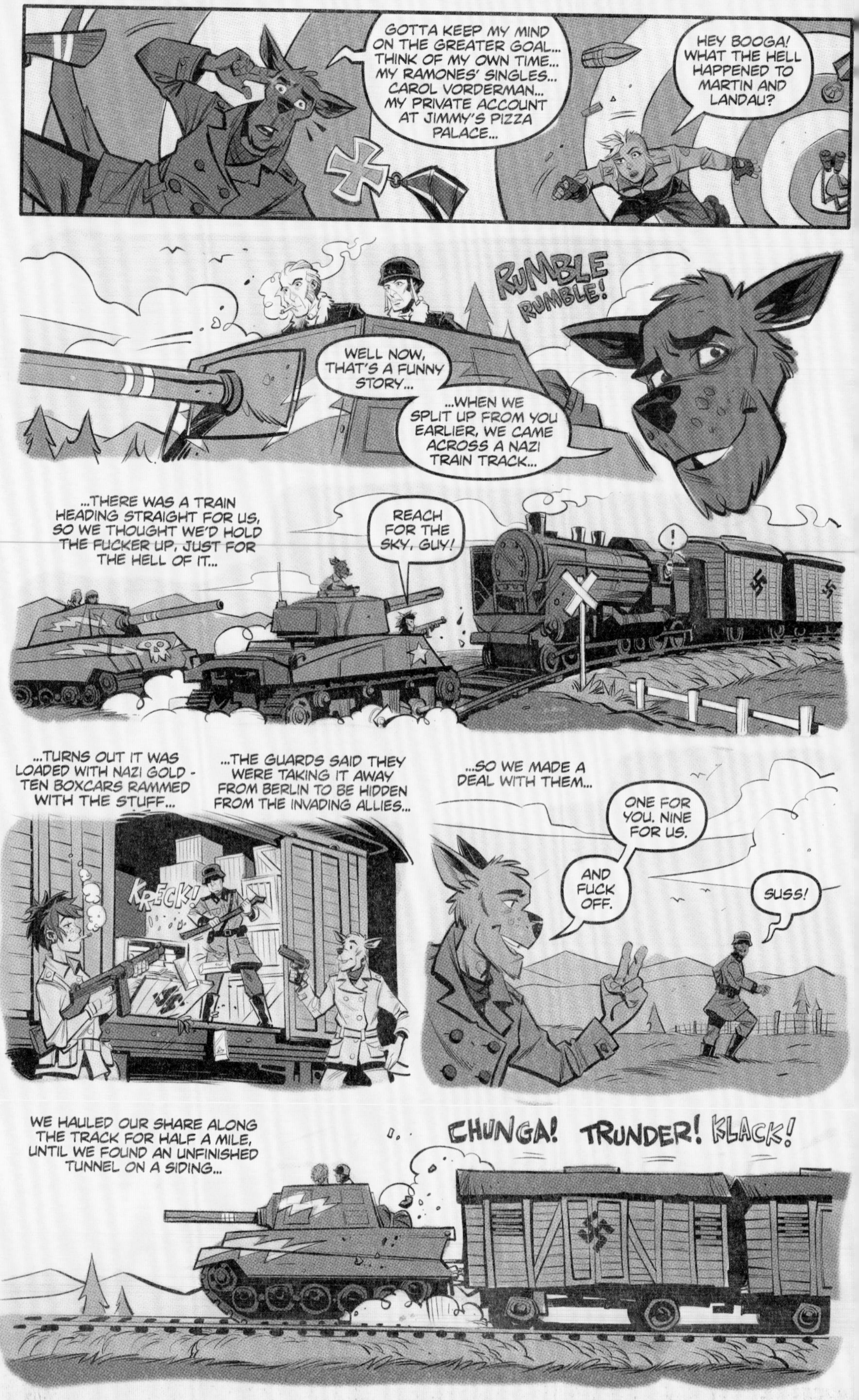

GOTTA KEEP MY MIND ON THE GREATER GOAL... THINK OF MY OWN TIME... MY RAMONES' SINGLES... CAROL VORDERMAN... MY PRIVATE ACCOUNT AT JIMMY'S PIZZA PALACE...
HEY BOOGA! WHAT THE HELL HAPPENED TO MARTIN AND LANDAU?
RUMBLE RUMBLE!
WELL NOW, THAT'S A FUNNY STORY...
...WHEN WE SPLIT UP FROM YOU EARLIER, WE CAME ACROSS A NAZI TRAIN TRACK...
...THERE WAS A TRAIN HEADING STRAIGHT FOR US, SO WE THOUGHT WE'D HOLD THE FUCKER UP, JUST FOR THE HELL OF IT...
REACH FOR THE SKY, GUY!
!
...TURNS OUT IT WAS LOADED WITH NAZI GOLD - TEN BOXCARS RAMMED WITH THE STUFF...
...THE GUARDS SAID THEY WERE TAKING IT AWAY FROM BERLIN TO BE HIDDEN FROM THE INVADING ALLIES...
KRECK!
...SO WE MADE A DEAL WITH THEM...
ONE FOR YOU. NINE FOR US.
AND FUCK OFF.
SUSS!
WE HAULED OUR SHARE ALONG THE TRACK FOR HALF A MILE, UNTIL WE FOUND AN UNFINISHED TUNNEL ON A SIDING...
CHUNGA! TRUNDER! KLACK!

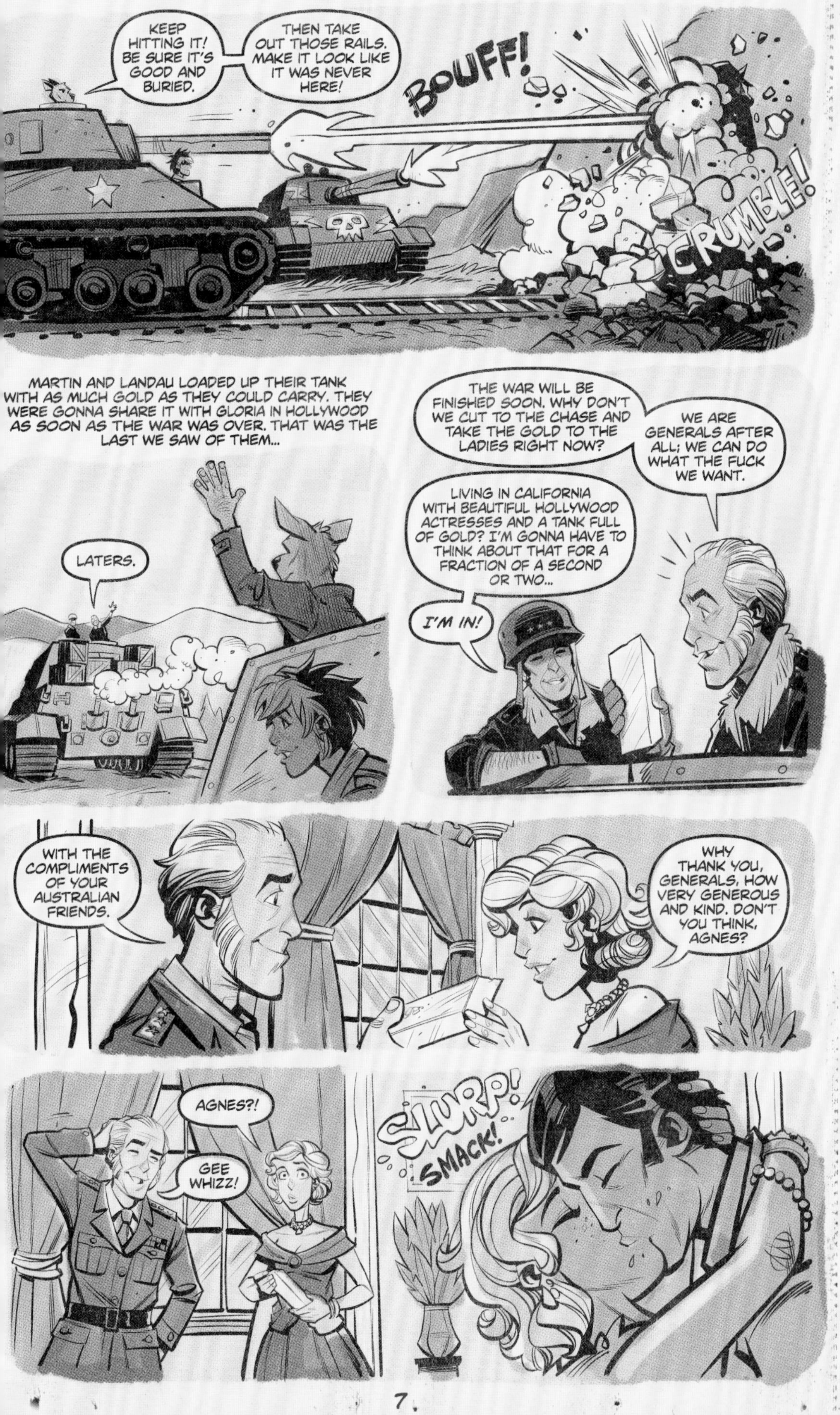
KEEP HITTING IT! BE SURE IT'S GOOD AND BURIED.
THEN TAKE OUT THOSE RAILS. MAKE IT LOOK LIKE IT WAS NEVER HERE!
BOUFF!
CRUMBLE!
MARTIN AND LANDAU LOADED UP THEIR TANK WITH AS MUCH GOLD AS THEY COULD CARRY. THEY WERE GONNA SHARE IT WITH GLORIA IN HOLLYWOOD AS SOON AS THE WAR WAS OVER. THAT WAS THE LAST WE SAW OF THEM...
LATERS.
THE WAR WILL BE FINISHED SOON. WHY DON'T WE CUT TO THE CHASE AND TAKE THE GOLD TO THE LADIES RIGHT NOW?
WE ARE GENERALS AFTER ALL; WE CAN DO WHAT THE FUCK WE WANT.
LIVING IN CALIFORNIA WITH BEAUTIFUL HOLLYWOOD ACTRESSES AND A TANK FULL OF GOLD? I'M GONNA HAVE TO THINK ABOUT THAT FOR A FRACTION OF A SECOND OR TWO...
I'M IN!
WITH THE COMPLIMENTS OF YOUR AUSTRALIAN FRIENDS.
WHY THANK YOU, GENERALS, HOW VERY GENEROUS AND KIND. DON'T YOU THINK, AGNES?
AGNES?!
GEE WHIZZ!
SLURP!
SMACK!

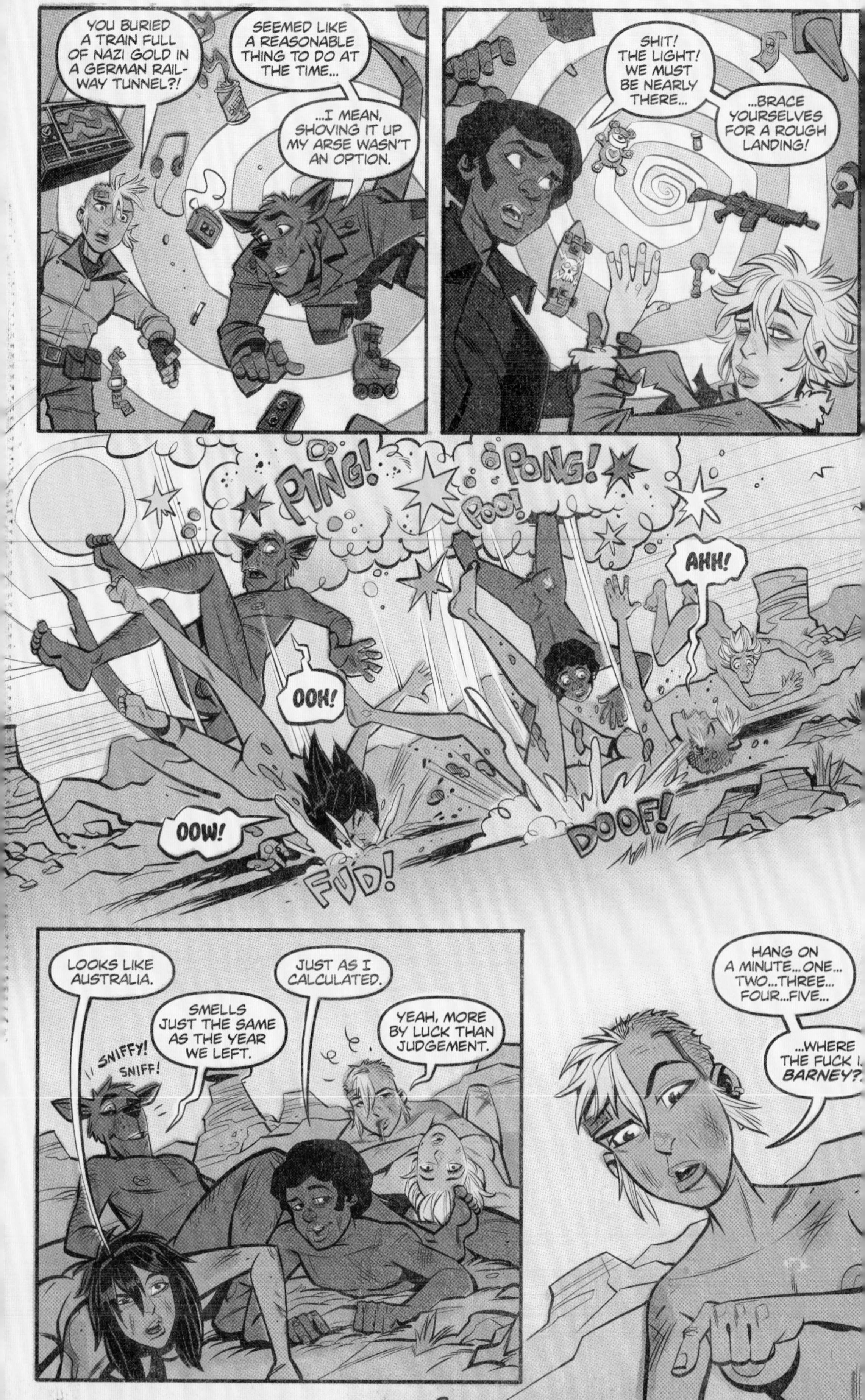
YOU BURIED A TRAIN FULL OF NAZI GOLD IN A GERMAN RAIL-WAY TUNNEL?!
SEEMED LIKE A REASONABLE THING TO DO AT THE TIME...
...I MEAN, SHOVING IT UP MY ARSE WASN'T AN OPTION.
SHIT! THE LIGHT! WE MUST BE NEARLY THERE...
...BRACE YOURSELVES FOR A ROUGH LANDING!
PING!
PONG!
POO!
AHH!
OOH!
OOW!
DOOF!
FUD!
LOOKS LIKE AUSTRALIA.
SMELLS JUST THE SAME AS THE YEAR WE LEFT.
SNIFFY! SNIFF!
JUST AS I CALCULATED.
YEAH, MORE BY LUCK THAN JUDGEMENT.
HANG ON A MINUTE...ONE... TWO...THREE... FOUR...FIVE...
...WHERE THE FUCK I. BARNEY?

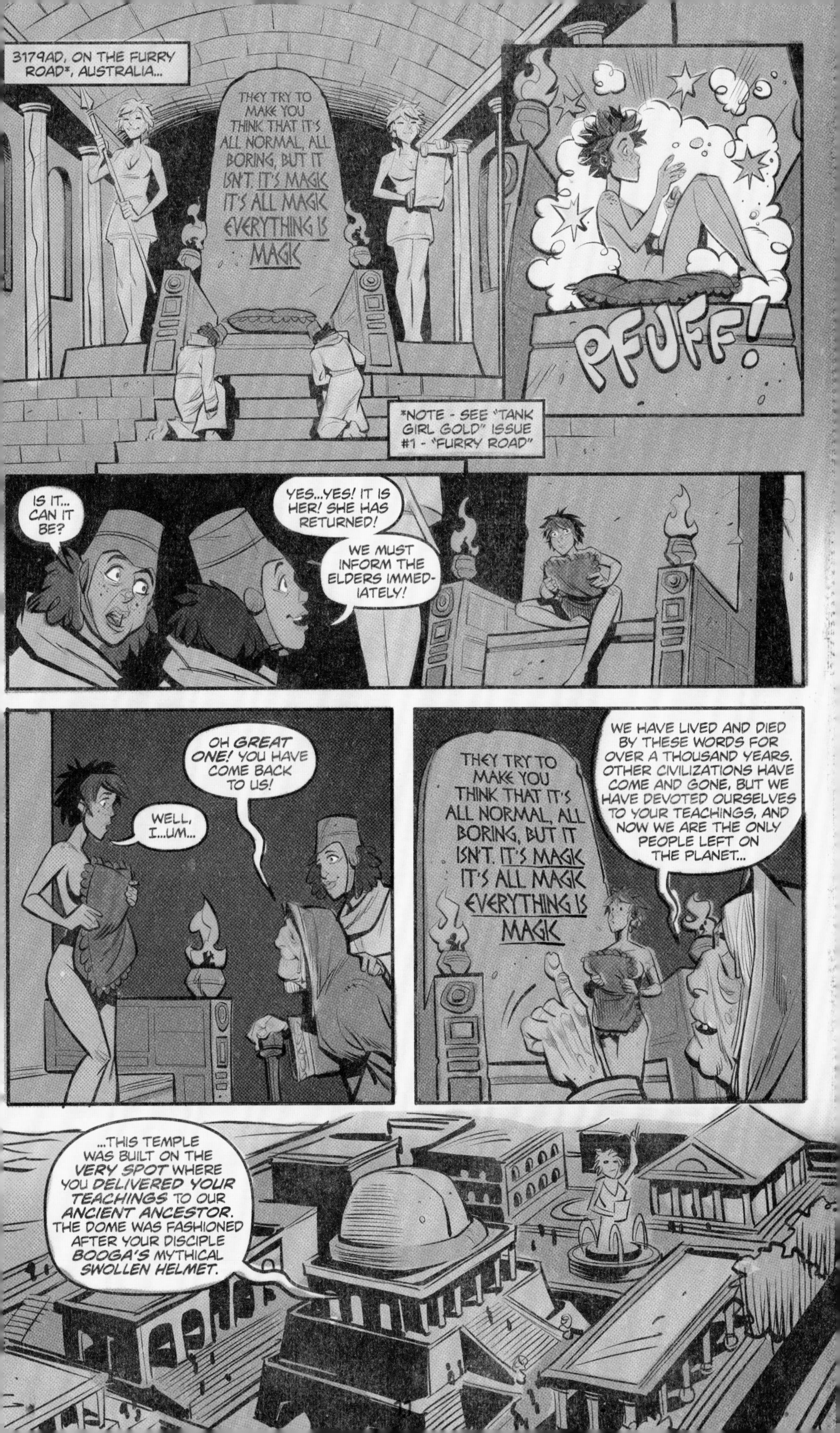
3179AD, ON THE FURRY ROAD*, AUSTRALIA...
THEY TRY TO MAKE YOU THINK THAT IT'S ALL NORMAL, ALL BORING, BUT IT ISN'T. IT'S MAGIC IT'S ALL MAGIC EVERYTHING IS MAGIC
PFUFF!
*NOTE - SEE "TANK GIRL GOLD" ISSUE #1 - "FURRY ROAD"
IS IT... CAN IT BE?
YES...YES! IT IS HER! SHE HAS RETURNED!
WE MUST INFORM THE ELDERS IMMEDIATELY!
OH GREAT ONE! YOU HAVE COME BACK TO US!
WELL, I...UM...
THEY TRY TO MAKE YOU THINK THAT IT'S ALL NORMAL, ALL BORING, BUT IT ISN'T. IT'S MAGIC IT'S ALL MAGIC EVERYTHING IS MAGIC
WE HAVE LIVED AND DIED BY THESE WORDS FOR OVER A THOUSAND YEARS. OTHER CIVILIZATIONS HAVE COME AND GONE, BUT WE HAVE DEVOTED OURSELVES TO YOUR TEACHINGS, AND NOW WE ARE THE ONLY PEOPLE LEFT ON THE PLANET...
...THIS TEMPLE WAS BUILT ON THE VERY SPOT WHERE YOU DELIVERED YOUR TEACHINGS TO OUR ANCIENT ANCESTOR. THE DOME WAS FASHIONED AFTER YOUR DISCIPLE BOOGA'S MYTHICAL SWOLLEN HELMET.

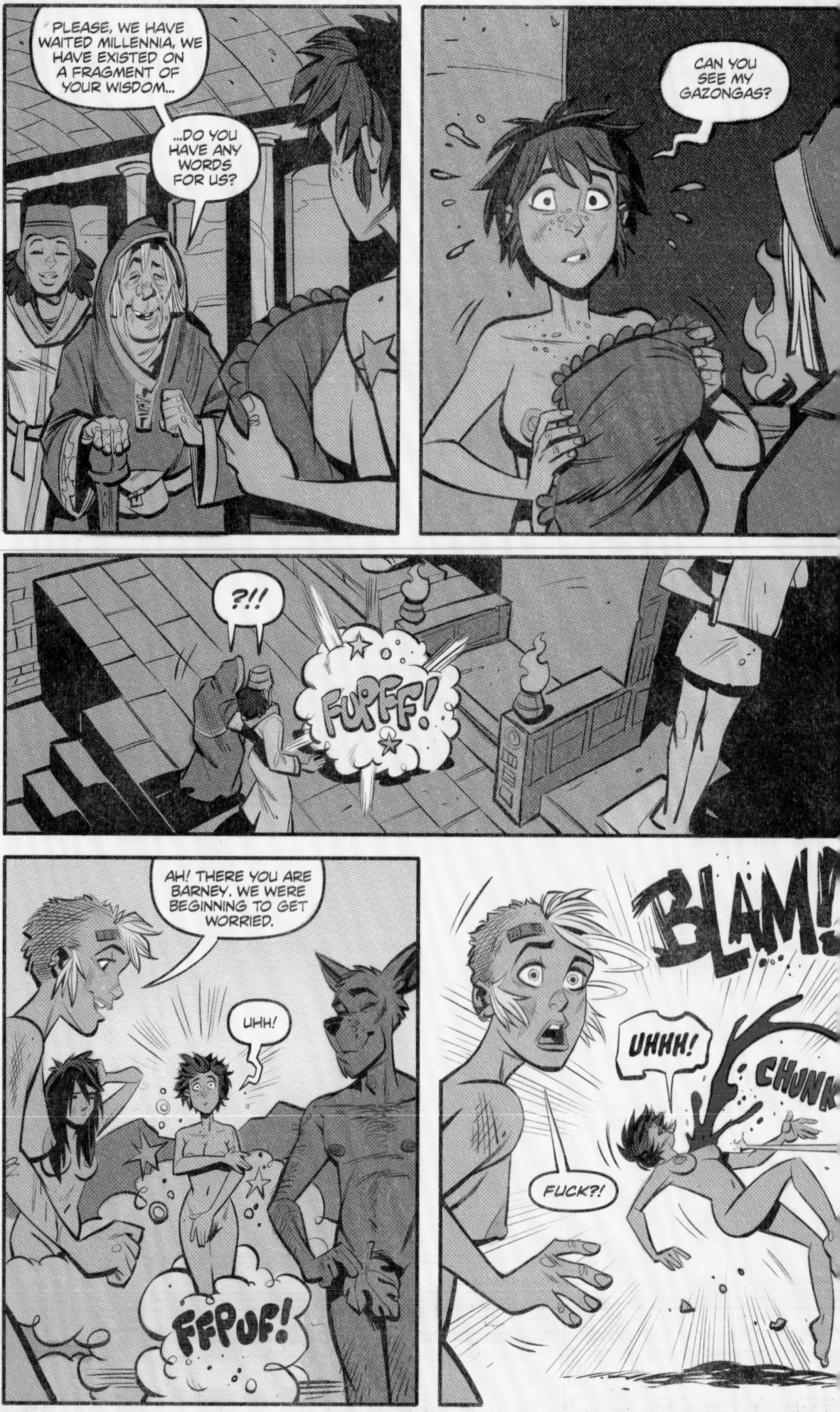
PLEASE, WE HAVE WAITED MILLENNIA, WE HAVE EXISTED ON A FRAGMENT OF YOUR WISDOM...
...DO YOU HAVE ANY WORDS FOR US?
CAN YOU SEE MY GAZONGAS?
?!!
FUPFF!
AH! THERE YOU ARE BARNEY. WE WERE BEGINNING TO GET WORRIED.
UHH!
FFPUF!
BLAM!
UHHH!
CHUNK
FUCK?!

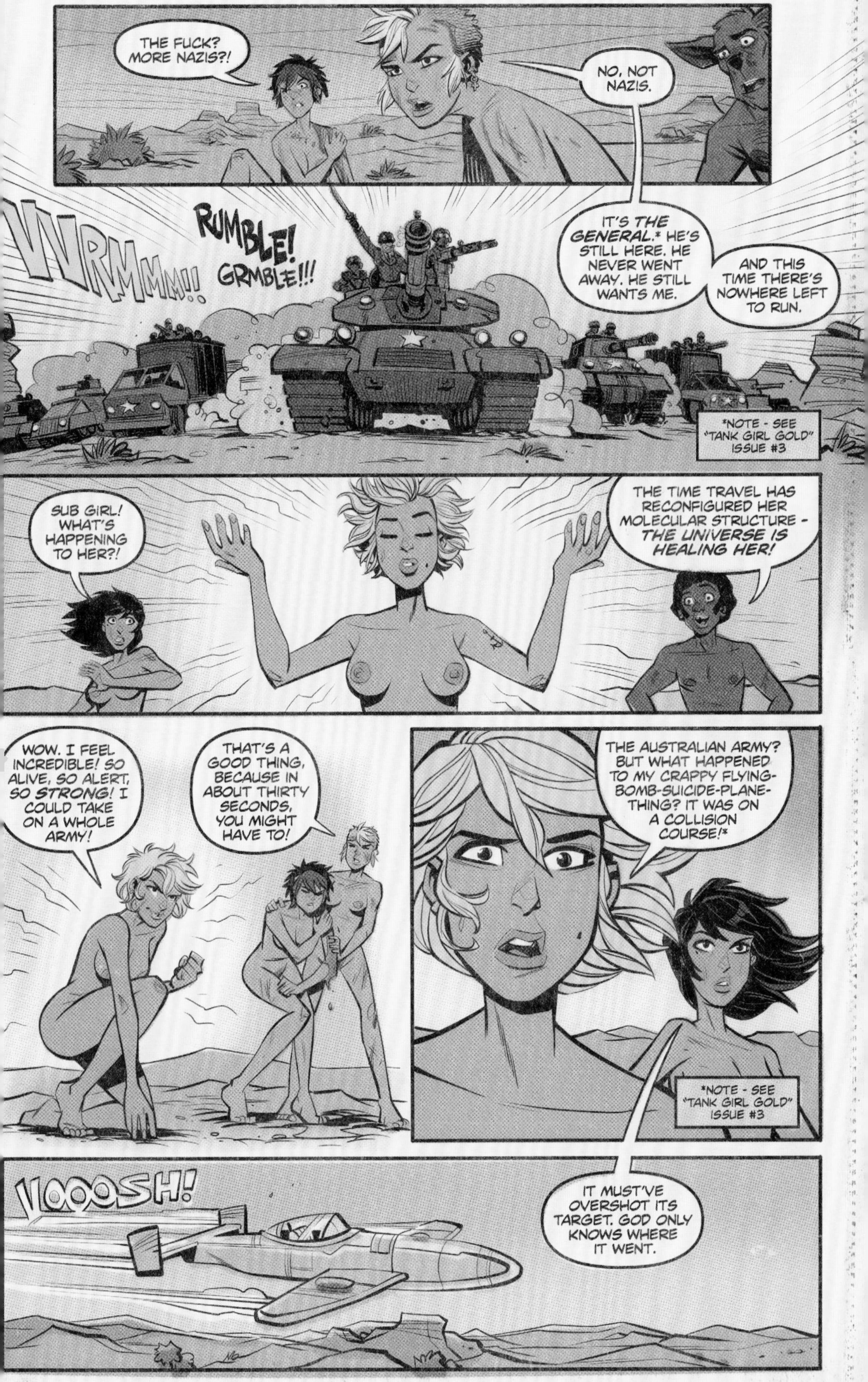
THE FUCK? MORE NAZIS?!
NO, NOT NAZIS.
IT'S *THE GENERAL*.* HE'S STILL HERE. HE NEVER WENT AWAY. HE STILL WANTS ME.
AND THIS TIME THERE'S NOWHERE LEFT TO RUN.
VVRMMMM!!
RUMBLE! GRMBLE!!!
*NOTE - SEE "TANK GIRL GOLD" ISSUE #3
SUB GIRL! WHAT'S HAPPENING TO HER?!
THE TIME TRAVEL HAS RECONFIGURED HER MOLECULAR STRUCTURE - *THE UNIVERSE IS HEALING HER!*
WOW. I FEEL INCREDIBLE! SO ALIVE, SO ALERT, SO *STRONG*! I COULD TAKE ON A WHOLE ARMY!
THAT'S A GOOD THING, BECAUSE IN ABOUT THIRTY SECONDS, YOU MIGHT HAVE TO!
THE AUSTRALIAN ARMY? BUT WHAT HAPPENED TO MY CRAPPY FLYING-BOMB-SUICIDE-PLANE-THING? IT WAS ON A COLLISION COURSE!*
*NOTE - SEE "TANK GIRL GOLD" ISSUE #3
IT MUST'VE OVERSHOT ITS TARGET. GOD ONLY KNOWS WHERE IT WENT.
VOOOSH!

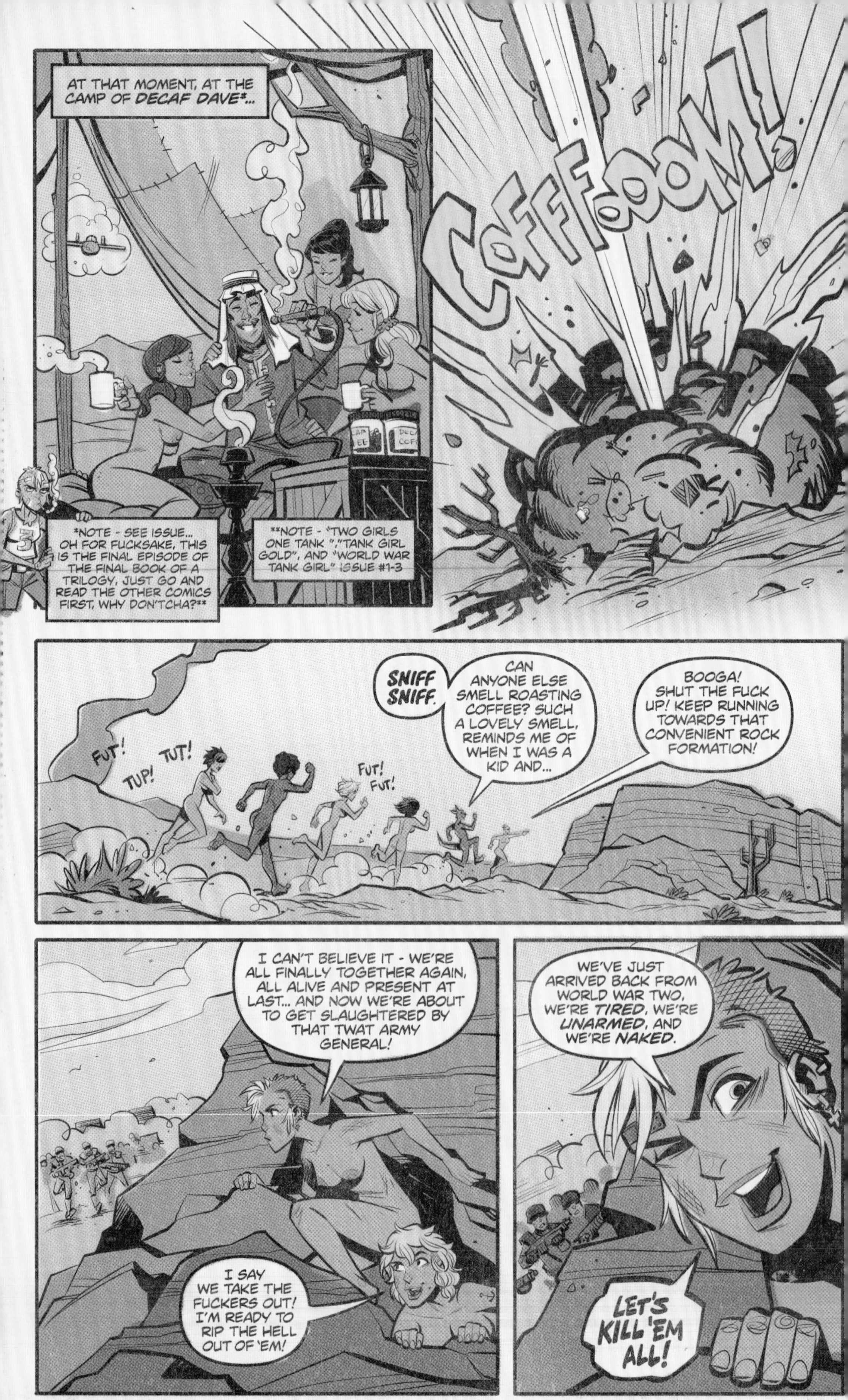
AT THAT MOMENT, AT THE CAMP OF DECAF DAVE*...
*NOTE - SEE ISSUE... OH FOR FUCKSAKE, THIS IS THE FINAL EPISODE OF THE FINAL BOOK OF A TRILOGY, JUST GO AND READ THE OTHER COMICS FIRST, WHY DON'TCHA?**
**NOTE - "TWO GIRLS ONE TANK","TANK GIRL GOLD", AND "WORLD WAR TANK GIRL" ISSUE #1-3
COFFFOOOM!!
FUT! TUP! TUT!
FUT! FUT!
SNIFF SNIFF.
CAN ANYONE ELSE SMELL ROASTING COFFEE? SUCH A LOVELY SMELL, REMINDS ME OF WHEN I WAS A KID AND...
BOOGA! SHUT THE FUCK UP! KEEP RUNNING TOWARDS THAT CONVENIENT ROCK FORMATION!
I CAN'T BELIEVE IT - WE'RE ALL FINALLY TOGETHER AGAIN, ALL ALIVE AND PRESENT AT LAST... AND NOW WE'RE ABOUT TO GET SLAUGHTERED BY THAT TWAT ARMY GENERAL!
I SAY WE TAKE THE FUCKERS OUT! I'M READY TO RIP THE HELL OUT OF 'EM!
WE'VE JUST ARRIVED BACK FROM WORLD WAR TWO, WE'RE TIRED, WE'RE UNARMED, AND WE'RE NAKED.
LET'S KILL 'EM ALL!

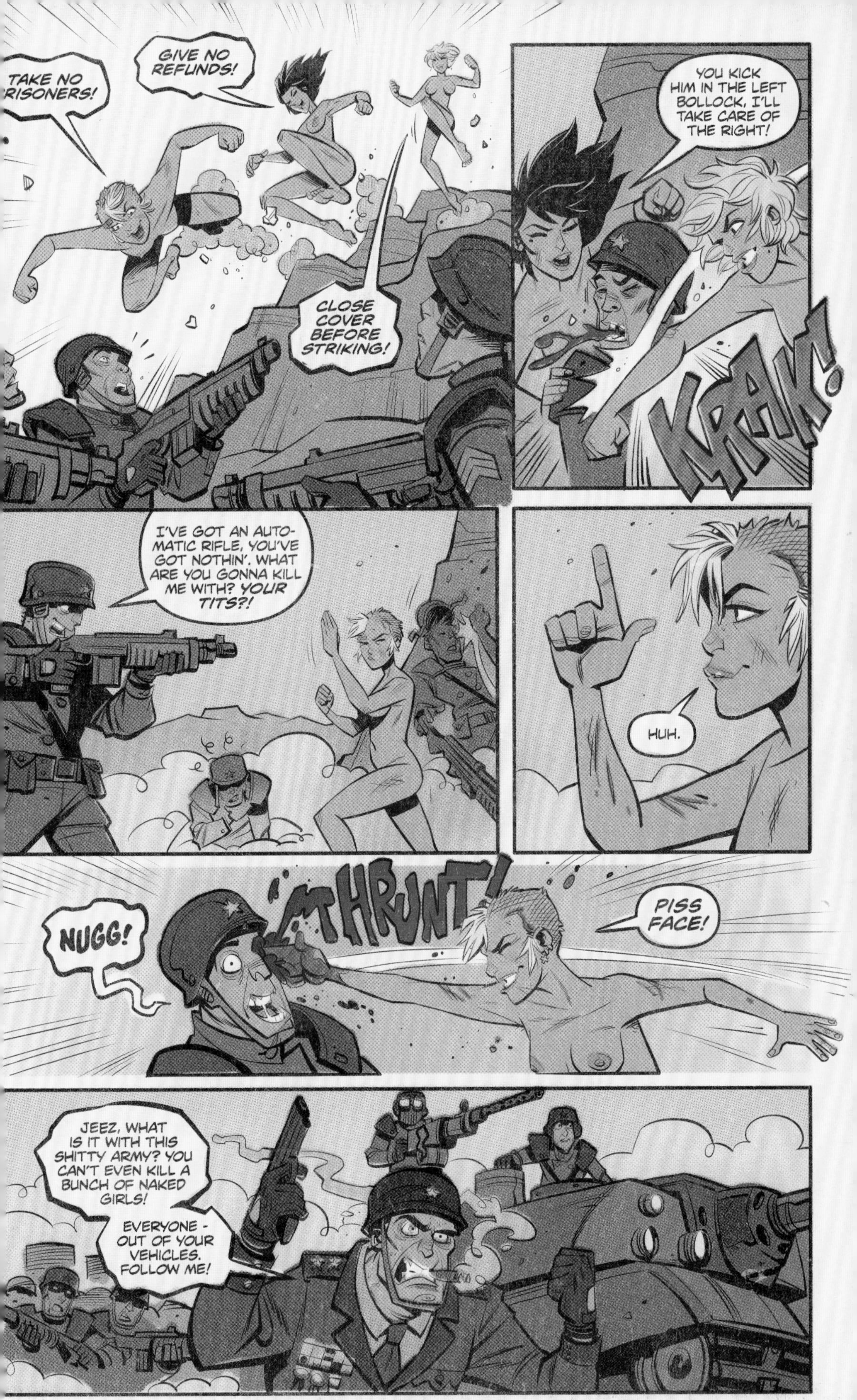
TAKE NO RISONERS!
GIVE NO REFUNDS!
CLOSE COVER BEFORE STRIKING!
YOU KICK HIM IN THE LEFT BOLLOCK, I'LL TAKE CARE OF THE RIGHT!
KRAK!
I'VE GOT AN AUTO-MATIC RIFLE, YOU'VE GOT NOTHIN'. WHAT ARE YOU GONNA KILL ME WITH? YOUR TITS?!
HUH.
'MTHRUNT!
NUGG!
PISS FACE!
JEEZ, WHAT IS IT WITH THIS SHITTY ARMY? YOU CAN'T EVEN KILL A BUNCH OF NAKED GIRLS!
EVERYONE - OUT OF YOUR VEHICLES. FOLLOW ME!

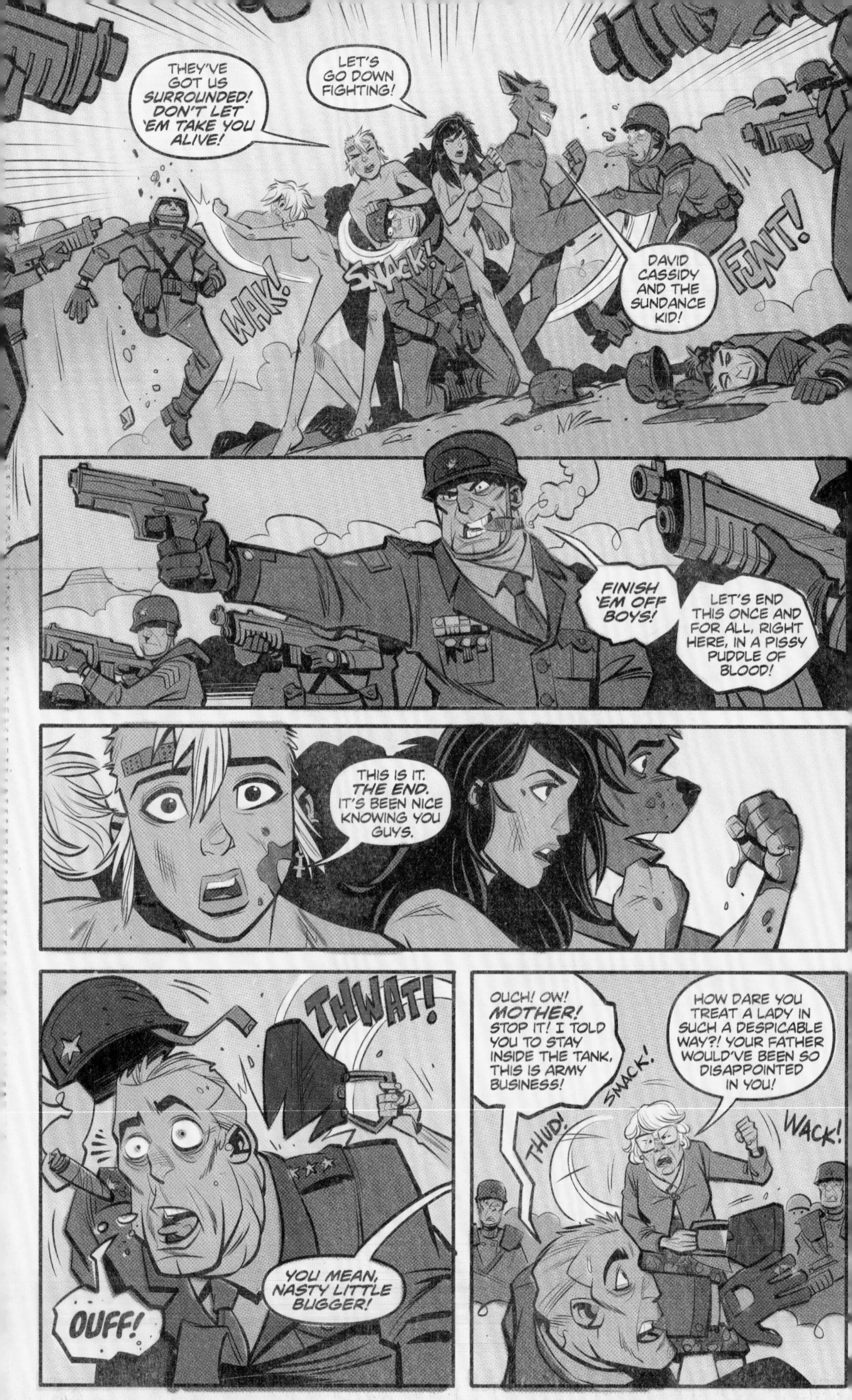
THEY'VE GOT US SURROUNDED! DON'T LET 'EM TAKE YOU ALIVE!
LET'S GO DOWN FIGHTING!
WAK!
SMACK!
DAVID CASSIDY AND THE SUNDANCE KID!
FWNT!
FINISH 'EM OFF BOYS!
LET'S END THIS ONCE AND FOR ALL, RIGHT HERE, IN A PISSY PUDDLE OF BLOOD!
THIS IS IT. THE END. IT'S BEEN NICE KNOWING YOU GUYS.
THWAT!
YOU MEAN, NASTY LITTLE BUGGER!
OUFF!
OUCH! OW! MOTHER! STOP IT! I TOLD YOU TO STAY INSIDE THE TANK, THIS IS ARMY BUSINESS!
HOW DARE YOU TREAT A LADY IN SUCH A DESPICABLE WAY?! YOUR FATHER WOULD'VE BEEN SO DISAPPOINTED IN YOU!
SMACK!
THUD!
WACK!

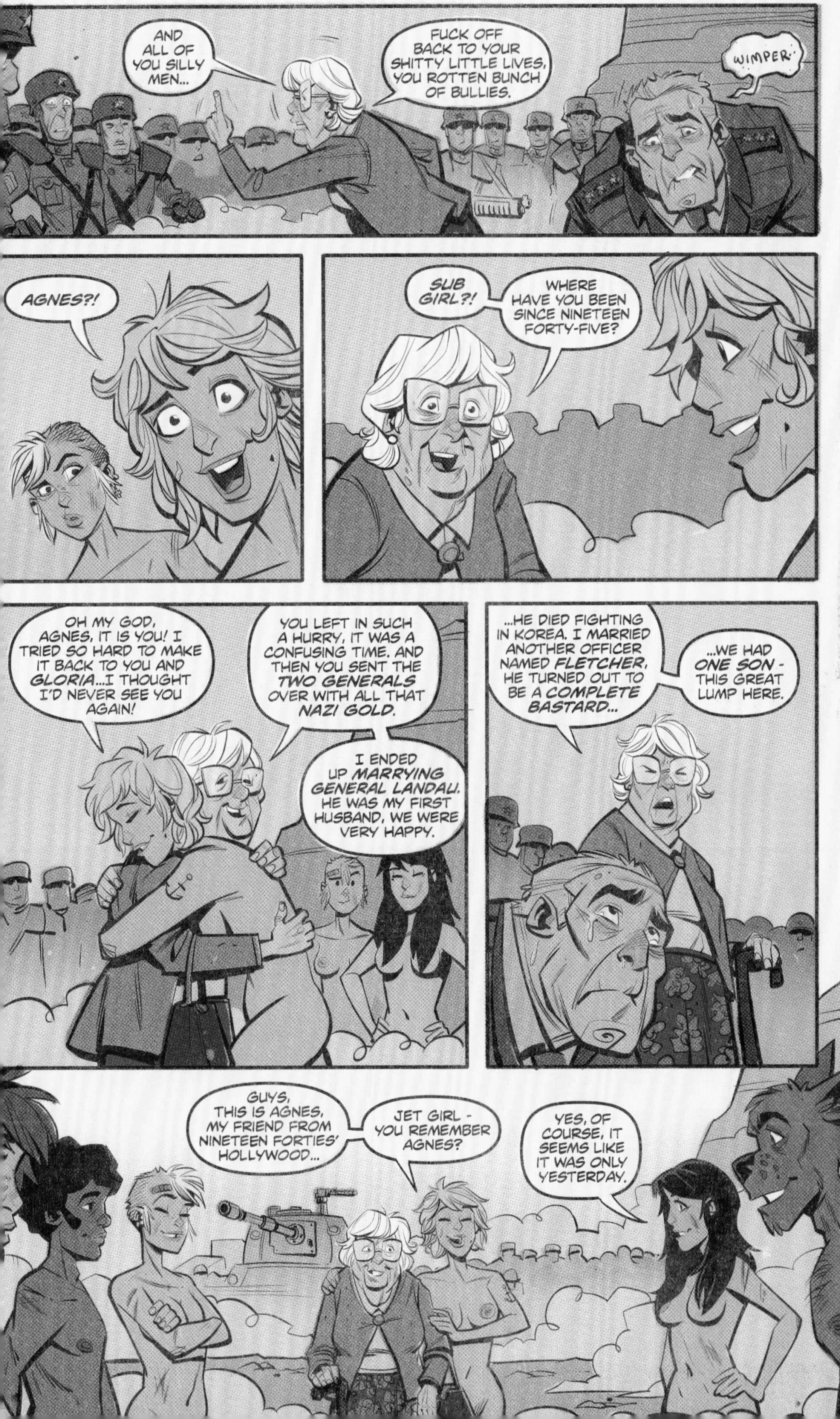
AND ALL OF YOU SILLY MEN...
FUCK OFF BACK TO YOUR SHITTY LITTLE LIVES, YOU ROTTEN BUNCH OF BULLIES.
WIMPER
AGNES?!
SUB GIRL?!
WHERE HAVE YOU BEEN SINCE NINETEEN FORTY-FIVE?
OH MY GOD, AGNES, IT IS YOU! I TRIED SO HARD TO MAKE IT BACK TO YOU AND GLORIA...I THOUGHT I'D NEVER SEE YOU AGAIN!
YOU LEFT IN SUCH A HURRY, IT WAS A CONFUSING TIME. AND THEN YOU SENT THE TWO GENERALS OVER WITH ALL THAT NAZI GOLD.
I ENDED UP MARRYING GENERAL LANDAU. HE WAS MY FIRST HUSBAND, WE WERE VERY HAPPY.
...HE DIED FIGHTING IN KOREA. I MARRIED ANOTHER OFFICER NAMED FLETCHER, HE TURNED OUT TO BE A COMPLETE BASTARD...
...WE HAD ONE SON - THIS GREAT LUMP HERE.
GUYS, THIS IS AGNES, MY FRIEND FROM NINETEEN FORTIES' HOLLYWOOD...
JET GIRL - YOU REMEMBER AGNES?
YES, OF COURSE, IT SEEMS LIKE IT WAS ONLY YESTERDAY.

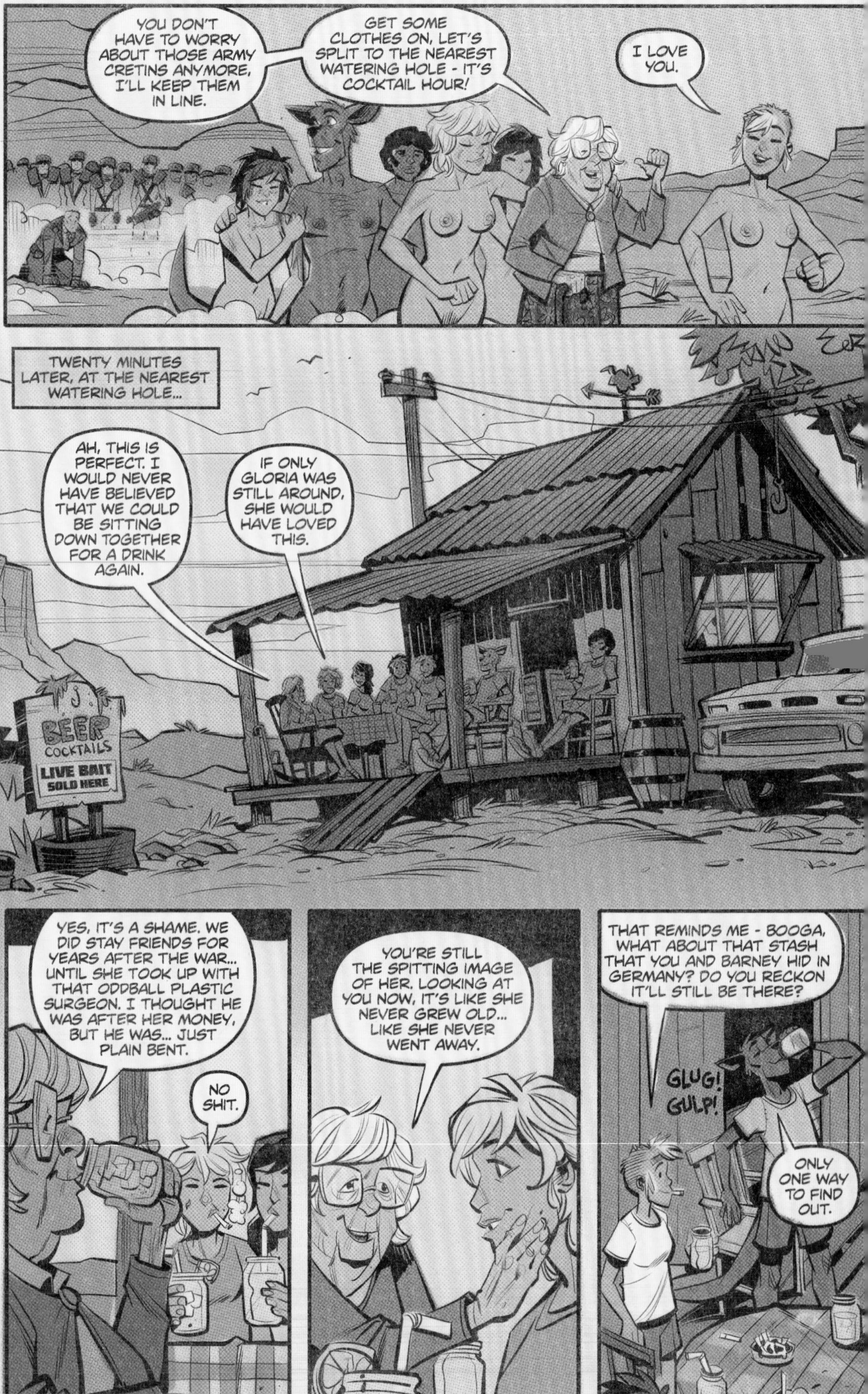
YOU DON'T HAVE TO WORRY ABOUT THOSE ARMY CRETINS ANYMORE, I'LL KEEP THEM IN LINE.
GET SOME CLOTHES ON, LET'S SPLIT TO THE NEAREST WATERING HOLE - IT'S COCKTAIL HOUR!
I LOVE YOU.
TWENTY MINUTES LATER, AT THE NEAREST WATERING HOLE...
AH, THIS IS PERFECT. I WOULD NEVER HAVE BELIEVED THAT WE COULD BE SITTING DOWN TOGETHER FOR A DRINK AGAIN.
IF ONLY GLORIA WAS STILL AROUND, SHE WOULD HAVE LOVED THIS.
BEER
COCKTAILS
LIVE BAIT
SOLD HERE
YES, IT'S A SHAME. WE DID STAY FRIENDS FOR YEARS AFTER THE WAR... UNTIL SHE TOOK UP WITH THAT ODDBALL PLASTIC SURGEON. I THOUGHT HE WAS AFTER HER MONEY, BUT HE WAS... JUST PLAIN BENT.
NO SHIT.
YOU'RE STILL THE SPITTING IMAGE OF HER. LOOKING AT YOU NOW, IT'S LIKE SHE NEVER GREW OLD... LIKE SHE NEVER WENT AWAY.
THAT REMINDS ME - BOOGA, WHAT ABOUT THAT STASH THAT YOU AND BARNEY HID IN GERMANY? DO YOU RECKON IT'LL STILL BE THERE?
GLUG! GULP!
ONLY ONE WAY TO FIND OUT.

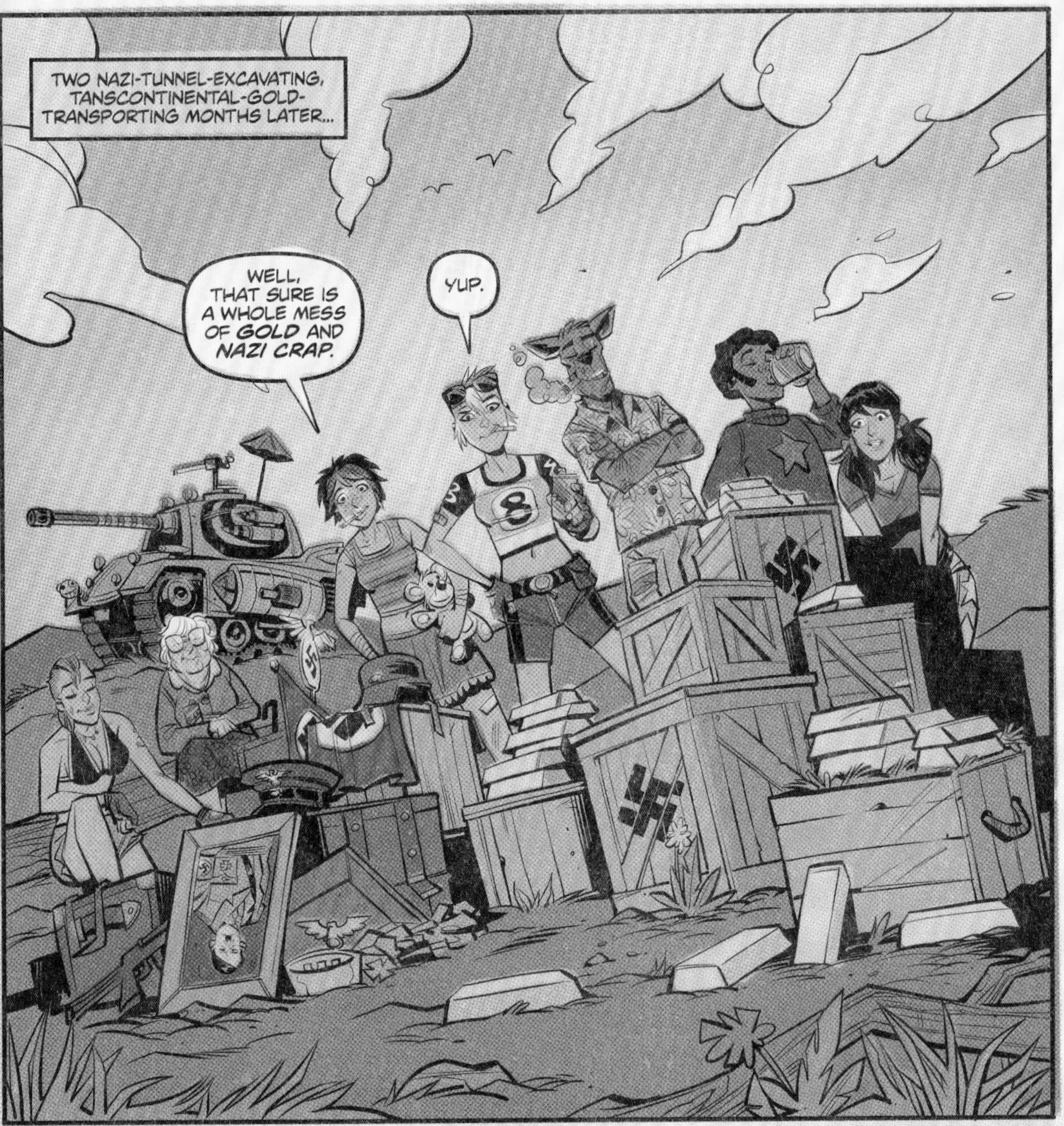
TWO NAZI-TUNNEL-EXCAVATING, TANSCONTINENTAL-GOLD-TRANSPORTING MONTHS LATER...
WELL, THAT SURE IS A WHOLE MESS OF GOLD AND NAZI CRAP.
YUP.

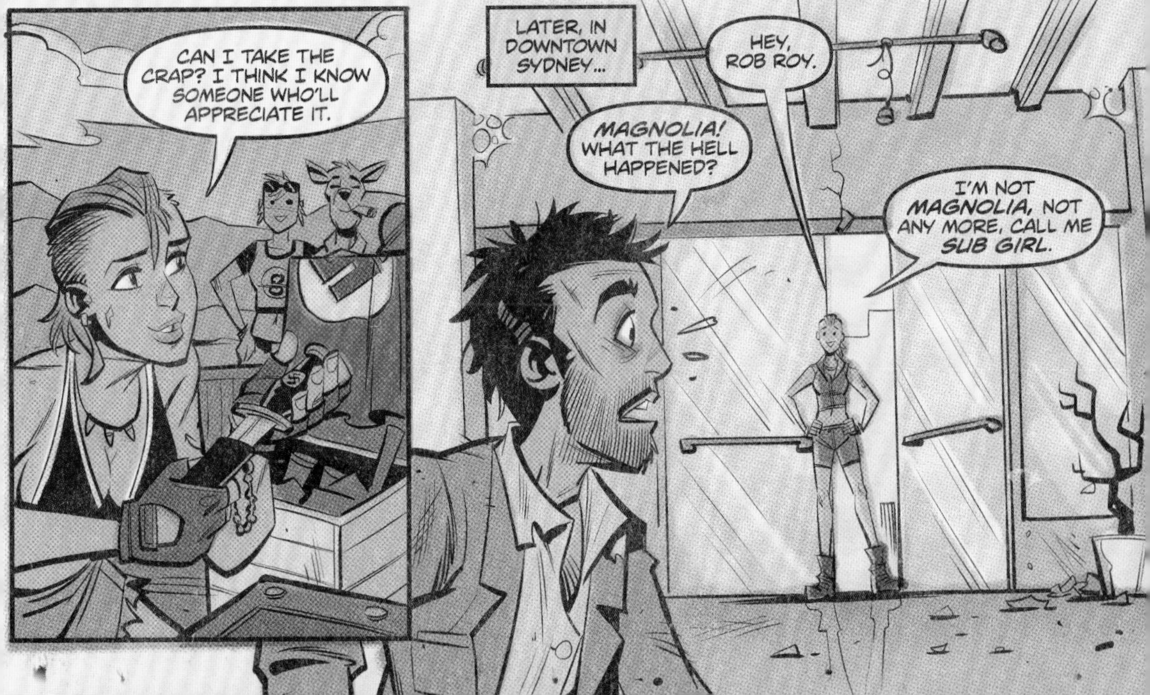
CAN I TAKE THE CRAP? I THINK I KNOW SOMEONE WHO'LL APPRECIATE IT.
LATER, IN DOWNTOWN SYDNEY...
HEY, ROB ROY.
MAGNOLIA! WHAT THE HELL HAPPENED?
I'M NOT MAGNOLIA, NOT ANY MORE, CALL ME SUB GIRL.

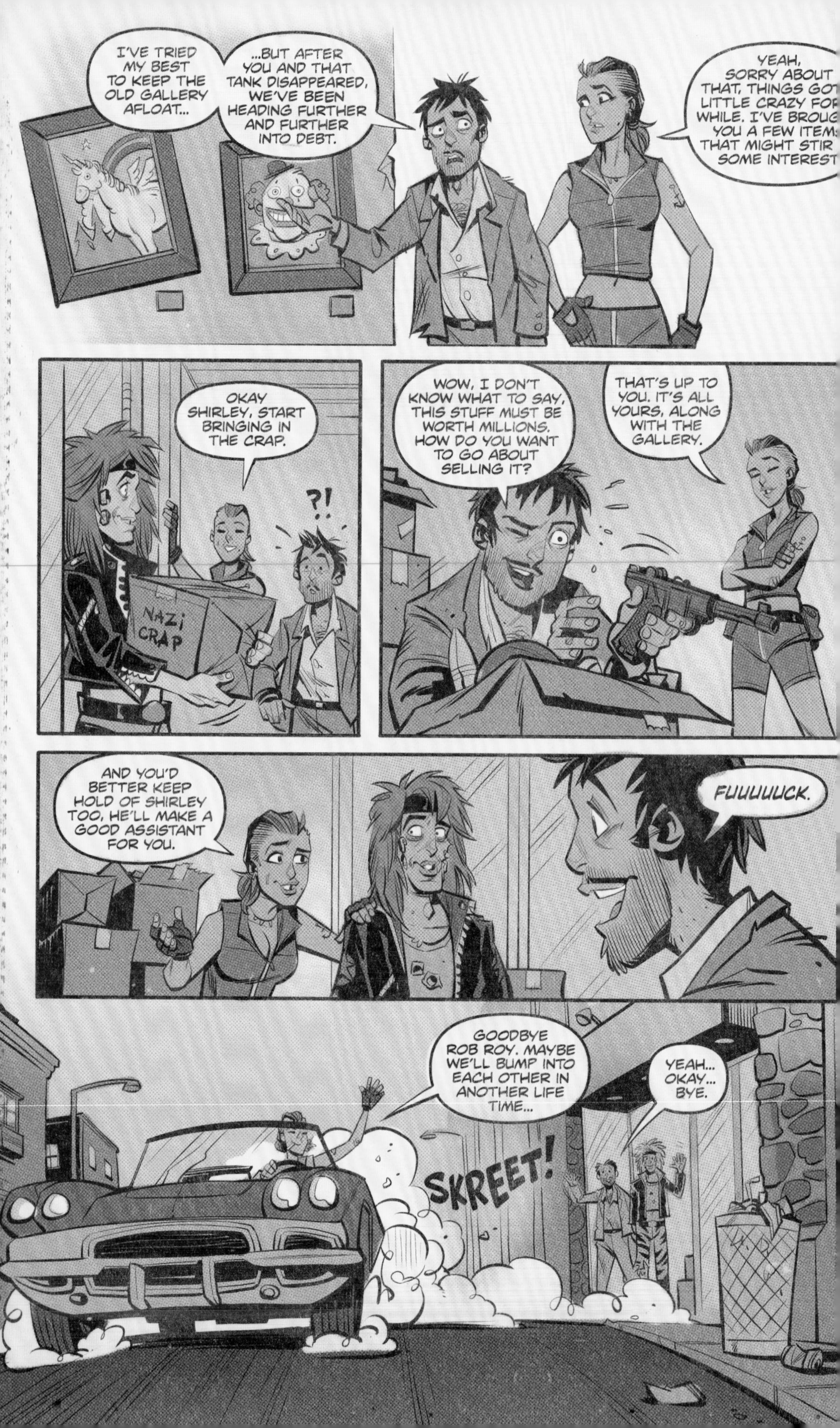
I'VE TRIED MY BEST TO KEEP THE OLD GALLERY AFLOAT...
...BUT AFTER YOU AND THAT TANK DISAPPEARED, WE'VE BEEN HEADING FURTHER AND FURTHER INTO DEBT.
YEAH, SORRY ABOUT THAT, THINGS GOT LITTLE CRAZY FOR WHILE. I'VE BROUG YOU A FEW ITEMS THAT MIGHT STIR SOME INTEREST
OKAY SHIRLEY, START BRINGING IN THE CRAP.
?!
NAZI CRAP
WOW, I DON'T KNOW WHAT TO SAY, THIS STUFF MUST BE WORTH MILLIONS. HOW DO YOU WANT TO GO ABOUT SELLING IT?
THAT'S UP TO YOU. IT'S ALL YOURS, ALONG WITH THE GALLERY.
AND YOU'D BETTER KEEP HOLD OF SHIRLEY TOO, HE'LL MAKE A GOOD ASSISTANT FOR YOU.
FUUUUUCK.
GOODBYE ROB ROY. MAYBE WE'LL BUMP INTO EACH OTHER IN ANOTHER LIFE TIME...
YEAH... OKAY... BYE.
SKREET!

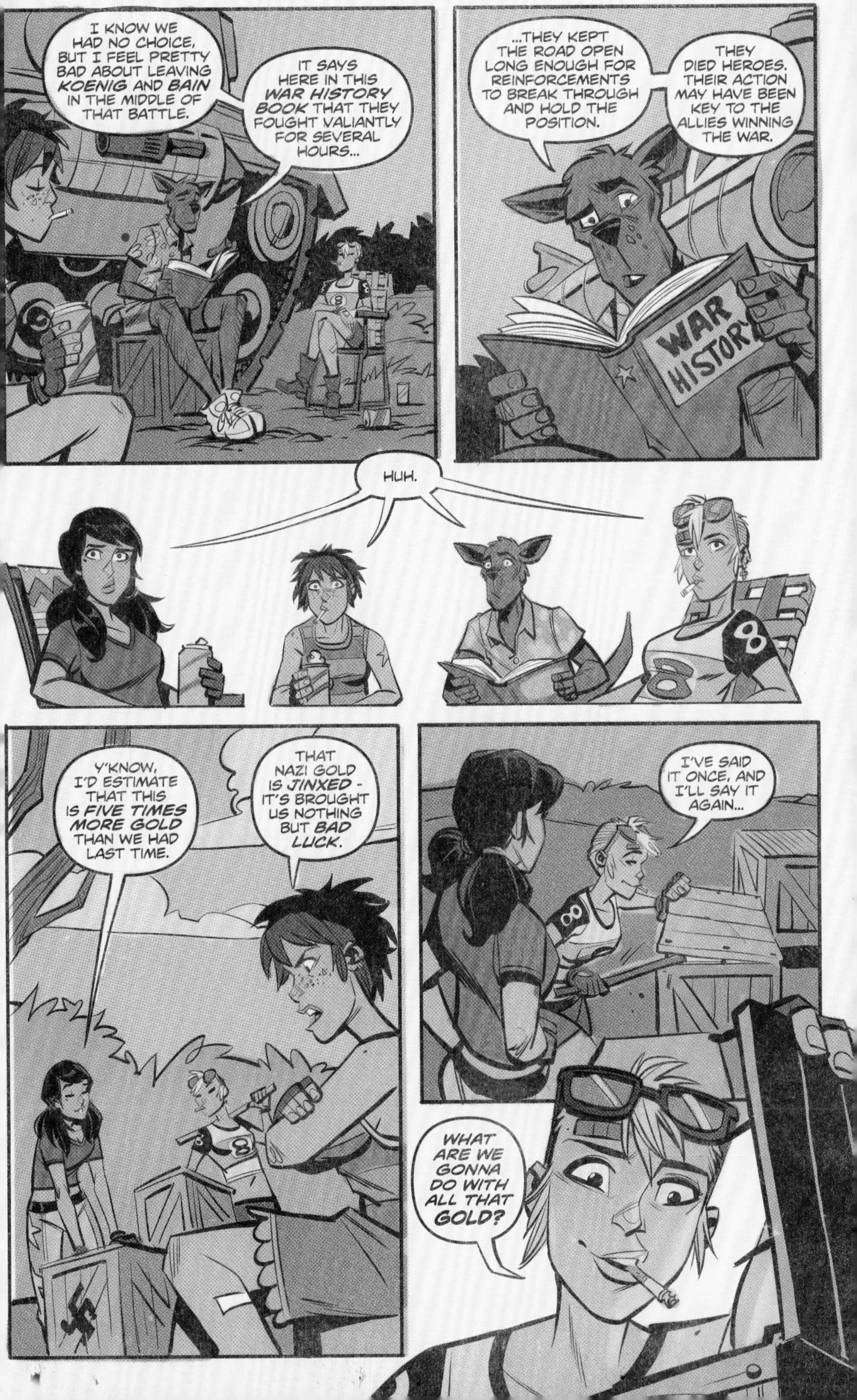

I KNOW WE HAD NO CHOICE, BUT I FEEL PRETTY BAD ABOUT LEAVING KOENIG AND BAIN IN THE MIDDLE OF THAT BATTLE.
IT SAYS HERE IN THIS WAR HISTORY BOOK THAT THEY FOUGHT VALIANTLY FOR SEVERAL HOURS...
...THEY KEPT THE ROAD OPEN LONG ENOUGH FOR REINFORCEMENTS TO BREAK THROUGH AND HOLD THE POSITION.
THEY DIED HEROES. THEIR ACTION MAY HAVE BEEN KEY TO THE ALLIES WINNING THE WAR.
WAR HISTORY
HUH.
Y'KNOW, I'D ESTIMATE THAT THIS IS FIVE TIMES MORE GOLD THAN WE HAD LAST TIME.
THAT NAZI GOLD IS JINXED - IT'S BROUGHT US NOTHING BUT BAD LUCK.
I'VE SAID IT ONCE, AND I'LL SAY IT AGAIN...
WHAT ARE WE GONNA DO WITH ALL THAT GOLD?

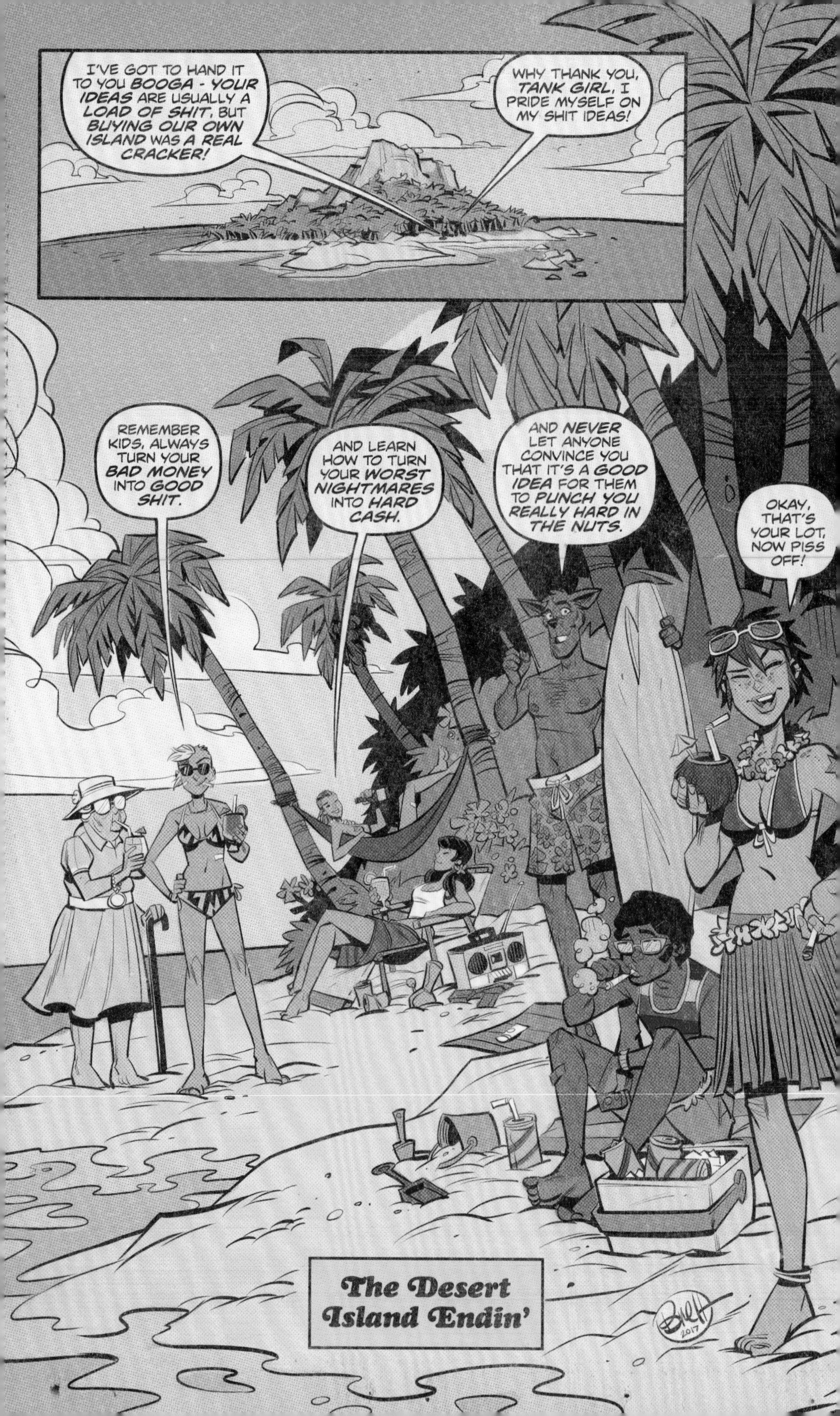

I'VE GOT TO HAND IT TO YOU BOOGA - YOUR IDEAS ARE USUALLY A LOAD OF SHIT, BUT BUYING OUR OWN ISLAND WAS A REAL CRACKER!
WHY THANK YOU, TANK GIRL, I PRIDE MYSELF ON MY SHIT IDEAS!
REMEMBER KIDS, ALWAYS TURN YOUR BAD MONEY INTO GOOD SHIT.
AND LEARN HOW TO TURN YOUR WORST NIGHTMARES INTO HARD CASH.
AND NEVER LET ANYONE CONVINCE YOU THAT IT'S A GOOD IDEA FOR THEM TO PUNCH YOU REALLY HARD IN THE NUTS.
OKAY, THAT'S YOUR LOT, NOW PISS OFF!
The Desert Island Endin'
2017

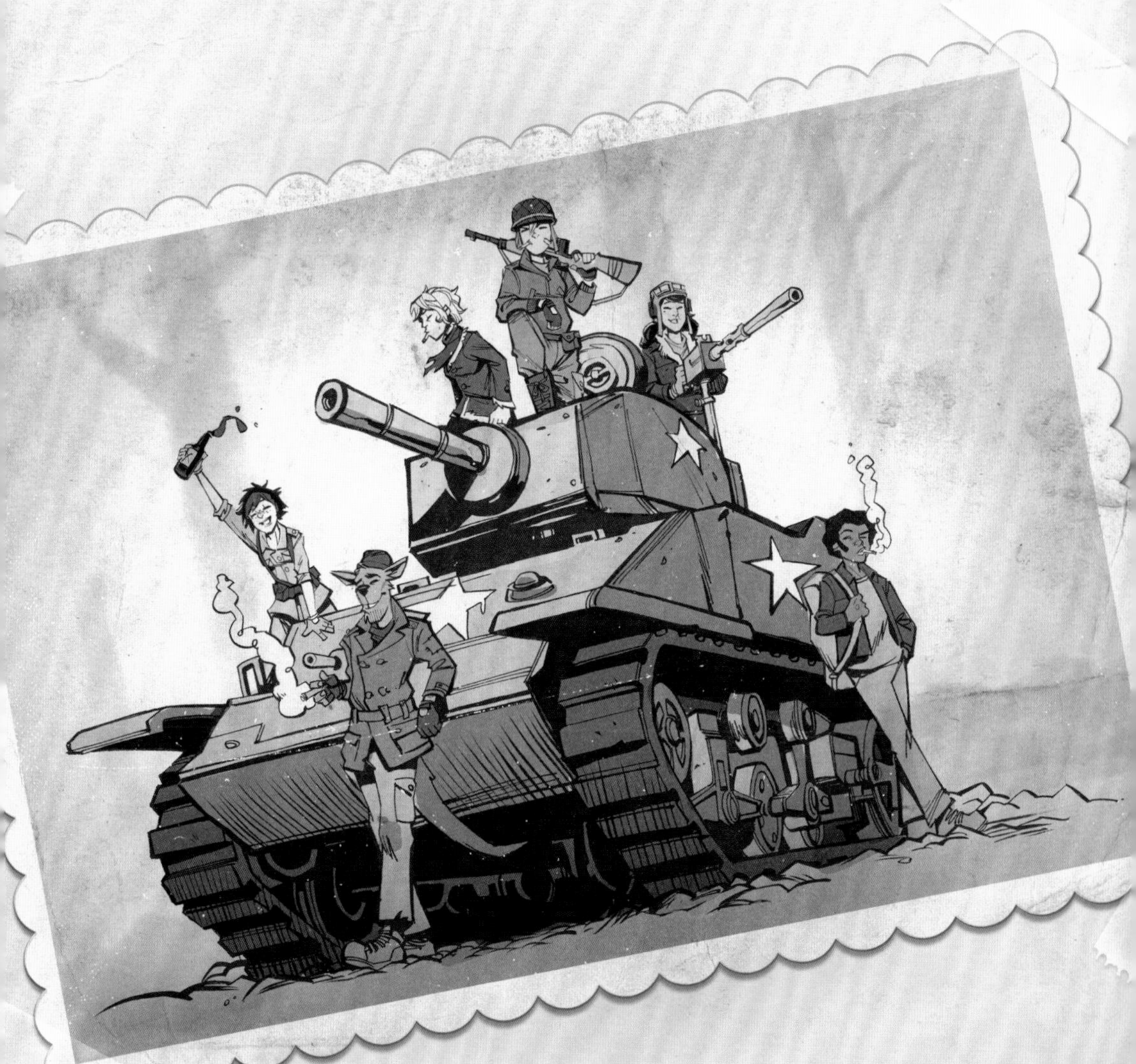

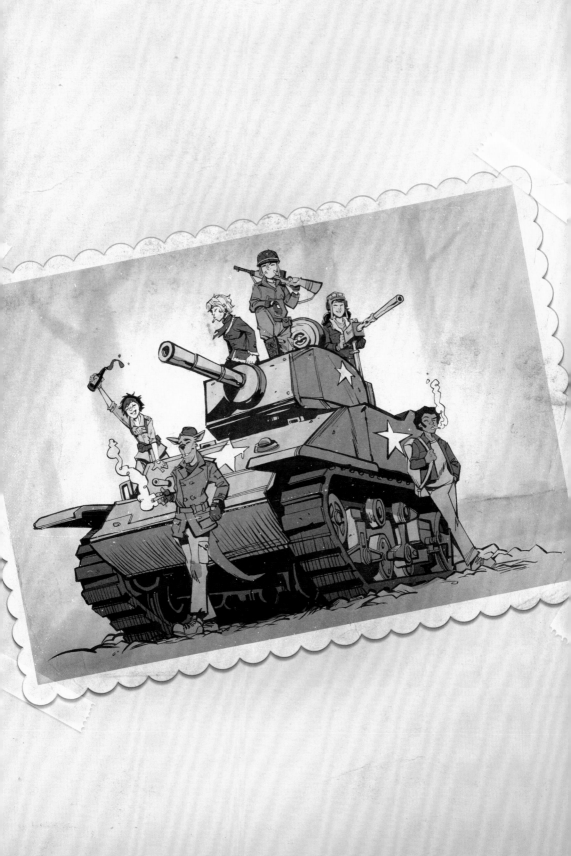

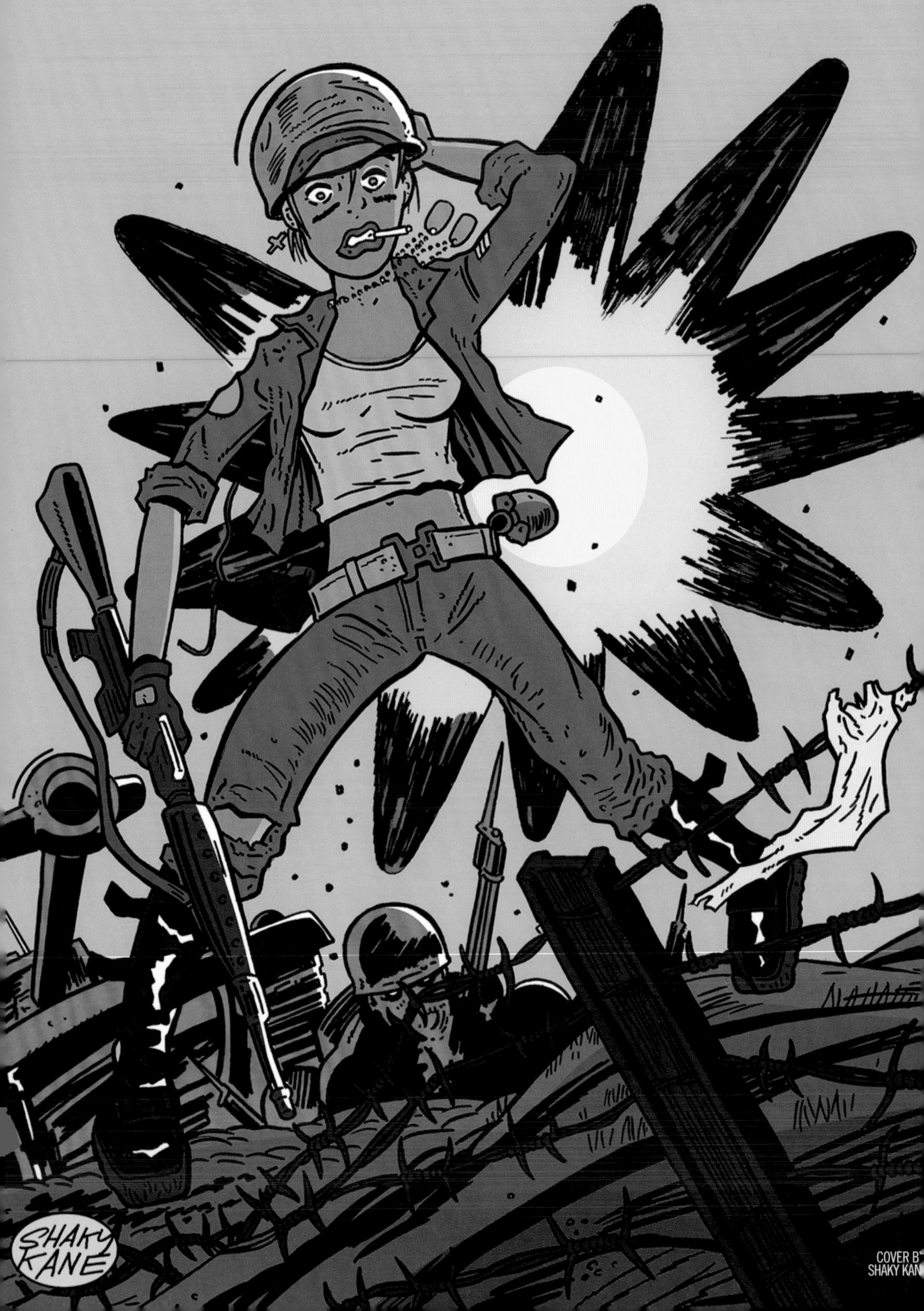
SHAKY KANE

COVER B
SHAKY KAN

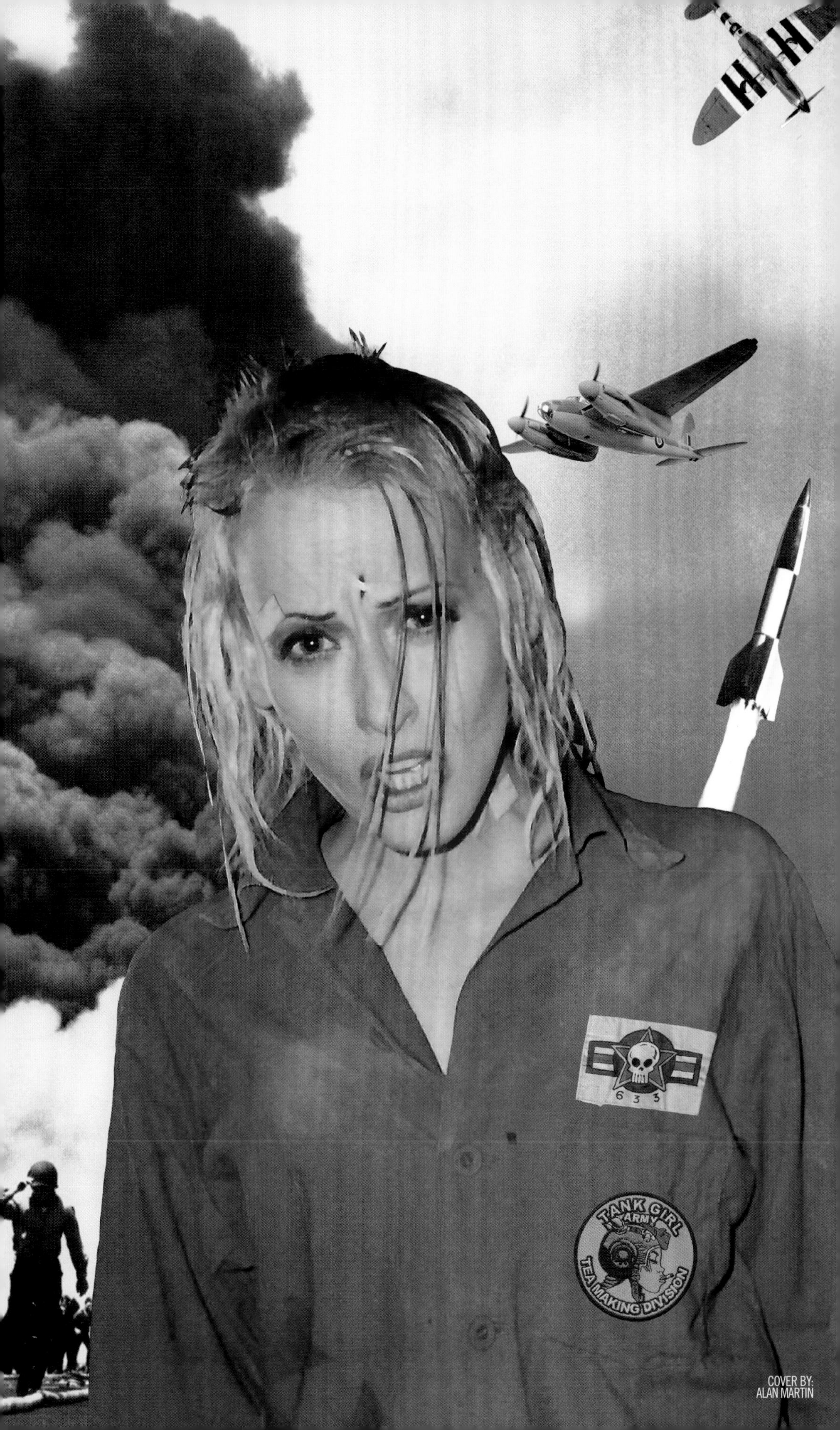
633
TANK GIRL
ARMY
TEA MAKING DIVISION

COVER BY:
ALAN MARTIN

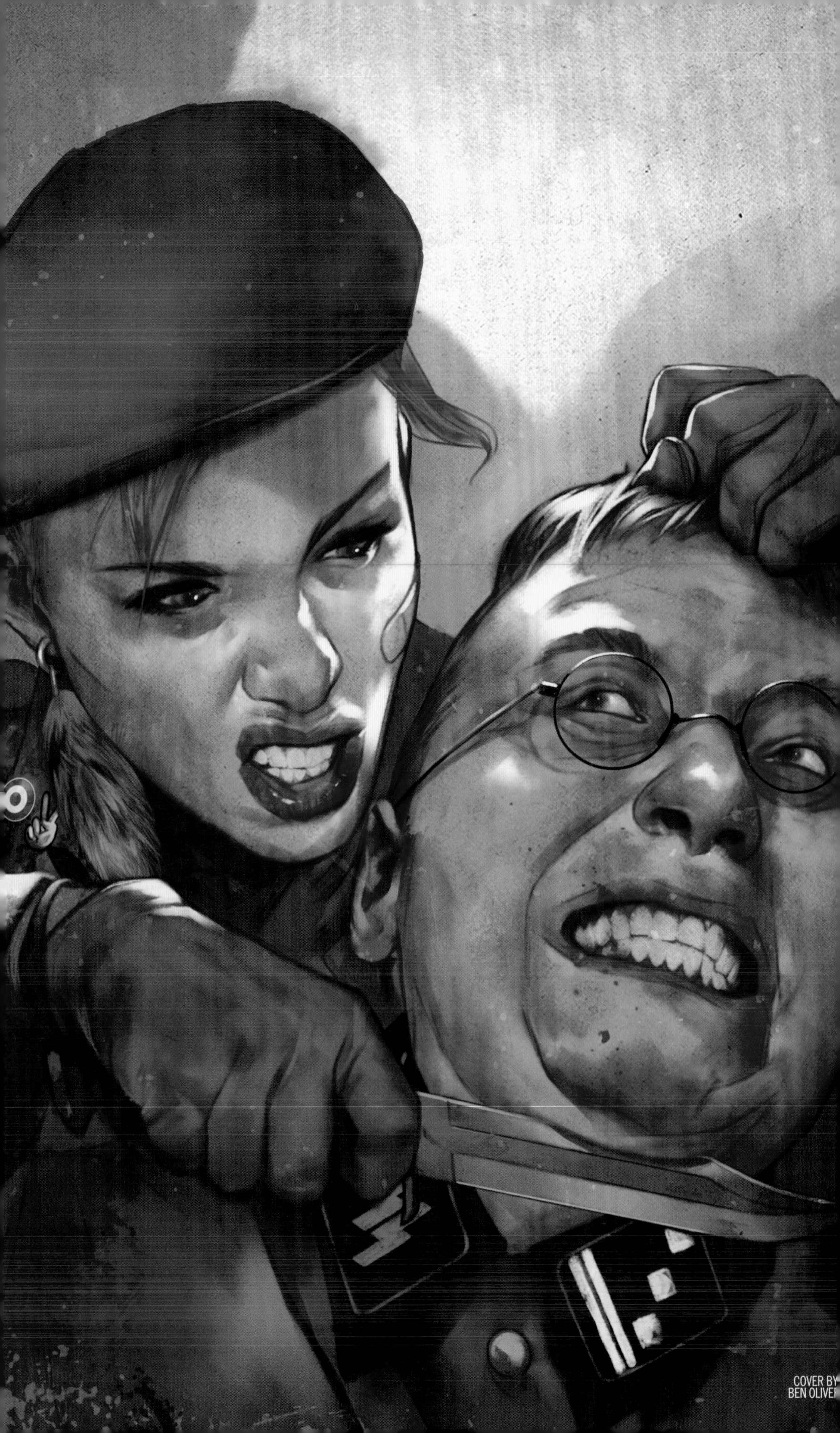
COVER BY
BEN OLIVE

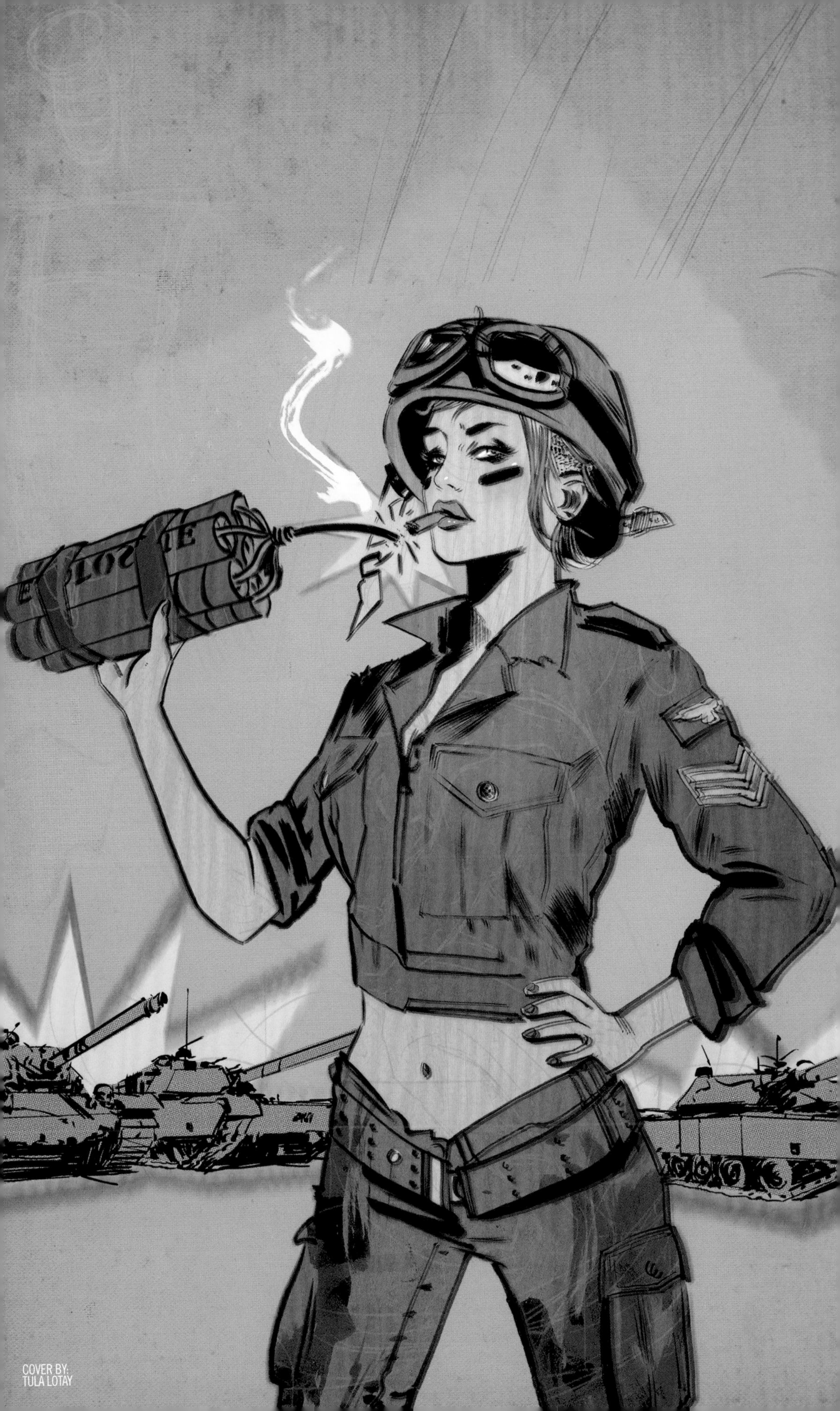

COVER BY:
TULA LOTAY

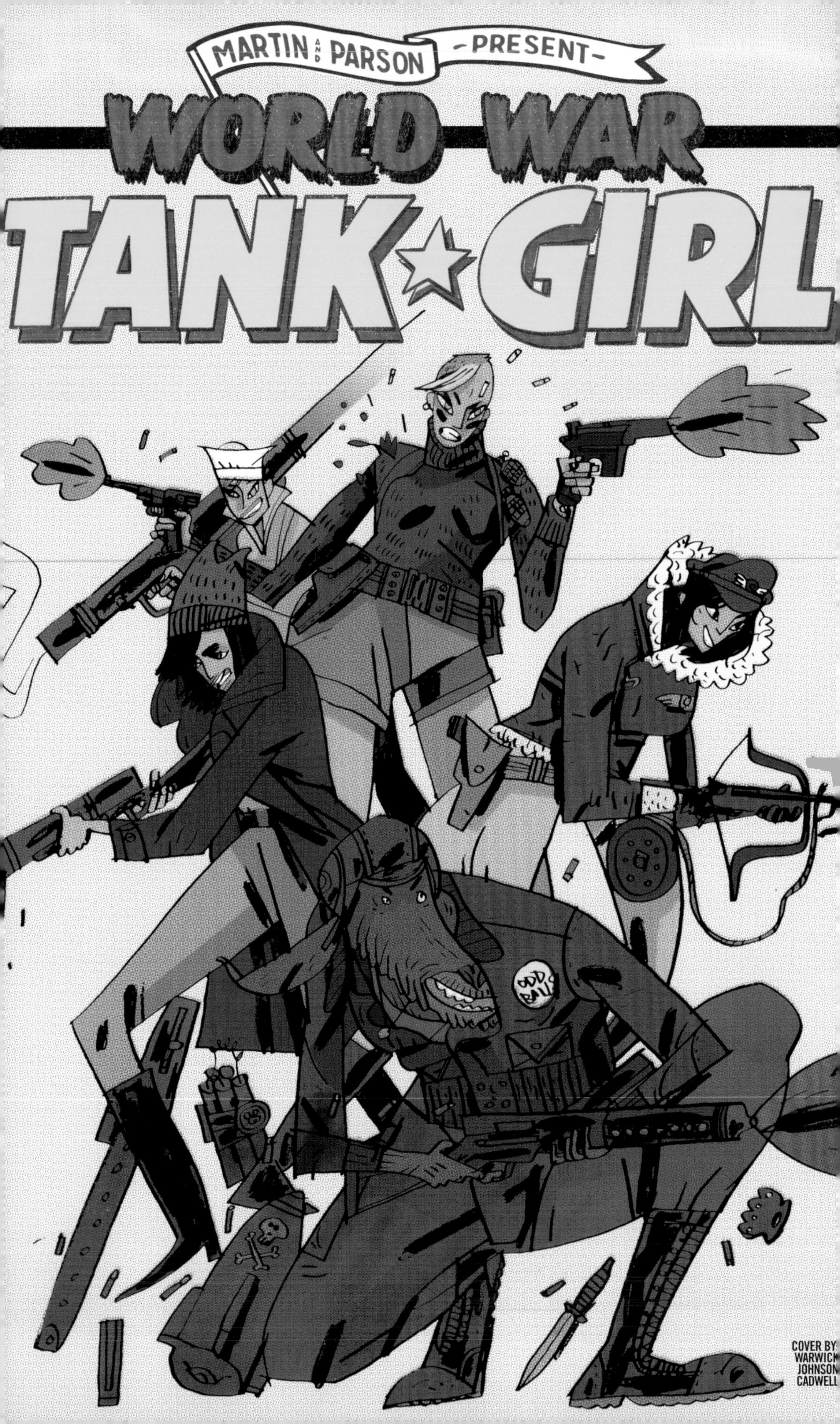
MARTIN AND PARSON -PRESENT-
WORLD WAR
TANK GIRL
ODD BALLS
COVER BY WARWICK JOHNSON CADWELL

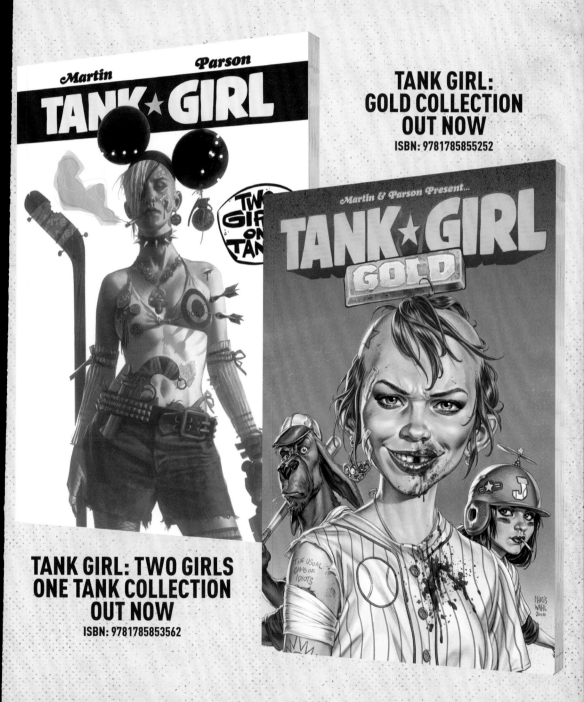

NOW GO AND READ THE OTHER TWO PARTS OF THE TRILOGY!

Martin
Parson
TANK★GIRL

TANK GIRL: TWO GIRLS ONE TANK COLLECTION OUT NOW

ISBN: 9781785853562

TANK GIRL: GOLD COLLECTION OUT NOW

ISBN: 9781785855252

Martin & Parson Present...
TANK★GIRL
GOLD
THE USUAL GANG OF IDIOTS
CHRIS WAHL 2016

AVAILABLE NOW

TITAN-COMICS.COM

TITAN COMICS

TANK GIRL
NEEDS YOU!

Join the exclusive ranks of the Tank Girl Army Tea Making Division today! All you need is a kettle, some good quality tea, optional milk and sugar, and this (now legendary) sew-on patch!

ONLY AVAILABLE FROM THE TANK GIRL SHOP

Check our store for t-shirts, hand-signed posters and prints, badges, stickers, beer mats, promotional give-aways, and much, much more!

WWW.TAN 3 1901 10093 7251 CARTEL.COM